IMPLEMENTING THE SOCIAL MODEL OF DISABILITY: THEORY AND RESEARCH

Edited by

Colin Barnes and Geof Mercer

The Disability Press
Leeds

First published 2004
The Disability Press
Centre for Disability Studies
School of Sociology and Social Policy
University of Leeds
Leeds LS2 9JT.

Output from disk supplied and printed by University Print Services, a
division of Media Services, at Leeds.

British Library Cataloguing in Publication Data
A catalogue record for this book is available from the British Library

Library of Congress Cataloguing in Publication Data
A catalogue record of this book has been requested

ISBN 0-9528450-8-3 (pbk)

Contents

The Disability Press

The Disability Press aims to provide an alternative outlet for work in the field of disability studies. The Disability Press draws inspiration from the work of all those countless disabled individuals and their allies who have, over the years, struggled to put this particular issue onto the political agenda. Its establishment is a testament to the growing recognition of 'disability' as an equal opportunities and human rights issue within the social sciences.

Funding for this volume has been provided by the Centre for Disability Studies. The editors also wish to record their thanks to the School of Sociology and Social Policy at the University of Leeds for its continuing support.

Acknowledgements

As the Editors of this volume, we are pleased to record our appreciation to the Economic and Social Research Council for a grant to help with the funding of a seminar series on 'Implementing the Social Model of Disability: from Theory to Practice' organised by the Centre for Disability Studies (CDS) at the University of Leeds.

Our thanks also to the participants at the first two seminars, and those presenting papers, who set the series off to such an excellent start.

Not least, we are very grateful to Marie Ross, who has contributed so much to the preparation of this volume for publication, including the compilation of the Index.

Contributors

Bill Armer is a postgraduate research student in the Centre for Disability Studies at the University of Leeds.

Katy Bailey is a PhD student in the Centre for Disability Studies in Leeds. She continues to meet up with other disabled people in groups to do research about disability and parenting.

Colin Barnes is Professor of Disability Studies at the Centre for Disability Studies, School of Sociology and Social Policy, University of Leeds.

Peter Beresford is Professor of Social Policy and Director of the Centre for Citizen Participation and Chair of Shaping Our Lives, the national user-controlled organisation, and a long-term user of mental health services.

Angie Carmichael is an independent disability researcher who has worked on a number of studies and projects, many of which have been either service user led, or initiated by disabled people.

John Davis is Co-ordinator of the BA Childhood Studies in the Department of Educationsal Studies at the Moray House School of Education, and Senior Consultant at the Children and Social Inclusion Consultancy, Edinburgh.

John Hogan is Children's Participation Officer, Liverpool Children's Fund (seconded from The Children's Society). He was previously Senior Worker in the Liverpool Bureau for Children and Young People.

Geof Mercer is a Senior Lecturer in the School of Sociology and Social Policy and a member of the Centre for Disability Studies at the University of Leeds.

Mike Oliver is recently retired, and Emeritus Professor of Disability Studies at the University of Greenwich.

Donna Reeve is a PhD student in the Department of Applied Social Science, Lancaster University.

Mairian Scott–Hill is Senior Research Fellow at King's College, London, and the University of Central Lancashire.

Carol Thomas is Senior Lecturer with the Institute for Health Research at Lancaster University.

Claire Tregaskis is a researcher in Applied Disability Studies at the School of Education, University of Sheffield.

Nick Watson is Senior Lecturer in the School of Health, University of Edinburgh.

CHAPTER 1

Theorising and Researching Disability from a Social Model Perspective

Colin Barnes and Geof Mercer

Introduction

The late 1960s and 1970s was a period when economic and political upheavals produced an extraordinary level of political activism among disadvantaged groups around the world. In Britain, the politicisation of disabled people and their organisations moved into a new, more militant, phase (Campbell and Oliver 1996; Barton 2001). Disabled activists became increasingly discontented with 'pressure group' activity as a means of achieving social change. A further grievance was the 'colonisation' of disability organisations by non-disabled 'experts'. Such concerns encouraged moves towards a 'grassroots' politics, with organisations controlled by disabled people playing an increasingly central role, and a challenge to traditional assumptions that disability was a 'personal tragedy'.

Disability activists began to explore an alternative, 'social interpretation' of the 'disabling society' and the sources of the widespread disadvantages and discrimination experienced by people with impairments (Hunt 1966; UPIAS 1976). These ideas provided the foundations for the 'social model of disability' (Oliver 1981, 1990) that has exercised such a powerful influence on organisations of disabled people and disability politics and also underpinned the growth of academic teaching and research on disability in Britain. Now is an opportune moment to reflect on the contribution of early social model thinking to disability studies, and to explore how far it might continue to inspire attempts to understand disability into the twenty first century.

Towards a social interpretation of disability

One of the key organisations instrumental in bringing disability on to the political agenda was the Disablement Income Group (DIG), formed in 1965. It opted to pursue traditional pressure group activity in order to advance the social and economic conditions of disabled people. Other groups initiated campaigns on specific issues such as accessible housing, supported living in the community, and integrated education.

However, some disability activists, disenchanted with the direction and speed of social change, began to explore innovative forms of disability politics. Undoubtedly, one of the most influential of the new political groups set up and controlled by disabled people was the Union of the Physically Impaired Against Segregation (UPIAS). Its origins lay in a letter from Paul Hunt published in *The Guardian* on 20th September 1972 that called on disabled people to form their own organisation. UPIAS functioned mainly through confidential correspondence and circulars circulated amongst its members, many of whom were living in residential institutions (Campbell and Oliver 1996). These exchanges led to the production of a *Policy Statement* and constitution in 1974. Two years later, it expanded on its thinking in the *Fundamental Principles of Disability* (UPIAS 1976).

The orthodox view of disability, accepted by academic writers, policy makers and service providers, stressed the problems caused by an individual's flawed mind or body. In complete contrast, UPIAS focused on the ways in which the current organisation of society created and perpetuated diverse social barriers to the inclusion of people with impairments:

> it is society which disables physically impaired people. Disability
> is something imposed on top of our impairments, by the way
> we are unnecessarily isolated and excluded from full participation
> in society (UPIAS 1976: 3).

This recast disability as a historically contingent relationship in which people with impairments became a socially oppressed group, as has occurred with women, black and ethnic minorities, lesbians and gay men.

A key architect of the UPIAS document was Vic Finkelstein, who had moved to Britain after being banished from South Africa because of his involvement in the anti-apartheid protest movement. He drew strong parallels with the experiences of discrimination among disabled people. While biological inferiority was used routinely to justify discriminatory practices, the analytical spotlight was now re-directed towards a socio-political explanation.

Social models and social theories

The ideas advanced by UPIAS were subsequently re-presented by Mike Oliver (1981, 1990) as the 'social model of disability'. The emphasis on disabling social and environmental barriers was contrasted with the current orthodoxy that viewed disability as a 'personal tragedy', and disabled people as in need of 'care'. Oliver drew on contemporary debates in the social sciences to explain this individualised approach to disability as a social creation of industrial capitalism. Moreover, the 'social model' approach pointed to areas where political action might bring about the social changes necessary to overturn the social exclusion of disabled people. Initially, this social model was used in training social workers and professionals, and later it became the principal mechanism for delivering Disability Equality Training (Gillespie Sells and Campbell 1990; Rieser and Mason 1990).

However, both Vic Finkelstein (2002) and Mike Oliver (1996) insisted that UPIAS' 'social interpretation' and the 'social model' were not equivalent to a theory of disability. Instead, they emphasised that the importance of the social model was primarily as a 'heuristic device' or an aid to understanding:

> A good model can enable us to see something which we do not understand because in the model it can be seen from different viewpoints (not available to us in reality) and it is this multi-dimensioned replica of reality that can trigger insights which we might not otherwise develop (Finkelstein 2002: 13).

Indeed, others were encouraged to create their own models in order to conceptualise and illuminate the different components of the 'disablement' process (Finkelstein 1996).

Several of the most influential early attempts by British writers to theorise the disabling society were located within broadly Marxist perspectives. Thus, Finkelstein offered a 'historical materialist' account of the emergence and reproduction of disability and helper/helped relations in his short monograph *Attitudes and Disabled People* (1980). Other noteworthy attempts to theorise disability drawing on neo-Marxist ideas that incorporated cultural and ideological factors were set out by Paul Abberley (1987) and Mike Oliver (1990). Even when not adopting a Marxist analysis, accounts immersed in social model thinking typically prioritised structural factors in explaining disabled people's social exclusion (Barnes 1991).

The UPIAS re-definition of disability exerted a powerful impact on the wider disabled people's movement. The social model has been adopted by organisations controlled and run by disabled people across the UK (Barnes, Mercer and Morgan 2000). The identification of disabling barriers acted as a significant stimulus and gave a precise focus for disabled people's campaigns (Campbell and Oliver 1996). Notable examples over the last decade include the struggles for anti-discrimination legislation by disabled people (Barnes 1991), and to legalise and extend direct payments to enable disabled people to organise their own personal assistance support (Zarb and Nadash 1994).

The social model was also adopted by the British Council of Organisations of Disabled People (BCODP), now the British Council of Disabled People, which is the national umbrella for organisations controlled and run by disabled people.

In the process, the social model acquired an explicit 'rights now' focus. As Jenny Morris recently argued:

> The social model of disability gives us the words to describe our inequality. It separates out (disabling barriers) from impairment (not being able to walk or see or having difficulty learning)…. Because the social model separates out disabling barriers and impairments, it enables us to focus on exactly what it is which denies us our human and civil rights and what action needs to be taken (Morris 2000: 1–3).

Mainstream thinking on disability

The academic focus within the social sciences and humanities prior to the 1990s represented disability in terms of individual 'functional limitations' or 'flaws', caused by 'chronic illness' and/or the complex interplay between the 'abnormal' body/mind, individual coping strategies and wider societal attitudes (Barnes and Mercer 1996).

Despite the occasional public outrage at the horrors of residential life for so many disabled people, politicians, policy makers, and service providers saw little reason to depart from established ways of dealing with disability. To illustrate this point, Eric Miller and Geraldine Gwynne (1972), after investigating the experiences of disabled people living in institutions, accepted that 'severely' disabled people had little prospect of inclusion in mainstream society. As a result, the quality of disabled people's lives was reduced to a 'social death', but despite this the researchers only felt able to recommend an 'enlightened guardianship' approach. In practice, this 'solution' comprised a re-working of traditional policy intervention at the individual level.

Understandably, such studies attracted hostile criticism from disabled activists because they reinforced the personal tragedy standpoint, and confirmed the general approach to disability within the social sciences and humanities (Hunt 1981). The gathering politicisation of disabled people, coupled with socio-political analyses of disability and disabling barriers, had made little impression on academic or policy debates. This was in sharp contrast to the radical analyses of racism and sexism that quickly won favour.

Nevertheless, by the 1990s, the social model of disability was attracting increasing interest even among those hitherto hostile to radical campaigns led by disabled people. A social model allegiance was claimed by a broad range of organisations dealing with disability and related issues in both the statutory and voluntary sectors. Examples included the Leonard Cheshire Foundation (Carmichael, Brown and Doherty 2000), NHS Trusts such as Liverpool NHS Primary Care Trust (Clarke 2002), local authority social service departments, as illustrated by Leeds City Council (LSSD 2001, 2003), and the Disability Rights Commission (DRC 2002). Yet, in practice, some of these have continued with traditional 'care' policies or done little to implement policies in line with social model thinking on disabling social and environmental barriers (GLAD 2000; Thomas, P. 2002).

A social model approach also attracted support on the world stage. Disabled People's International (DPI) agreed the significance of re-interpreting 'disability' in 1981, although it rejected the UPIAS formulation of 'impairment' and 'disability' in favour of 'disability' and 'handicap'. This was because of difficulties and disagreements over translation and interpretation. Subsequently, DPI Europe reversed this decision because of unease over the term 'handicap', but the choice of terminology remains highly contentious and fuels continuing debates about the cross-national applicability of the social model.

Notwithstanding such issues, the focus on social barriers has been introduced into various documents produced by the United Nations. A primary illustration is the *Standard Rules on the Equalisation of Opportunities for People with Disabilities* (United Nations 1993). A further influence has been identified on social policy in Europe (Oorshot and Hvinden 2001). Additionally, a broad social model perspective underpinned *Rethinking Care from Disabled People's Perspectives* sponsored by the World Health Organization's (WHO 2001) Disability and Rehabilitation Team. This comprised a two-year project and conference that involved professionals, disabled people, and their families from around the world. Moreover, WHO decided to replace the much maligned *International Classification of Impairments, Disabilities and Handicaps* (ICIDH) with the *International Classification of Functioning* (ICF) also known as ICIDH-2, that explicitly aims to integrate traditional medical and social model insights (WHO 1998).

ICF replaces the ICIDH use of impairment, disability and handicap with another three-fold framework – impairment, activity, and participation. It acknowledges that participation is the outcome of the inter-relationship between the 'features of the person' and 'social and physical environments' (Üstün et al. 2001: 6-7). While the importance attached to the social and physical environment in the ICF ties in with social model thinking, and it recognises the cultural influences on perceptions of disability, its classification system remains firmly grounded in western scientific concepts (Finkelstein 1998; Pfeiffer 2000; Miles 2001). Equally, the 'bio-psychosocial' approach retains the individual as the starting point for the analysis of bodily function and activity. Its concept of 'participation' is underdeveloped and linked to individual circumstances rather than grounded in social and political inclusion. Although potential users are encouraged to classify environmental factors, it fails to suggest effective tools to accomplish this task or to assess the disabling tendencies of government policies and practices, physical environments and cultural contexts (Baylies 2002).

Enter disability studies

In Britain, as elsewhere, the first signs that a social interpretation of disability was gaining credibility in higher education appeared in the 1970s. The Open University (OU) paved the way with a course entitled *The Handicapped Person in the Community*. This broke with the traditional designation of teaching on disability as solely concerned with health issues. Instead, its central aim was to provide professionals and practitioners with the knowledge and skills to support disabled people's quest for greater autonomy. A later change in title - *The Disabling Society* – made explicit its social model foundations. Although discontinued in 1994, the course inspired the development of disability studies within other educational institutions, particularly through its 'course readers' (Brechin and Liddiard 1981; Swain *et al*. 1993). In addition, academic and policy debates were stimulated by the launch in 1986 of the first journal devoted exclusively to social approaches to disability issues - *Disability, Handicap and Society* - re-named *Disability and Society* in 1993 – under the editorship of Len Barton and Mike Oliver. By the mid-1990s, disability studies programmes were gaining acceptance in a number of Universities and Colleges around the UK. Indeed, the first undergraduate course with the title 'disability studies' was introduced in 1992, and a complete MA programme a year later, by the Department of Sociology and Social Policy at the University of Leeds.

Disability studies as an academic subject area also took off internationally. In the United States, the first disability studies programme was established in 1977 following pressure from disabled activists and academics. The setting up of the American Disability Studies Association quickly followed in 1981 (Pfeiffer and Yoshida 1995). American writers were in the vanguard of (non-Marxist) socio-political analyses of disability (for example, Hahn 1987; Longmore 1987; Albrecht 1992). Moreover, the primary disciplinary location for disability studies in America was education and the humanities (notably cultural and literary studies, philosophy and law) rather than the social sciences, as in the UK (Linton 1998; Barnes *et al*. 1999; Snyder *et al*. 2002). In Canada, social model thinking has been more conspicuous in the disability literature, as illustrated by critical contributions from writers such as Marcia Rioux and Michael Bach (1994), Shelley Tremain (1996), and Rod Michalko (2002).

In Britain, early advocates of the social model perspective were critical of established social science disciplines; in particular, medical sociologists, both for their acceptance of the IDIDH, and their focus on 'disease' and 'chronic illness' as the cause of 'disability' which was defined as individual functioning. Moreover, medical sociologists largely ignored or dismissed early writings around the social model. Indeed, there was a considerable chasm separating the Marxist and structuralist accounts of disability theorists and the prevailing interactionist and interpretative affiliations of the most influential contributions to the sociological literature on 'chronic illness and disability' (Bury 1996; Barnes, Mercer and Shakespeare 1999; Williams 1999).

Over the last decade, the range of disciplinary interests involved in disability studies has become much more cosmopolitan. In addition, the implementation of the social model has come under intense scrutiny from both activists and academics. The Marxist influences evident in early attempts to analyse disability in the British literature have been challenged by an increasingly disparate set of perspectives. These include interpretative and phenomenological approaches, feminism, and most recently, post-modernism and post-structuralism, with Michel Foucault (1980) a notable powerful influence (Davis 1995; Mitchell and Snyder 1997; Stiker 1999; Corker and Shakespeare 2002; Snyder *et al.* 2002). The materialist account of disability history (at least, as outlined by Finkelstein and revised by Oliver) was criticised as overly simplistic, for downplaying the role of culture and other 'non-structural' factors in the oppression/everyday lives of disabled people, and for ignoring impairment and recent debates around embodiment (Corker and Shakespeare 2002).

Nevertheless, attempts to develop a materialist or 'political economy' of disability to ground the changing relationship between impairment and disability have gained a new currency: for example, in studies of non-capitalist 'modes of production', and against the changing character of capitalism. Such issues have been pursued in contrasting ways by a number of writers, including Marta Russell (1998) in America, and Brendan Gleeson (1999) in Australia. In a further variation of this theme, Carol Thomas (1999) has explored disability within a framework of feminist materialism. Indeed, debates within feminism have exercised a wider impact on disability studies, particularly in the transfer of issues raised in theoretical debates around sex and gender.

Critics also called for a social interpretation of impairment (as well as disability), and social modellists have acknowledged the force of this argument (Abberley

1987; Oliver 1996). In fact, the changing meaning attached to medical labels such as 'mental illness' and 'mental impairment' has attracted considerable sociological interest (Ryan with Thomas 1980; Foucault 1980). A further issue has been whether the social model is applicable to the circumstances of people across the range of impairments, particularly people with learning difficulties (Chappell 1998) and mental health system users (Beresford and Wallcraft 1997). The critics claimed that social model writings were responsible for the neglect of impairment-related experiences, the body and diversity – particularly in terms of gender, ethnicity, age and sexuality (though not surprisingly, social class).

These issues divide writers on disability as well as highlighting the unease many disabled people feel about whether such academic debates have any positive material impact on their lives, and particularly their social exclusion. Indeed, as disability studies becomes more established as an academic discipline there is a risk that its engagement with disabled people and the issues with which they identify will diminish. At the same time, it is important not to underestimate the necessity and complexity of theorising disability that goes beyond any social model (Finkelstein 1996).

Re-thinking disability research

The challenge to the dominant 'personal tragedy' approach was reinforced in a critique of mainstream research on disability (Barnes and Mercer 1997). In a withering attack, Oliver (1992) condemns it as a 'rip-off' that has done little, if anything, to confront the social exclusion experienced by disabled people or initiate policies for social change. The roots of this suspicion can be traced back at least to the 1960s and the denunciation of academic researchers as 'parasites' on disabled people (Hunt 1981). This example illustrated the potential for tension between disabled people's interest in challenging social and environmental barriers and the concerns of those focusing on disability in academic and research institute settings (Germon 1998).

An alternative approach began to take shape as social model thinking on social oppression was absorbed into research practice (Oliver et al. 1988; Morris 1989; Barnes 1990). 'Critical theory' was a formative influence, with its emphasis on emancipatory goals, and a commitment to openly partisan inquiry. A crucial stimulus to taking these ideas forward was provided by a series of seminars funded by the Joseph Rowntree Foundation in the late 1980s and early 1990s. These led to a national conference and a special issue of the journal *Disability, Handicap and Society* in 1992. In this, Mike Oliver (1992) set out the rationale for 'emancipatory disability research'. This encompassed a political commitment to confront disability by changing: the social relations of research production, including the role of funding bodies and the relationship between researchers and those being researched; and the links between research 'findings' and policy responses.

The asymmetrical relationship between researcher and researched in mainstream social research was identified as a major reason for the alienation of disabled people from the research process. A few key funding bodies control what research is undertaken, while researcher-experts control the research design, implementation and dissemination. As a consequence, the 'subjects' of research have little positive input or sense of active 'ownership' of the research process (Zarb 1992). Oliver suggests that emancipatory disability research should be distinguished by its stress on 'reciprocity, gain and empowerment' (1992: 111). This is highlighted in demands that researchers place their skills and knowledge at the disposal of disabled people.

Needless to say, debates among disability theorists have found expression in the disability research literature. A particularly contentious issue has been how far and in what ways research should focus on subjective experiences of disability and impairment, such as physical pain, fatigue, and depression (Morris 1989; Shakespeare et al. 1996). A further issue is the extent to which emancipatory disability research engages with wider social research debates about the merits of different methodologies and methods. There has been relatively little debate of the criteria that differentiate 'emancipatory' from other forms of disability research, or of the merits or appropriateness of specific methods of data collection and analysis. Disability researchers have however raised important questions about issues in undertaking research with people from different impairment groups, particularly people with learning difficulties, and mental health users (Beresford and Wallcraft 1997; Ward 1997).

Yet cautionary tales abound. The 'textbook' way of conducting emancipatory disability research is as likely to confront difficulties in practice as has been the experience of mainstream social research (Barnes and Mercer 1997). As Sarah Beazley, Michele Moore and David Benzie (1997) discovered, the lack of time and resources, the involvement of other 'stakeholders' with differing interests and commitments, not to mention unforeseen 'interruptions', threaten to confound even the most resourceful researcher. Not all people so labelled consider themselves 'disabled' or are united on a theoretical and research agenda guided by the social model. This reinforces the need to ensure that emancipatory disability research is 'reflexive' and self-critical.

Debating the social model

This book contains twelve chapters on the social model of disability. These were first delivered as papers in a seminar series entitled 'Implementing the Social Model of Disability: from Theory to Practice' organised by the

Centre for Disability Studies (CDS) at the University of Leeds. Funding was provided by the Economic and Social Research Council and CDS. The primary aim of the first two seminars (held in November 2002 and February 2003) was to reflect on theoretical and research debates since the 1980s. While social model thinking has provided a firm foundation for the development of disability politics and academic studies of disability, continuing debate is necessary if it is to maintain its relevance for disabled people.

In Chapter 2 Mike Oliver, chronicles the social model's history from its UPIAS origins through its use in training of social workers and other professionals in the early 1980s and, later, its adoption by the British Disabled People's Movement as a practical tool in the development of Disability Equality Training (DET). He notes how the social model has attracted criticism from some disability writers. Oliver insists that the social model should not be regarded as a social theory but rather as a practical tool for challenging disablism. He illustrates this potential in a review of the implementation of one local authority's policies for disabled people.

The theoretical underpinnings of a social model perspective are analysed in Chapter 3 by Carol Thomas. She contends that the 'social relational' implications of the biological/societal distinction central to the UPIAS reinterpretation of disability led to substantial progress in identifying disabling barriers: economic, political, social and cultural. The theoretical challenge is to understand what gives form to and sustains these relationships – in such diverse areas as social structures, inter-personal relations, organisational practices, ideologies and discourses. She outlines a theoretical agenda and way forward for disability studies that spans: the political economy of disability; the psycho-emotional dimensions of disability; theorising difference; and, theorising impairment and impairment effects.

In Chapter 4, Bill Armer examines what he describes as the apparent contradictions of the 'radical' materialist account elaborated by Vic Finkelstein. He draws on a range of sources both within and outside the disability studies literature to criticise the emphasis on economic determinism as the primary cause of disabled people's oppression in late capitalist society. Instead, he argues for an account that prioritises the cultural dynamic of the normality/abnormality divide. While he accepts that Finkelstein's socio-political approach has proved an invaluable basis for understanding the production of disability, he outlines doubts over its utility in encompassing the economic and socio-cultural aspects of the disablement process.

Disability theory and the interface between disabled and non-disabled people are the primary concern of Claire Tregaskis' discussion in Chapter 5. She utilises her experience working as a disabled consultant with a mainstream environmental conservation agency to examine the often overlooked possibilities for disability theory to make connections with non-disabled people, rather than presenting disabled and non-disabled people as in continuous and unchanging opposition, in order to initiate social change and more inclusive practice. She stresses the importance of disabled people securing their (multiple) identity, acknowledging difference without assimilating to the majority viewpoint, developing their understanding of power relations, and enhancing their communication and negotiation skills.

In Chapter 6, Donna Reeve argues that the social model must address both the structural and psycho-emotional dimensions of disability. She explores how the systematic exclusion from the mainstream of economic and social life has an adverse effect on the psycho-emotional well being of people with impairments. Internalised oppression or the negative reactions of others can 'disable' as effectively as any environmental barrier. She claims that the structural and psycho-emotional dimensions of disability are intertwined and mutually reinforcing. Since these psycho-emotional consequences of disability are particularly severe for many disabled people, their analysis should be accorded greater attention than hitherto in the disability studies literature.

Nick Watson extends the critique of the social model in Chapter 7. He focuses on its failure to examine the complex interplay between impairment and disability in the everyday experiences of disabled people. He argues for the development of a pluralistic approach to the development of disability theory and research. Citing the work of the German philosopher Axel Honneth, Watson challenges approaches to disability that view it exclusively in structural terms (following the UPIAS example), and advocates analyses of disablement as the withholding of social and cultural recognition grounded in the experiences of disabled people. Only then will disability politics be 're-invented' as a democratic movement.

In Chapter 8, Geof Mercer reviews the ways in which social model thinking has influenced the emergence of emancipatory disability research. In tracing its trajectory over the past decade with reference to both disability studies and a wider social science literature, he identifies key issues and concerns for doing disability research. These extend to greater engagement with methodological debates within social research. He argues that those following an emancipatory research agenda must explore and explain disablism in all its forms in order to make a meaningful contribution to debates about how such knowledge can be used to advance the social inclusion of disabled people.

While Katy Bailey acknowledges the importance of the socio-political interpretation of disability in Chapter 9, she argues that social model accounts have become 'de-contextualised' by downplaying the socio-cultural environment in which these ideas were developed. This separation of the social model of disability from its social origins threatens a one-sided interpretation that has potentially negative implications for the development of a social theory of disability and emancipatory disability research. She highlights the potential and centrality of participatory methods in research that supports group-based discussion of the links between experience with knowledge production, and generally opening up and collectivising the processes of data analysis and theory development.

In Chapter 10, Mairian Scott-Hill foregrounds the complex issues of language and meaning in the research process. She warns against the uncritical acceptance of what she categorises as social model orthodoxy in disability theory and research. She illustrates with reference to several diverse case studies how the 'communicative' paradigm can enable us to research the 'messy side' of social life in all its complexity and subtlety. This, she maintains, represents a more rigorous and reflexive approach to disability research that is more appropriate for the investigation of social relations across difference, collec- tivisation, and the mechanisms and structures of inclusive societies.

Research with children is the central focus for John Davis and John Hogan in Chapter 11. The authors report on their experiences in conducting a participatory research project with disabled children and young people in Liverpool. Besides documenting their participant's views on crucial issues such as the effectiveness of social services, respite care, education, health care, leisure activities, career services and disabled role models, Davis and Hogan reflect critically on the theoretical and practical issues that arose during their study. They emphasise the value and variety in participatory approaches, and the important contribution made by children and young people in the implementation of the project.

User involvement in research and policy formulation is the principal area of concern for Angie Carmichael in Chapter 12. She draws on a range of studies including her own small-scale empirical project that gave voice to disabled people with first hand experience of user consultation and involvement. She identifies some of the main barriers to the implementation of user involvement, and the significance of developing an equal partnership between disabled people, professionals and various agencies. She also explores key issues relevant to the future development of emancipatory disability research, in particular, the relationship between research, the disabled people's movement, and the on-going struggle for meaningful inclusion.

Finally, in Chapter 13, Peter Beresford reviews research and social model approaches within the mental health system users' or survivors' movement

in comparison with the disabled people's movement. He identifies key
similarities and differences between the two movements, particularly with
reference to the social model, partnerships with professionals, and user-led
initiatives. In articulating the history of the mental health system users'/survivors'
movement, their involvement in 'user led' research, he argues for the urgent
development of a 'social model of madness' along similar lines to that of the
social model of disability including its 'transformatory' aspirations, but which
highlights issues of personal experience and social oppression.

Over the last three decades disability activists have established the social
model of disability as a comprehensive critique of mainstream academic theories,
and policy approaches. The contributors to this volume cover many issues
central to theorising and researching disability. Taken together these provide
ample testimony to the continuing vitality of debates around the social
model in disability studies. We hope that they will prove a positive addition
to the growing body of knowledge that underpins disabled people's struggles
for a fair and just society.

Bibliography

Abberley, P. 1987: The Concept of Oppression and the Development of
a Social Theory of Disability. In L. Barton, and M. Oliver (eds),
Disability Studies: Past Present and Future. Leeds: The Disability
Press.

Albrecht, G. L. 1992: *The Disability Business.* London: Sage.

Barnes, C. 1990: *Cabbage Syndrome: The Social Construction of
Dependence.* Lewes: Falmer.

Barnes, C. 1991: *Disabled People in Britain and Discrimination: the case
for anti-discrimination legislation.* London: Hurst and Co. in Association
with the British Council of Organizations of Disabled People.

Barnes, C. and Mercer, G. 1996: Introduction: Exploring the Divide. In C.
Barnes and G. Mercer (eds), *Exploring the Divide: Accounting for
Illness and Disability.* Leeds: The Disability Press.

Barnes, C. and Mercer, G. 1997: Breaking the Mould: an introduction to
doing disability research. In C. Barnes and G. Mercer (eds), *Doing Disability
Research.* Leeds: The Disability Press.

Barnes, C. and Mercer, G. 2003: *Disability: An Introduction.* Cambridge:
Polity Press.

Barnes, C., Mercer, G. and Morgan, H. 2000: *Creating Independent Futures:
Stage One Report.* Leeds: The Disability Press.

Barnes, C., Mercer, G. and Shakespeare, T. 1999: *Exploring Disability.*
Cambridge: Polity.

Barton, L. (ed.) 2001: *Disability, Politics and the Struggle for Change.* London: David Fulton Publishers.

Baylies, C. 2002: Disability and the Notion of Human Development: questions of rights and responsibilities. *Disability and Society,* 17 (7), 725-740.

Beazley, S., Moore, M. and Benzie, D. 1997: Involving Disabled People in Research: A study of inclusion in environmental activities. In C. Barnes and G. Mercer (eds), *Doing Disability Research.* Leeds: The Disability Press.

Beresford, P. and Wallcraft, J. 1997: Psychiatric System Survivors and Emancipatory Research: Issues, overlaps and differences. In C. Barnes and G. Mercer (eds), *Doing Disability Research.* Leeds: The Disability Press.

Bury, M. 1996: Defining and researching disability: challenges and responses. In C. Barnes and G. Mercer (eds), *Exploring the Divide: Illness and Disability.* Leeds: The Disability Press.

Brechin, A., Liddiard, P. with Swain, J. (eds) 1981: *Handicap in a Social World.* Sevenoaks: Hodder and Stoughton in association with the Open University.

Campbell, J. and Oliver, M. 1996: *Disability Politics: Understanding our Past, Changing our Future.* London: Routledge.

Carmichael, A., Brown, L. and Doherty, M. 2000: *Exploring the Future Accommodation and Support Needs of Disabled People.* Bath: Leonard Cheshire and the University of Bath.

Chappell, A. L. 1998: Still out in the cold: people with learning difficulties and the social model of disability. In T.Shakespeare (ed.), *The Disability Reader: Social Science Perspectives.* London: Cassell.

Clarke, L. 2002: *Liverpool Central Primary health Care Trust Accessible Health Information: Project Report.* Liverpool: Liverpool Central Primary Health Care Trust. ⋆

Corker, M. and Shakespeare, T. (eds) 2002: *Disability/postmodernity. Embodying disability theory.* London: Continuum.

Davis, L. J. 1995: *Enforcing Normalcy: Disability Deafness and the Body.* London: Verso.

DRC. 2002: *Independent Living and the DRC Vision.* London: Disability Rights Commission.

Finkelstein, V. 1980: *Attitudes and Disability.* Geneva: World Rehabilitation Fund. ⋆

Finkelstein, V. 1996: Modelling Disability. Paper presented at the 'Breaking the Moulds' Conference, Dunfermline, Scotland, 16-17 May. ⋆

Finkelstein, V. 1998: The Biodynamics of Disablement. Paper presented at the Disability and Rehabilitation Research Workshop, Harare, Zimbabwe, 29 June. *

Finkelstein, V. 2002: The Social Model of Disability Repossessed. *Coalition: the Magazine of the Greater Coalition of Disabled People.* Manchester: The Greater Manchester Coalition of Disabled People, February, 10-16. *

Foucault, M. 1980: *Power/Knowledge* (ed. C. Gordon). Brighton: Harvester Press.

Germon, P. 1998: Activists and Academics: part of the same or a world apart. In T. Shakespeare (ed.), *The Disability Reader: social science perspectives.* London: Cassell.

Gillespie-Sells, K. and Campbell, J. 1991: *Disability Equality Training.* London: Disability Resource Team.

GLAD. 2000: *Reclaiming the Social Model of Disability: Conference Report.* London: Greater London Action on Disability. *

Gleeson, B. 1999: *Geographies of Disability.* London: Routledge.

Hahn, H. 1987: Civil rights for disabled Americans: the foundation of a political agenda. In A. Gartner and T. Joe (eds) *Images of the Disabled, Disabling Images.* New York: Praeger.

Hunt, P. 1966: A Critical Condition. In P. Hunt (ed.), *Stigma: The Experience of Disability.* London: Geoffrey Chapman.

Hunt, P. 1981: Settling Accounts With The Parasite People: A Critique of 'A Life Apart' by E. J. Miller and G. V. Gwynne. *Disability Challenge,* 1, 37-50.

Linton, S. 1998: *Claiming Disability: knowledge and identity.* New York: New York University Press.

Longmore, P. 1987: Screening stereotypes: images of disabled people in television and motion pictures. In A. Gartner and T. Joe (eds), *Images of the Disabled, Disabling Images.* New York: Praeger.

LSSD. 2001: *Developing a Joint Investment Plan for People with Physical Impairments in Leeds.* Leeds: Leeds Social Services Department, Modernisation Team.

LSSD. 2003: *Adult Services Strategy 2003-5.* Leeds: Leeds Social Services Department.

Michalko, R. 2002: *The Difference that Disability Makes.* Philadelphia: Temple University Press.

Miles, M. 2001: ICIDH, Meets Postmodernity, or 'incredulity towards meta-terminology'. *Disability World,* 7 (March-April). Available at: http://www.disabilityworld.org/03-04_01/resources/icidh.html (Accessed 24th February 2003).

Miller E. J. and Gwynne G.V. 1972: *A Life Apart.* London: Tavistock.

Mitchell, D.T. and Snyder, S. L. 1997: *The Body and Physical Difference: discourses of disability.* Ann Arbor: University of Michigan Press.

Morris, J. 1989: *Able Lives,* London. The Women's Press.

Morris, J. 2000: Summary of Presentations, *Reclaiming the Social Model of Disability: Conference Report.* London: Greater London Action on Disability.

Oliver, M. 1981: A New Model of the Social Work Role in Relation to Disability. In J. Campling (ed.), *The Handicapped Person: a New Perspective for Social Workers?* London: RADAR.

Oliver, M. 1990: *The Politics of Disablement.* Basingstoke: Macmillan.

Oliver, M. 1992: Changing the Social Relations of Research Production? *Disability, Handicap & Society,* 7 (2),101-114.

Oliver, M. 1996: *Understanding Disability.* Basingstoke: Macmillan.

Oliver, M., Zarb, G., Silver, J., Moore, M. and Sainsbury, V. 1988: *Walking into Darkness.* London: Macmillan.

Oorschot, V. and Hvinden, B. (eds.) 2001: *Disability Policies in European Societies.* The Hague: Kluwer Law International.

Pfeiffer, D. 2000: The Devils are in the Detail: the ICIDH2 and the Disability Movement. *Disability and Society,* 15 (7), 1079-1082.

Pfeiffer, D. and Yoshida, K. 1995: Teaching Disability Studies in Canada and the USA. *Disability and Society,* 10 (4), 475-500.

Rieser, R. and Mason M. (eds.) 1990: *Disability Equality in the Classroom: a Human rights Issue.* London: Inner London Education Authority.

Rioux, M. H. and Bach, M. 1994: *Disability is Not Measles,* Ontario: Roeher Institute, York University.

Russell, M. 1998: *Beyond Ramps. Disability at the End of the Social Contract.* Monroe, Maine: Common Courage Press.

Ryan, J. with Thomas, F. 1980: *The Politics of Mental Handicap.* Harmondsworth: Penguin.

Shakespeare, T., Gillespie-Sells, K. and Davies, D. 1996: *The Sexual Politics of Disability: Untold Desires.* London: Cassell.

Snyder, S.L., Brueggemann, B.J. and Garland-Thomson, R. (eds) 2002: *Disability Studies: enabling the humanities.* New York: Modern Language Association of America.

Stiker, H-J. 1999/1982: *A History of Disability,* trans. W.Sayers. Ann Arbor: University of Michigan Press.

Stone, E. 1999: Disability and development in the majority world. In E.Stone (ed.), Disability and Development. Leeds: The Disability Press.

Swain, J. Finkelstein, V. French, S. and Oliver, M. (eds) 1993: **Disabling Barriers - Enabling Environments.** London: Sage in Association with the Open University.

Thomas, C. 1999: **Female Forms: Experiencing and Understanding Disability.** Buckingham: Open University Press.

Thomas, P. 2002: The Social Model of Disability is Generally Accepted. **Coaliton, The Magazine of the Greater Manchester Coalition of Disabled People.** Manchester: The Greater Manchester Coalition of Disabled People, February,17-21.

Tremain, S. 1996: **Pushing the Limits: Disabled Dykes Produce Culture.** Toronto: The Women's Press.

United Nations. 1993: **Standard Rules on the Equalization of Opportunities for Persons with Disabilities.** New York: United Nations.

UPIAS. 1976: **Fundamental Principles of Disability.** London: Union of Physically Impaired Against Segregation. ★

Üstün, T.B. et al. (eds) 2001: **Disability and Culture. Universalism and Diversity.** Seattle: Hogrefe & Huber, in association with WHO.

WHO. 1998: **Introduction (ICIDH-2).**
www.who.ch/programmes/mnh/mnh/ems/icidh/introduction

WHO. 2001: **Rethinking Care from Disabled People's Perspectives.** Geneva: World Health Organization.

Williams, S. 1999: Is anybody there? Critical realism, chronic illness and the disability debate. **Sociology of Health and Illness,** 21 (6), 797-819.

Zarb, G. 1992: On the road to Damascus; first steps towards changing the relations of disability research production. **Disability, Handicap & Society,** 7(2), 125-38.

Zarb, G. and Nadash, P. 1994: **Cashing in on Independence.** Derby: The British Council of Disabled People.

★ Available on www.leeds.ac.uk/disability-studies/archiveuk/index

CHAPTER 2

The Social Model in Action:
if I had a hammer

Mike Oliver

Introduction

A little while ago, Prime Minister Tony Blair stated that the Labour
Government's aim is: 'To take down the barriers that hold people back from
fulfilling their potential'. It is tempting to suggest that we are all social
modellists now! It certainly seems that it is not just disabled people who recognise
the potential and usefulness of the social model. However, its rising popularity
has coincided with it becoming increasingly contested, not just its definition
but also in terms of its usefulness and applicability.

In this chapter, I want to argue that, as the title implies, in the last
twenty years we have spent too much time talking about the social model
and its usefulness and indeed its limitations and not devoted enough attention
to actually implementing or attempting to implement it in practice. This criticism
applies both to the disabled people active in the Disability Movement and
those academics who have been central to the ongoing progress of disability
studies.

In order to develop this viewpoint, firstly, I will provide a brief history
of the social model from my own personal perspective as someone who was
centrally involved in its elaboration, almost from the beginning. Secondly,
I will explore the main criticisms of the social model that have emerged from
the Movement and from disability studies. I do not intend to engage with
the disapproving analyses that have been offered from those outside the Movement
or in other parts of the academy. Thirdly, I will examine examples of the
application of the social model with which, in one way or another, I have
been involved. I will focus primarily on a recent project undertaken with
Birmingham City Council (Oliver and Bailey 2002).

Origins of the social model

The starting point for the social model was the publication of *The Fundamental Principles of Disability* by the Union of the Physically Impaired Against Segregation (UPIAS) in 1976. It stated that:

> In our view it is society which disables physically impaired people.
> Disability is something imposed on top of our impairments by
> the way we are unnecessarily isolated and excluded from full
> participation in society (UPIAS 1976:14).

This turned the understanding of disability completely on its head by arguing that it was not impairment that was the main cause of the social exclusion of disabled people but the way society responded to people with impairments.

The more detailed elaboration of the social model stemmed from attempts to apply this insight into practice: firstly, in training of social workers, and secondly, in the design and delivery of disability equality training. More precisely, it emerged out of a course that I was teaching at the time that was the first postgraduate course in what would now be called disability studies. This was based at the University of Kent and was aimed primarily at qualified social workers, although some occupational therapists and others including a few disabled people also enrolled. Essentially, I was trying to provide my students with a way of applying the idea that it was society and not people with impairments that should be the target for professional intervention and practice. This approach was first introduced to a wider audience at a Royal Association for Disability and Rehabilitation (RADAR) conference in 1982. Subsequently, it was advanced in my book *Social Work with Disabled People* (Oliver 1983).

In recent years there has been a great deal of discussion about different models of disability and what they mean for disability politics, policy and services as well as how adequate they are as an explanation for the experiences that disabled people have. We have seen the emergence of individual and social models, the medical model, the charity model, the welfare and administrative models among others (Finkelstein 1993). As the person who invented the term 'the social model of disability', though not the ideas behind it, I find the arrival of all these different models confusing rather than helpful.

For my part, I prefer to understand disability in terms of two models: the individual and the social. Models are ways of translating ideas into practice and the idea underpinning the individual model was that of personal tragedy, while the idea behind the social model was that of externally imposed restriction. I do not deny the influence (some positive, some negative) of medicine, charity and welfare in the lives of disabled people but none of these offer a sufficient foundation for building a distinctive model of disability.

For too long, this individual, medicalised model of disability has dominated disability policy and service provision (Oliver 1996a, 1996b). The medical view of disability tends to regard disabled people as 'having something wrong with them' and hence the source of the problem. Despite this, disabled people are widely given a low priority when placed against the competing needs of other groups. This is particularly surprising given that, according to the Government's own figures, disabled people are a significant minority who make up approximately 15% of the population (Oliver 1996a). It was not until the arrival of the social model that the necessary radical change in direction was outlined.

I want to make three general points about the social model. Firstly, it is an attempt to switch the focus away from the functional limitations of individuals with an impairment on to the problems caused by disabling environments, barriers and cultures. Secondly, it refuses to see specific problems in isolation from the totality of disabling environments: hence the problem of unemployment does not just entail intervention in the social organisation of work and the operation of the labour market but also in areas such as transport, education and culture. Thirdly, endorsement of the social model does not mean that individually based interventions in the lives of disabled people, whether they be medically, rehabilitative, educational or employment based, are of no use or always counter-productive (Oliver 1996b).

From a social model perspective, too much is invested in individually based interventions with ever diminishing returns. As a consequence, modifications to environments tend to be neglected or under resourced despite the greater potential benefits of such investments. To put it simply, providing a barrier free environment is likely to benefit not just those with a mobility impairment but other groups as well (e.g. mothers with prams and pushchairs, porters with trolleys) whereas physical rehabilitation will only benefit those privileged enough to be able to access it. This is not a criticism of rehabilitation *per se*, but more about the efficient use of scarce resources.

Additionally, the traditional voice for disabled people had been the big charities that are still largely run and controlled by non-disabled people. Recent Government initiatives like the establishment of the Disability Rights Commission (DRC) have done little to change this situation although the number of organisations controlled and run by disabled people has grown steadily at both local and national levels. This trend must be sustained as the voice of disabled people is crucial to delivering on the social model.

From theory to practice

We can see how this has been applied in examining current welfare to work policies in respect of disabled people. There is universal agreement that disabled people do not have the same access to jobs as the rest of the population. Estimates of the unemployment rates amongst disabled people suggest that they are between two and five times more likely to be unemployed and that this huge discrepancy cannot be accounted for solely on the grounds of impaired performance. However, government policies are, by and large, targeted at equipping impaired individuals for the unchanging world of work rather than changing the way work is carried out in order that more people might access it. Hence, much greater resources are currently spent on employment rehabilitation, training and so on (individual model) rather than on removing the barriers to work or on attempting to prevent the labour market from operating in a non-discriminatory manner (social model).

For example, the Government is promoting disabled people's inclusion in the paid labour market with policies to revise the benefits system, and make radical changes in the operation of the labour market. All these sound like social model solutions to the problem of high unemployment rate amongst disabled people. However, when the government talks about mechanisms to implement these changes, it focuses on two things: a small number of special schemes, and job coaches for individual disabled people. So while the government accepts that the problems are external to disabled people, its solutions target individual disabled people.

In the broadest sense, the social model of disability is about nothing more complicated than a clear focus on the economic, environmental and cultural barriers encountered by people who are viewed by others as having some form of impairment – whether physical, sensory or intellectual. The barriers disabled people encounter include inaccessible education systems, working environments, inadequate disability benefits, discriminatory health and social support services, inaccessible transport, houses and public buildings and amenities, and the devaluing of disabled people through negative images in the media – films, television and newspapers. Hence, the cultural environment in which we all grow up usually sees impairment as unattractive and unwanted. Consequently, parent's feelings towards, and treatment of, a child born with an impairment are dependent upon what they have learned about disability from the world around them. Moreover, people who acquire impairment later in life have already been immersed in the personal tragedy viewpoint and it is not therefore surprising that many of these individuals find it difficult to know how to respond in any other way.

The social model of disability does not ignore questions and concerns relating to impairment and/or the importance of medical and therapeutic treatments. It acknowledges that in many cases, the suffering associated with disabled lifestyles is due primarily to the lack of medical and other services. It is similarly recognised that for many people coming to terms with the consequences of impairment in a society that devalues disabled people and disabled lifestyles is often a personal tragedy. But the real misfortune is that our society continues to discriminate, exclude and oppress people with impairments viewed and labelled as disabled.

As a consequence, in Britain, there began a remarkable growth in organisations of disabled people in the 1980s, along with the appearance of Disability Equality Training. Furthermore, the social model became the primary means of taking forward the idea of disability equality, across a whole range of trainers and organisations. The next stage in its development came when the Disabled People's Movement, notably the British Council of Organisations of Disabled People (BCODP), adopted the social model. If you read the book by Jane Campbell and myself (Campbell and Oliver 1996) you will see quite clearly that it played a crucial role in enhancing the collective consciousness of disabled people and in the emergence of the Disability Movement.

But it was not just amongst disabled people that the social model idea gained recognition. It gradually became incorporated into the State and there were a number of reports, the first in 1988 was called *A Wider Vision* (DHSS 1988), which advocated the idea of the social model as the way forward in providing services for blind and partially sighted people. Thus, by the 1990s the social model was being colonised by a range of organisations, interests and individuals, some of whom had bitterly opposed its appearance less than 10 years previously.

Criticisms of the social model

There are five main criticisms of the social model that have come from within the Disability Movement and disability studies. The first of these is that the social model ignores or is unable to deal adequately with the realities of impairment. This is based upon a conceptual misunderstanding because the social model is not about the personal experience of impairment but the collective experience of disablement (Oliver 1996b). This critique has sometimes turned into personal attacks and a few have suggested that it is only fit, white men in wheelchairs who are able to ignore their impairments.

As a severely disabled tetraplegic, who everyday of my life needs to make the necessary arrangements to be able to get up in the morning and go to bed at night and indeed use the toilet, I find such suggestions galling, particularly when they come from non-disabled people or those disabled people who have no idea what it is like to be at the mercy of State services for personal survival, let alone social functioning. Of course, white men in wheelchairs are aware of the limitations that impairments impose, and of course we struggle with the difficulties they create for us. But as I have indicated elsewhere (Oliver 1990), the limitations that our functional impairments impose upon us are an inadequate basis for building a political movement.

A second, related criticism contends that our subjective experiences of the 'pain' of both impairment and disability are ignored by the social model. Again, I find this censure partial and hard to countenance. If I simply focus on my own work, I co-wrote a book on male experiences of spinal cord injury (Oliver et al. 1988) and undertook another study of the experiences of disability and ageing (Zarb and Oliver 1993). More generally, I cannot accept assertions that the social model is not based upon disabled people's experiences. Quite the reverse, it emerged out of the experiences of disabled activists in the 1970s.

The third criticism of the social model states that it is unable to incorporate other social divisions, e.g. 'race', gender, ageing, sexuality and so on. The fact that the social model has not so far adequately integrated these dimensions does not mean that it cannot ever do so. In my view it is not that the social model cannot cope with these issues. Far better, if the critics had spent less of their time criticising the social model for its perceived failures and instead put more effort into attempting to apply it in practice.

A fourth criticism centres on the issue of 'otherness'. From this perspective, it is not the physical and environmental barriers that we face but the way our cultural values position disabled people as 'other'. This viewpoint is buttressed by recent developments in the theory of postmodernism and ideas about representation being crucial to disabled people. It is wrong to assert that, in principle, the social model ignores cultural values. More importantly, at the present time most disabled people in the world live in abject poverty, and do not have enough food and drink, while the two main causes of impairment internationally are war and poverty. As a consequence of this, any attempt to try to move disability politics exclusively into the realm of representation is fundamentally misguided and inappropriate when so many disabled people continue to experience life threatening material deprivation.

The final criticism of the social model is that it is inadequate as a social theory of disablement. Now the problem with this is that I do not think that those of us involved in the early discussions around the social model ever claimed that it was equivalent to a theory of disability. Indeed, most of us explicitly said these theoretical debates still needed to take place (Oliver

1996b). And yet, a recent collection (Corker and French 1998) spends a lot of time in the first and last chapters criticising what are termed 'social model theorists' for their inadequacies before finally acknowledging that the social model is not a theory. It seems superfluous to criticise the social model for not being something that it has never claimed to be.

These criticisms should not be seen merely as academic disputes, however heated and vitriolic they have become at times. They have also been part of the political terrain over which disability activists have fought in the last ten years. There have been those who have been critical of the alleged formal or informal policing that has supposedly taken place. For example, the journal *Disability and Society* has been accused of only publishing articles on the social model that were ultimately sympathetic to it. However, a count of articles published between the first number in 2000 and the last number in 2002 demonstrates that the Journal published more than twenty papers which sought to criticise, refine, review or even abandon the social model.

There is less dispute that some disability equality trainers, like some racism awareness and sexism awareness trainers, have been over zealous in their promotion of the social model and have perhaps spent their time trying to make non-disabled people feel guilty that they were not disabled. However, that is clearly a problem with the application of the model by some individuals rather than a flaw in the model itself. Further, there is no doubt that the Disability Movement itself has sometimes been over-sensitive about its 'big idea', but that has to be seen in the context of the way in which throughout our history our ideas have been taken by others, used and indeed even claimed for their own. Something like that pattern has occurred with respect to the social model. Speaker after speaker from non-representative organisations *for* disabled people claimed the social model as their own in the Trafalgar Square demonstrations of 1994. Additionally, the Disability Rights Commission established in 1997 by the New Labour Government declares that it is guided in everything it does by the social model of disability.

This has recently led some parts of the Movement to attempt to reclaim the social model, whatever that means. My argument is that we do not have the time, the energy or the resources to reclaim it, even if such a thing was possible. That would reduce disability activism to the kind of intellectual masturbation in which academics sometimes engage. Instead we need to work out and promote political strategies that are in line with the principles of the social model. Never mind yet more talk about how we might reclaim it, we need to get on and use it. We must not waste the gift that was bestowed upon by those disability activists who were struggling against the oppressive structures that kept disabled people out of society in the 1970s.

The social model in action

For the remainder of this chapter I want to focus on three areas or projects which I have been involved in over the last twenty years that have sought to apply the social model, although I will concentrate on a recent study of its implementation in Birmingham City Council.

The first project was my attempt to reconstruct social work with disabled people in accordance with the social model principles. It was intended to provide a counter to individualised casework that positioned disabled people as tragic victims in need of personalised therapeutic intervention. My book *Social Work with Disabled People* (Oliver 1983) sought to switch social work intervention away from impaired individuals and target the disabling society. Moreover, the British Association of Social Workers adopted it in 1986 as the way ahead for building a relationship between disabled people and social workers. In practice, this failed to materialise and disability issues have remained a poor relation in equal opportunities social work training, and disabled people's needs have ranked very low down the agenda of most social service departments. There is little doubt that the hegemony of the individual model still endures within social work, as in other professions (Oliver and Sapey 1999).

The social model then, has had no real impact on professional practice, and social work has failed to meet disabled people's self-articulated needs. Twenty years ago, I predicted that if social work was not prepared to change in terms of its practice towards disabled people it would eventually disappear altogether (Oliver 1983). Given the proposed changes by the New Labour Government in respect of modernising social services, it seems likely that that forecast is about to come true. We can probably now announce the death of social work at least in relation to its involvement in the lives of disabled people.

A second illustration of the application of the social model was very evident in research on disability politics undertaken by Jane Campbell and myself. The social model of disability had become the 'big idea' of the Disability Movement. A central reason for its impact was that it provided a shorthand way of linking up the many diverse experiences among people with a whole range of different impairments (Campbell and Oliver 1996). Prior to the late 1970s and early 1980s disabled people's attempts at self-organisation had always floundered on the conflicts between the specific impairments and the different experiences of disablement that they generated.

The social model was a way of getting us all to think about the things we had in common, and the barriers that we all faced. Of course, some of those barriers were impairment specific; for example, blind people might have information barriers, people with mobility restrictions might have access barriers, deaf people communication barriers and so on. But nevertheless the social model became a way in which to link up all of those kinds of experiences and enabled the Movement to develop a collective consciousness that enabled it to expand at a rapid rate throughout the 1980s.

Yet, in the 1990s, independent living and disabled people's rights have emerged as key ideas to sit alongside the social model. This coupled with the increasing disputes about the meaning of the social model has led some activists, notably Vic Finkelstein, to claim that the Movement has lost its way and needs to return to its roots. What is clear is that as we move into the twenty first century, the social model of disability is no longer the glue that binds the Movement together in the way that it did in the 1980s. Instead, it has been relegated to the back burner, and its radical potential has been put on hold while the disability leadership has become involved in parliamentary campaigns to improve disabled people's rights and to enhance the services necessary to support 'independent living'.

The third social model project that I want to discuss, and the most recent one that I have been involved with, was carried out with Birmingham City Council (Oliver and Bailey 2002). While many local authorities (and indeed other agencies) have signed up to the social model, none has successfully implemented it as the means to providing services to disabled people. There are no blueprints to guide its implementation and there is not a substantial body of experience on how to do it. This is not necessarily a bad thing, however, because the social model is nothing more than a practical tool to facilitate the restructuring of services and hence can be adapted to specific local contexts, needs and circumstances.

In 1996, Birmingham City Council adopted the social model as a guide to service provision for disabled people. However, like many organisations that claim to endorse the social model, when it was reviewed five years later nothing much had happened. In 2001, I was commissioned to provide a report suggesting ways in which the City Council could take forward its renewed commitment to the social model. I worked with a disabled colleague Peter Bailey and conducted a wide range of visits, meetings and consultations.

We concluded that the influence of the social model of disability varied greatly: with evidence of its impact in some areas, but in many others, it was perceived as largely irrelevant, if not flawed. In discussions, it was possible to identify three broad approaches to service provision among providers, what we term humanitarian, compliance, and citizenship.

(1) The humanitarian approach

In this perspective, services are provided out of goodwill and the desire to help individuals and groups perceived as less fortunate. This means that a medical model is all-pervasive, with the professional experts in control of service provision, while the disabled person is regarded as 'the problem'. Hence, users are expected to be grateful for receiving these services. A characteristic outcome is that producers think they are doing a good job even though users, when asked, are often critical. Disabled people do not like being patronised or not valued as human beings. As a result, the relationship between service providers and disabled users is characterised by conflict, with a lack of trust, and dissatisfaction with existing services because they are unreliable and inadequate.

As an illustration, the Ring and Ride service has been set up as a way of compensating disabled people for the lack of accessible transport. Thus, the Council funds an alternative service, but control remains firmly with the provider. What is available falls far short of meeting disabled people's needs, and many complain that the service has been set up for second-class citizens, which they feel powerless to change. Another example of the humanitarian approach exists in the provision of residential care places. This is usually arranged out of a genuine desire to help disabled people but with staff again in effective control disabled users fear that the residential 'solution' will be long-term. With little autonomy in how they lead their lives, disabled inmates are at risk of becoming institutionalised, and invariably end up with a poorer quality of life than they have the right to expect.

(2) The compliance approach

From the 'compliance' perspective, government policy and legislation drive service provision. Obviously the Disability Discrimination Act (DDA) 1995 is of prime importance in respect of services to disabled people but earlier legislation such as the Chronically Sick and Disabled Act 1970, the NHS and Community Care Act 1990 and the Direct Payments Act 1996 are also relevant. Despite the stated objectives of such initiatives, producers have typically seen their role as doing the minimum amount required complying with the law or government regulations. Needless to say, service users often feel disgruntled because they do not think that services are being organised according to disabled people's support needs or rights. It is the producers who interpret the laws, rules and regulations, often adopting a check-list, or task-oriented approach, that simply satisfies basic standards and demonstrates little sense of commitment to wider service goals or to a partnership with disabled users. As a result, the compliance approach is characterised by conflict, a denial of entitlements and expectations, inadequate services and low levels of user satisfaction.

An illustration of the compliance approach is provided in the Home Care or Home Support service, where disabled people should receive personal support to maintain an appropriate degree of control, independence and autonomy for users in their own homes. In practice, staff provide a service to help disabled users go to bed at the end of the day, yet they have to fit in with when staff are available to provide such support. As a consequence, the service does not meet users' needs, but they dare not complain for fear of damaging important relationships. Conversely, the providers are so focussed on their problems that they find it hard to see users as equals, or align themselves with the aim of user empowerment.

(3) The citizenship approach

In this approach, disabled people are regarded as equal citizens with full rights and responsibilities. Three main dimensions are identified:

(a) Economic: disabled people are seen as contributing members of society as both workers and valued customers or users.

(b) Political: disabled people are recognised as empowered individuals, and voters, and a powerful, interest group.

(c) Moral: disabled people are seen as active citizens with all that implies in terms of rights and responsibilities.

Only when all three dimensions are met will the relationship between providers and users of services be a truly harmonious one.

An example of the citizen approach is evident in the direct payments system. It stresses the following points:

- the user makes direct payments to the person of their choice to provide personal support;
- the support worker identifies the disabled person as the person with the power to end the relationship and the income source;
- the support worker identifies with the overall aims of the relationship not specific tasks, like getting someone to bed;
- the user expects the support worker to turn up on time and therefore can take on work and other commitments;
- the user makes the decisions about how they want to be treated by support staff.

A citizenship approach contrasts with traditional practices such as giving discounts to disabled people for some council services, including leisure services like swimming. The basis on which a discount is applied is often lost in history and continued simply because disabled people are relatively poorer as a group.

However, this is the application of a stereotype unthinkable in a 'race' or gender context. An alternative rationale might be that full access to the service is not available to some disabled people. However, this sustains the compensatory culture that has for so long undermined disabled people's struggle for equality. Such compensation is not consistent with the social model or a citizenship approach. What disabled people are seeking is as end to social oppression and discrimination.

We concluded that services for disabled people in Birmingham are still largely provided under the humanitarian and compliance approaches. However, the Council is moving towards a citizenship approach in terms of services to its ethnic minorities and there is no reason why it cannot do the same in respect of disabled people.

Implementing a citizenship approach

Departmental services in Birmingham had no single driver, and the formal corporate commitment to the social model in 1995 was widely ignored. The Disability Discrimination Act (1995) was having some effect on services but the compliance was mostly fairly limited and partial. It was evident that beyond a generalised commitment to the humanitarian approach, few elected members showed any real commitment to disability issues.

We know that the main disability charities that drove the humanitarian-based disability agenda for so many years had limited aspirations for disabled people. These could be summed up as a need for good medical care, a comfortable place to live, and to be protected from those that might take advantage of them. More recently the welfare agenda has been driven by professionals, both within charities and the voluntary sector and within the state, and has moved towards a compliance approach. This contrasts starkly with disabled people's agenda that focuses on issues such as employment and social inclusion, independent living and civil rights.

Recently the Government has made it clear that its idea of citizenship encompasses rights and entitlements as well as duties and responsibilities. Thus, disabled people should be given fair and equal opportunities to compete in the labour market. Despite a number of important and innovative initiatives aimed at getting disabled people into the workforce, only 0.8% of the City Council workforce is disabled. In contrast, the Council has set a target of 20% for people from ethnic minority communities. We believe that adopting a firm target and formulating appropriate plans for the employment of disabled people will have a positive impact and help to overcome the poor response rate amongst disabled people when jobs are advertised. Finally, it is important that those disabled employees already in post are afforded opportunities for promotion and advancement equal to that of the rest of the population. This further presumes that disabled people secure an education and training that provides them with the necessary qualifications and skills.

Of course, other factors like race, gender, age and sexuality also have a considerable impact on how disability is experienced. We found little evidence to suggest that service providers or planners are aware of, or sensitive to, the need to recognise such diversity. Again, the only way to ensure that services do not institutionally discriminate against minority groups of disabled people is to consult widely about their needs. While Council departments assured us that they consulted regularly with users and in a meaningful way, disabled people often told a different story. Some felt that consultation was tokenistic and even where there were well-established user groups, only 'the chosen few' were consulted and this usually resulted in the department concerned implementing policies that it had already decided on.

The social model is incompatible with taking an impairment specific approach to disabled people. However, we did make an exception in the case of deaf people in Birmingham, many of whom do not see themselves as part of a disabled community but as a linguistic minority. This is in line with the way deaf people nationally see themselves and there is considerable pressure on Government to recognise British Sign Language as a language in its own right. That said, the social model of disability recognises that the communication problems faced by deaf people are not because they are unable to speak but because the rest of us do not speak their language.

Whether action will be taken on our report that will improve the lives of disabled people in Birmingham is unknown at this particular time, but it is the only basis on which it can be judged. There is little point in asking whether the social model was an adequate framework for revamping disability services in Birmingham or whether we accurately translated the principles of the social model as recommendations for action. The real test will be in five or ten or fifteen years when it should be possible to determine its impact in improving the lives of disabled people in Birmingham.

Conclusion

Throughout this chapter I have argued that the social model of disability is a practical tool, not a theory, an idea or a concept. Furthermore, I have suggested that too much time has been spent discussing it rather than attempting to use it to produce social and political change. If we imagine that throughout human history the carpenters and builders of the world had spent their time talking about whether the hammer was an adequate tool for the purpose of building houses, we would still be living in caves or roaming the plains. Finally,

I have tried to demonstrate that we do have a hammer in the Disability Movement and that, if properly used, the social model of disability could become the means of achieving justice and freedom for disabled people 'all over this land'.

Bibliography

Barnes, C., Oliver, M., and L. Barton (eds) 2002: *Disability Studies Today.* Cambridge: Polity Press.

Campbell, J. and Oliver, M. 1996: *Disability Politics: Understanding Our Past, Changing Our Future.* London: Routledge.

Corker, M. and French, S. (eds) 1998: *Disability Discourse.* Buckingham: Open University Press.

Department of Health and Social Security. 1988: *A Wider Vision. A Report on the Inspection of the management and Organisation of Services who are Blind or Partially Sighted.* London: DHSS.

Finkelstein, V. 1993: Disability: a social challenge or an administrative responsibility? In J. Swain, V. Finkelstein, S. French and M. Oliver (eds), *Disabling Barriers – Enabling Environments.* London: Sage, in association with the Open University.

Oliver, M. 1983: *Social Work with Disabled People.* Basingstoke: Macmillan.

Oliver, M. 1990: *The Politics of Disablement.* Basingstoke: Macmillan.

Oliver, M. 1996a: *Understanding Disability.* Basingstoke: Macmillan.

Oliver, M. 1996b: A Sociology of Disability or a Disablist Sociology? In Barton (ed.), *Disability and Society, emerging issues and insights.* Harrow: Longman.

Oliver, M. and Bailey, P. 2002: *Report on the Application of the Social Model of Disability to the Services provided by Birmingham City Council.* Birmingham: Birmingham City Council

Oliver, M. and Barnes, C. 1998: *From Exclusion to Inclusion: Social Policy and Disabled People.* London: Longman.

Oliver, M. and Sapey, B. 1999: *Social Work with Disabled People.* 2nd edn. Basingstoke: Macmillan.

Oliver, M., Zarb, G., Moore, M., Silver, J. and Salisbury, V. 1988: *Walking Into Darkness: the experience of spinal cord injury.* Basingstoke: Macmillan.

UPIAS. 1976: *Fundamental Principles of Disability.* London: Union of the Physically Impaired Against Segregation.

Zarb, G. and Oliver, M. 1993: *Ageing With A Disability: what do they expect after all these years.* London: University of Greenwich.

CHAPTER 3

Developing the Social Relational in the Social Model of Disability: a theoretical agenda

Carol Thomas

Introduction

The emergence of the social model of disability in 1970s Britain placed new theoretical tasks on the agenda. By reformulating disability as social, the disabled peoples' movement and its academic wing, disability studies, opened up a black box of complex questions about this additional societal form of oppression. Important advances have been made in tackling some of the questions posed, but a great deal remains to be unravelled. It might be said that the journey has only just begun.

This chapter attempts to assist those on this journey by reflecting upon the terrain travelled so far and by working towards an agenda for further theoretical work. No doubt other writers' theoretical agendas would take a contrasting shape, but the one presented here, though only a starting point, may be of assistance. Of course, an agenda for social policy research would look very different, prioritising the immediate and pressing policy-related needs of disabled people in every area of social life. But disability studies needs a theoretical as well as a policy-oriented agenda, to secure the foundations for empirically related work.

At the core of the observations set out here is a conviction that the *social relational* kernel of the early UPIAS formulation of a social understanding of disability (UPIAS 1976) holds the key to unlocking both the questions and answers concerning the nature of disability - its ontology. It defined disability,

> as the disadvantage or restriction of activity caused by a contemporary social organisation which takes no or little account of people who have [impairments] and thus excludes them from the mainstream of social activities (UPIAS 1976: 14)

This lifted disability free from its traditional association with matters bio-medical and placed it on a new social terrain. The 'social model' of disability was born. Disability now resided in a nexus of social relationships connecting those socially identified as impaired and those deemed non-impaired or 'normal', relationships that worked to exclude and disadvantage the former while promoting the relative inclusion and privileging of the latter. The new challenge was to: i) describe this nexus of social relationships, that is, to make clear the manifestations of disability in the social world (in organisations, systems, policies, practices, ideologies and discourses), and ii) to explain it, by employing theoretical paradigms that generate ways of understanding what gives form to and sustains these relationships.

How far have we come?

Success in making the manifestations of disability apparent, or exposing disablism, in the social world is evident in the emergence of a research literature on the 'social barriers' faced by disabled people in arenas critical to material well-being and civil status: education, employment, transport, housing, health and welfare services, recreation, media and cultural representation, legislation and so forth (see the journal *Disability and Society*; Barnes 1991; Zarb 1995). These barriers have been uncovered and documented, highlighting key features of the landscape of social exclusion. Less attention has been paid to barriers in more 'intimate' life domains in which disablist social relationships operate, for example, familial and sexual attachments as well as in areas of reproduction, parenting and childrearing. However, research excavating disablism in these areas has also begun (Shakespeare *et al.* 1996; Thomas 1997, 1998, 1999). This success in bringing to the light the manifestations of oppressive social relationships between those designated impaired and those who qualify as non-impaired has been powerfully significant for disabled people. Experiences of inequity and exclusion have been named as such, perhaps for the first time, and as a consequence there have been important, if limited, shifts towards greater equality for disabled people in social policy, legislation and cultural imagery (Oliver and Barnes 1998).

Less of a success story, in my view, is the theorisation of disability as a social relational phenomenon, since the 1970s. Headway has certainly been made in a number of contrasting directions, three of which are now briefly reviewed.

First, historically materialist minded writers and activists like Vik Finkelstein (1980) and Mike Oliver (1990) have sought to locate the cause of the exclusionary nexus of social relationships that structure disability in the core workings of the capitalist economy. In late eighteenth and early nineteenth century Britain, the imperatives of a system of generalised commodity production demanded that non-owners of the means of production sell their labour-power, to be harnessed in the service of a fast moving and exhausting industrial labour process. Those who could not sell their labour-power on these terms faced exclusion from the opportunity to independently obtain the means of subsistence – the decisive arbiter of social standing and merit in modern society (Oliver 1990; Gleeson 1999). The rest is history: workhouses, institutionalised care, enforced dependency, 'special' education, 'sheltered' workshops, community care, supported employment, and so forth.

Second, feminist writers in disability studies have shown us that the social relationships that constitute disability articulate with those that constitute gender relations. This means that disabled women and disabled men are understood to occupy different, if sometimes overlapping, social spaces, and the theoretical task of explaining their social positioning is made more complex (Thomas 1999). However, simple formulae like 'disabled women are doubly oppressed because patriarchy operates in conjunction with disablism' have long since been dismissed by disabled feminist writers (Morris 1996). The task of examining the interplay of disability and gender became more challenging as feminist perspectives on the nature of gender relations themselves became fragmented and attuned to multiple 'differences' from the 1980s onwards, reflecting the arrival of anti-foundationalist epistemologies in the social sciences and humanities in the academy (Skeggs 1995). This feminist attention to social diversity has had a widespread impact, including in disability studies where dimensions of difference among disabled people, in addition to gender, are recognised as requiring theorisation: differences associate with 'race' and ethnicity, sexuality, age, impairment type, class, and so forth. While the identification of the social barriers faced by disabled people occupying these social locations of 'difference' has begun, the theorisation of the social relational foundations that feed their particular experiences of social exclusion or inclusion is in its infancy.

Third, writers heavily influenced by postmodernist and poststructuralist thought have called into question traditional parameters in the theorisation of disability. From a deconstructionist perspective, to assert that disability resides in a nexus of social relationships connecting the impaired and the non-impaired is to buy into the Enlightenment fallacy that such social categories and dichotomies (impaired/non-impaired, normal/abnormal) are 'real' (Price and Shildrick 1998; Corker and French 1999; Corker and Shakespeare 2002). In this view, to suggest that there are pre-social biological differences marking off the 'impaired' from the 'normal' is to commit the error of essentialist thinking. This sits alongside other errors of an Enlightenment strain such as trying to find the 'root causes' of oppression and, in some cases, trying to bring about 'progressive' change. From these anti-essentialist perspectives, disability theory centres on the interrogation of cultural categories, discourses, language, and practices in which 'disability', 'impairment' and 'being normal' come into being through their social performance, and on the power that these categories have in constructing subjectivities and identities of self and other.

These, and related, theoretical innovations have certainly energised our thinking about disability, and have consolidated the legitimacy of the claim that disability is a social question. But we remain on the cusp of significant developments in the realm of disability theory. What follows is a discussion of four themes, or areas, in which the social theorising of disability is urgently required. A short chapter on such complex questions means that the approach taken here is necessarily broad brush, but, hopefully, this will not detract from the utility of drawing together some priority themes for a theoretical agenda. My own feminist materialist perspective informs the agenda that emerges, but I try to suggest how linkages can be made with other epistemologies. Put another way, the argument presented here is in favour of developing the social relational ideas inherent in the UPIAS (1976) definition of disability, and thus in the social model of disability it inspired.

Theme 1: Disability in a global economy: towards a contemporary political economy of disability

In attempting to look for the causal mechanisms of disability in the core workings of the capitalist system of production and exchange, writers such as Finkelstein (1980), Oliver (1990) and Gleeson (1999) have followed a well-trodden path in Marxist historical materialism. The profound economic, political and cultural changes brought about by the transition from feudalism to capitalism in the West, and particularly from mercantile to industrial capitalism, offered fertile ground for thinking about the creation of classes of people, including 'the feebleminded', 'cripples', 'in-valids', deemed redundant and dependent on the grounds of their incapacity to present themselves as wage labourers. The consolidation of capitalist social relations of industrial production in nineteenth century Britain was a transformative force that altered all remnants of pre-capitalist social relationships at the micro and macro scales. In the new nexus of social relationships, children and adults with physical or cognitive characteristics that made them sufficiently at variance from the socially defined norms of embodiment found themselves not just dependent but, often, logistically separated and outcast in the warehouses that were the sanatoria, the asylums and workhouses (Braddock and Parish 2001). This approach to explaining the root cause of the social exclusions that constitute disability has, in my view, tremendous potential. It is a *political economy of disability,* but one that requires considerable development. The historical analysis itself requires verification in terms of empirical evidence: what did people with impairments 'do' in pre-capitalist and pre-industrial communities, what were their social roles and status? What proportion of people with impairments were employed in early industrial society? What proportion of people with impairments were institutionalised once industrial capitalism had taken hold? What were the particular experiences of girls and women with impairments, and how did this differ from the male experience? What difference did other markers of ascribed social identity (age, 'race', sexuality and class) and of impairment type make to disabled people's social positioning? These questions hint at the large theoretical and empirical agenda that begins to take shape when one embarks on an historical account of the political economy of disability.

A more imposing challenge, and one of greater significance to disabled people today, is to develop a contemporary political economy of disability. We read so much about our supposedly 'post-industrial' society, about the dominance of the consumerist imperative in today's world, including 'MacDonaldisation' (Ritzer 1995), about the rapidity of global cultural change, about our risk society and the informational age (Castells 1996; Bauman 1998; Beck 1999; Giddens 1999), that we can easily forget that the vast majority of the world's population remains impoverished. The global masses in the developing world scrape a living through subsistence agriculture, wage labour and petty commodity production (often in combination) (Greider 1997; Canterbery 2000; Gilpin 2000; Thomas 2001; Pilger 2002). This not to be forgotten truth about the predicament of billions of people in the transnational capitalist economy seems to me to set the agenda for a new political economy of disability. That is, the examination of the position that people occupy in the social relations of production and consumption in the globally skewed system of generalised commodity production and agriculture that penetrates every corner of the globe continues to hold the key to unlocking the social relational dynamics that construct disability. This is the case whether disabled people are in or out of the labour market. Of course, in any societal or regional context, close attention has to be paid to the particularities of the economic, political, cultural and historical profiles of those social spaces. But the basic task remains the same: to locate the tap-roots of contemporary disablism in the imperatives of the system(s) of production and exchange that exist in any region, functioning as they do under the tutelage of the World Bank, the International Monetary Fund and the US Treasury. One valuable resource for this work is the small but growing number of studies and accounts of disability in non-Western and developing societies (Charlton 1998; Stone 1999; Ingstad 2001; Priestley 2001).

The process of economic polarisation is important here, both on a global and local scale. Almost everywhere, poverty has become more extensive and deeply entrenched as wealth and access to resources is further concentrated in the hands of a minority (Thomas 2001; Pilger 2002). In Britain, for example, the last three decades have seen a sharp increase in poverty and income inequality, associated with changes in the occupational structure (the shift from manufacturing to service industries) and in marriage patterns and family structures, and with regressive Conservative Government policies on taxation and welfare expenditure in the 1980s and early 1990s (Graham 2002). How have disabled people fared in all of this? What are the gains, if any, and what are the losses? Which disabled people have joined the ranks of workers in the service sector, on what terms, and which have fallen into deeper poverty? What difference has 'New Labour' in Government made? Answering such questions requires an examination of the complex nexus of socio-economic relationships in which people with impairments are now located (Sapey 2000; Roulstone 2002). The rapid spread in the last quarter of the twentieth century of electronic and information technology is, of course, a key feature of the present socio-economic landscape in the world's economically developed societies, and has much wider implications than the narrowly economic for the quality of life of people with impairments (Roulstone 1998; Sapey 2000; Abberley, 2002). Many new questions are posed for the theoretical, policy and empirical research agendas in developing these aspects of the contemporary political economy of disability.

The kinds of issues reviewed above are of little direct interest to those working with postmodernist and poststructuralist epistemologies. These writers focus on the current global *cultural* landscape - whether this is seen as conjured up by, as instigating, or as just corresponding with, global economic change. Those far more expert than I on the questions posed about disability by the deployment of these perspectives will have to comment on the theoretical agenda that emerges in these connections (Corker and Shakespeare 2002).

Theme 2: The psycho-emotional dimensions of disability

Attention now turns from the macro level to the qualities that social relationships display on a micro scale. I have argued elsewhere (Thomas 1999) that our appreciation of the exclusions that constitute disability should include those that work along psychological and emotional pathways. The oppression that disabled people experience operates on the 'inside' as well as on the 'outside': it is about being made to feel of lesser value, worthless, unattractive, or disgusting as well it is about 'outside' matters such as being turned down for a job because one is 'disabled', not being able to get one's wheelchair into a shop or onto a bus because of steps, or not being offered the chance of a mainstream education because one has 'special needs'.

What is of particular interest here are the impacts and effects of the social behaviours that are enacted between the 'impaired' and the 'non-impaired', for example in familial relationships, in interactions in communities, and in encounters with health, welfare and educational services. Who has the power, and how is it wielded? What are the decisions made, the words said, the meanings conveyed, in these networks of relationships? And what are the effects on disabled individuals' sense of self, self-esteem, and existential security? In my own research on disabled women's life experiences (Thomas 1998; 1999), including those associated with becoming pregnant and having a baby (Thomas 1997), the operation of disablism along psycho-emotional pathways is a crucial dimension of being disabled. Some writers have touched on these matters using the concept 'internalised oppression' (Reeve 2002). This form of disability shapes in profound ways what people can *be*, as well as affecting what they can *do* as a consequence.

This concern to bring the psycho-emotional dimensions of disability onto the agenda is a consequence of my feminist interest in the experiential, the personal or private, the emotional and the intimate - to make these legitimate social subjects worthy of sociological attention in disability studies, an interest shared with writers like Jenny Morris (1996). I have written at length about the mistaken tendency within disability studies to reject what is seen to be public and 'confessional' dabbling in such 'personal or private' matters because this, supposedly, diverts attention away from the 'really important' disabling social barriers 'out there'. Such diversion is also feared because it appears to open up opportunities for the traditional 'personal tragedy' perspective on disability to re-establish its hold (Thomas 1999, 2001). My argument is that by relegating psycho-emotional consequences of living in a disabling world to the realms of 'private life' or 'the personal restrictions of impairment' (Oliver 1996: 48), key dimensions of *disability* are ignored. The manifestations of disability are thus mistaken for the psychological angst of 'personal troubles'.

The psycho-emotional dimensions of disability have yet to be theorised; I have merely drawn attention to them. Where can we find the tools and methods for a full theoretical engagement with the social interactions and embodied processes that are involved in this form of disability? At the very least we need to draw on what is helpful in the sociology of the emotions, social psychology, psychoanalysis, and the phenomenology of lived experience (Hevey 1992; Shakespeare 1997; Williams and Bendelow 1998; Williams 2001; Corker and Shakespeare 2002). That is, what is helpful in these disciplines and literatures needs to be put to work in the interests of disability studies. We also need to draw on the insights of cultural theorists who look at the wider discourses that circulate in the media, arts, science and other aspects of the cultural superstructure, since these incubate the meanings and messages about impairment and 'unacceptable difference' that inform the attitudes and behaviours of us all. Postmodernist and poststructuralist perspectives can play an important role here for at least two reasons. First, they show how the discourses that bring into being the categories 'disability' and 'impairment' can be critically deconstructed. Second, they remind us of the need to look at the mutually constitutive nature of meanings in social interactions (Price and Shildrick 2002): in talking about you as a disabled person I not only perform the act of constructing who you are, I am also performing the construction of myself as 'normal'.

Theme 3: Theorising difference

Disability studies, like feminism, queer studies and other arenas of thought directed towards a greater understanding of the social position of relatively excluded groups of people marked off, or self-identified, as possessing particular attributes and characteristics, soon ran into the need to confront questions of difference. The unifying category 'disabled people', while of utility as a rallying cry in political struggle, soon came to be seen as problematic under closer analytical scrutiny. Questions were raised, for example: What are the qualifying criteria of being 'disabled', or 'non-disabled' – where are the boundaries drawn? What makes deaf people and people with spinal injuries 'the same' in their cultural labelling as 'disabled people'? Why do people in the Deaf community choose not to call themselves disabled (Corker 1998)? In what ways are some people more impaired and disabled than others? Why are old people with impairments seen as 'just old' rather than as disabled (Priestley 2003)? For deconstructionists, these questions are principally about the meanings embedded in the categories and labels themselves, and about how these are socially constituted; for the more materialistically inclined they are about the relationship between categories of meaning and underlying realities.

Such questions have occupied many writers in disability studies in the last twenty years, and many dimensions of difference have been engaged with, either singly or in their intersection: gender, sexuality, 'race' and ethnicity, age and impairment type (see, for example, the journal *Disability and Society;*

and note the absence of 'class' from this list, something yet to be addressed). The processes shaping identity and disavowal are also drawn to the foreground, as is the im/possibility of a disability identity politics (Shakespeare 1996, 1997; Wendell 1996).

The degree to which differences and identities are understood to be socially constructed depends on the epistemological perspectives that are being brought to bear. As noted earlier, poststructuralist writers eschew the 'essentialist fallacy' of the pre-social fixity of social categories like 'disabled', 'women', or 'black', pointing instead to their ever-fluid and always-newly-created-in-cultural-practice character. In contrast, materialist or realist commentators look for what embeds differences in 'real' but changing socio-biological substances, while fully acknowledging that these are overlaid by social constructed categories of meaning – meanings that are formed in particular temporal and spatial contexts, and thus possess fluidity.

The further development of this area of theorising and research is essential if the potential of the social relational understanding of disability in the UPIAS (1976) formulation is to be unleashed. To suggest, as that formulation does, that disability resides in a nexus of social relationships connecting those socially identified as impaired and those deemed non-impaired or 'normal', is to invite questions about difference and sameness on all sides, such as those rehearsed above. It is also to invite questions about the intersection of dimensions of social oppression, for example: disability, age and gender. In my view, however, the postmodernist and poststructuralist pursuit of these matters, while insightful and of value in many ways, holds the dangers of falling into an all-consuming spiral of linguistic and discursive deconstruction. Such a spiral has little to offer those who want to obtain a theoretical grounding to support empirically and policy-oriented research and/or a disability praxis that holds out the possibility of making *real differences* in the lives of disabled people. But if that is a danger along a deconstructionist pathway, a danger for those informed by other theoretical perspectives is the down-playing of the significance of difference, both among disabled people and between disabled and non-disabled people (Oliver 1996; Oliver and Barnes 1998). Many challenges lie ahead for disability studies in adequately theorising the complex threads of social commonality and divergence (Thomas 1999).

Fresh approaches to thinking through difference are much to be welcomed – for example, Mark Priestley's engagement with disability over the life course (Priestley 1995, 2001, 2003). His operationalisation of a perspective that interrogates disability across the generations, paying attention to the dynamics of both social structure and agency over the life course, is a powerful way of engaging with difference, one that develops important conceptual insights for the theorisation of disability. More work of that ilk is required in disability studies.

Theme 4: Impairment and impairment effects

In my view, the argument that disability studies requires a theoretical engagement with impairment has been heard and widely accepted. One piece of evidence for this is the inclusion of a chapter on disability and the body, by Bill Hughes, in Barnes et al.'s recent edited collection, *Disability Studies Today* (2002). This development deserves much encouragement, not simply because it helps us to understand impairment *per se* in social terms, but because, in dialectical fashion, it can assist in deepening our understanding of disability.

To unpack that claim, let us return once again to the UPIAS formulation: disability is identified as:

> the disadvantage or restriction of activity caused by a contemporary social organisation which takes no or little account of people who have physical impairments and thus excludes them from participation in the mainstream of social activities (UPIAS 1976: 14).

Social modellist thinkers soon extended this definition to cover all impairments: physical, intellectual and sensory and, more recently, to mental illness (Barnes 1991; Barnes et al. 2002). The point here is that in this social relational proposition, disability and impairment are inextricably linked and interactive: *disability is social exclusion on the grounds of impairment.* Impairment does not cause disability, certainly not, but it is the raw material upon which disability works. It is the embodied socio-biological substance – socially marked as unacceptable bodily deviation – that mediates the social relationships in question. The particular character of the impairment plays a critical role in shaping the forms and degrees of disablism encountered (of course, impairments vary greatly in nature: physical, sensory, intellectual, cognitive, behavioural; visible or invisible; singular or multiple; stable or degenerative, and so forth). It follows that the theorisation of disability requires the theorisation of impairment, but in what directions?

There are many theoretical routes that can be taken. A poststructuralist deconstruction of the concept 'impairment' and of the 'impairment/disability' dichotomy has exercised some minds (Corker and French 1999; Corker and Shakespeare 2002). In contrast, materialistically oriented writers could usefully develop a political economy of impairment by building, for example, on the early work of Paul Abberley (1987). He considered the socio-economic origins of impairment in industrial capitalist societies, enabling us to appreciate that much impairment is created through industrial processes and accidents, through pollution, through medical advance as well as blunder, and through wars and famines. In my view this is an important line of analysis which could gain much by drawing on the voluminous published research undertaken by social epidemiologists, medical sociologists and others on the social aetiology of health inequalities (Graham 2001, 2002). Making links, on our own terms, between the disability studies agenda and health inequality scholarship is an important move that is yet to be made. This would throw important light on the generation and distribution of impairment, and hence of disability, and would underline the connection between socio-economic disadvantage, illness, impairment, and disability, over the life course. This is only one of many challenges facing those who want to develop a materialist ontology of impairment.

A theme that has attracted greater attention in disability studies is that of the rapid shifts in knowledge in the genetic and biological sciences, with its therapeutic and eugenic implications for medical practice (Shakespeare 1999; Shakespeare and Kerr 2002). Given the enormous significance of this 'brave new world' for disabled people, getting to grips with such developments must, surely, occupy a high ranking position in the theoretical agenda of those interested in both impairment and disability. This requires at least some engagement with the substance of the genetic, biological and medical sciences, as well as with the ideas of those who critique these sciences – as in the literature emanating from the sociology of science and technology (Varcoe et al. 1990; Law 1991; Franklin 1997). This is a daunting but necessary task. One problem, in my view, is that it is poststructuralist theoretical perspectives that occupy a hegemonic position in the contemporary critique of science. Materialist and realist approaches are sorely needed in this field.

I would suggest that theorising the socio-biological dynamics associated with different types of impairment should occupy a place on the disability studies agenda, something that writers in the learning difficulties field have drawn particular attention to (Goodley 2001). As indicated above, this assists in understanding the forms and degrees of disablism in operation in our society. In my own work (Thomas 1999), one feature of trying to think through impairment differences and consequences has involved the introduction of the concept 'impairment effects'. It seemed to me that such a concept was required to acknowledge that impairments do have direct and restricting impacts on people's social lives – 'restricting' as judged against socially defined age-norms. Such restrictions are, of course, to be distinguished from the restrictions, exclusions and disadvantages that people with impairments experience *as a result of disability*. In any one life, impairment effects and disability interlock in unique and complex ways. However difficult it may be to separate impairment effects and disability effects in someone's life, it is necessary to make such an analytical distinction within disability studies, but taking care not to mistake the former for the latter.

The concept 'impairment effects' requires considerable theoretical development. I have a particular interest in taking this into the domain of 'chronic illness and disability', an area currently under-conceptualised and researched in disability studies. This would include the study of cancer and disability, something barely touched upon to date. Once again, other literatures can be helpful here, not least the work of medical sociologists (Barnes and Mercer 1996; Thomas 1999, 2002; Williams 2001). In whatever ways it is taken forward, I suggest that the concept 'impairment effects' does have a place on the theoretical agenda.

Conclusion: developing the social-relational in the social model of disability

This chapter took as its starting point the social relational kernel in the proposition that disability is social exclusion on the grounds of impairment. This means that disability involves a nexus of social relationships between those designated impaired and those designated non-impaired or normal, relationships that work to exclude and disadvantage the former while promoting the relative inclusion and privileging of the latter. The theoretical challenge is to understand what gives form to and sustains these relationships, however and wherever they are manifest – in social structures, organisational practices, systems, policies, ideologies, discourses and inter-personal relationships.

Four themes have been identified to head-up a theoretical agenda in disability studies: the political economy of disability; the psycho-emotional dimensions of disability; theorising difference; and, theorising impairment and impairment effects. It has been shown that each theme contains many sub-themes and potential lines of analysis, but of course this brief chapter has only been able to hint at the richness of the theoretical questions that each theme embodies. Other writers would no doubt construct theoretical agendas of a different cast, their priorities being informed by perspectives other than the feminist materialist world-view that has shaped the one set out here. That is to be welcomed rather than lamented: disability studies is enriched by the dynamic exchange of ideas from a broad range of social scientific perspectives.

The attempt to craft a theoretical agenda in this chapter has not been done in the spirit of mere academic whimsy. On the contrary, I would suggest that disability studies has reached a point, certainly in the UK, where there is a pressing need to think strategically about the theoretical tasks that lie ahead – with the scope being global rather than local or regional. While it is perhaps too strong to suggest that this young discipline has lost some of its early vitality and radical edge, the time has come, in my view, for a re-energised engagement with the formulation of both theoretical and policy-related agendas. In saying this, it is taken as a given that the close liaison between disability studies and the disabled people's movement will continue to act as the necessary power-house and testing ground for action and ideas. In the final analysis, theoretical agendas and contributions are only of value if they can inform a rights-oriented disability praxis.

Bibliography

Abberley, P. 1987: The concept of oppression and the development of a social theory of disability, *Disability, Handicap and Society,* 2, 5-20.

Abberley, P. 2002: Work, Disability, Disabled People and European Social Theory. In C. Barnes, M. Oliver and L. Barton (eds), *Disability Studies Today.* Cambridge: Polity Press.

Barnes, C. 1991: *Disabled People in Britain and Discrimination.* London: Hurst & Co.

Barnes, C. and Mercer, G. (eds) 1996: *Exploring the Divide: Illness and Disability.* Leeds: The Disability Press.

Barnes, C., Oliver, M., and L. Barton (eds) 2002: *Disability Studies Today.* Cambridge: Polity Press.

Bauman, Z. 1998: *Globalization: The Human Consequences.* Cambridge: Polity Press.

Beck, U. 1999: *World Risk Society.* Cambridge: Polity Press.

Braddock, D.L. and Parish, S. L. 2001: An Institutional History of Disability. In G. Albrecht, K. Seelman and M. Bury (eds), *Handbook of Disability Studies.* London: Sage.

Canterbery, R.E. 2000: *Wall Street Capitalism: the theory of the bondholding class.* Singapore: World Scientific.

Castells, M. 1996: *The Rise of the Network Society.* Oxford: Blackwell Publishers.

Charlton, J.I. 1998: *Nothing about Us without US: Disability, Oppression and Empowerment.* Berkeley: University of California Press.

Corker, M. 1998: *Deaf and Disabled, or Deafness Disabled?* Buckingham: Open University Press.

Corker, M. and French, S. (eds) 1999: *Disability Discourse.* Buckingham: Open University Press.

Corker, M. and Shakespeare, T. (eds) 2002: *Disability/Postmodernity: Embodying Disability Theory.* London: Continuum.

Disability and Society. *Journal published by Carfax.*

Finkelstein, V. 1980: *Attitudes and Disabled People: Issues for Discussion.* New York: World Rehabilitation Fund.

Franklin, S. 1997: *Embodied Progress: a cultural account of assisted conception.* London: Routledge.

Giddens, A. 1999: *Runaway World: How Globalization is Shaping our Lives.* London: Profile Books.

Gilpin, R. 2000: *The challenge of global capitalism: the world economy in the 21st century.* Princeton, N.J.: Princeton University Press.

Gleeson, B.J. 1999: *Geographies of Disability.* London: Routledge

Goodley, D. 2001: 'Learning Difficulties', the Social Model of Disability and Impairment: challenging epistemologies. *Disability and Society,* 16 (2), 207-232.

Graham, H. (ed.) 2001: *Understanding health inequalities.* Buckingham: Open University Press.

Graham, H. 2002: Building an inter-disciplinary science of health inequalities: the example of lifecourse research. *Social Science and Medicine,* 55, 2005-2016.

Greider, W. 1997: *One world, ready or not: the manic logic of global capitalism.* Harmondsworth: Penguin.

Hevey, D. 1992: *The Creatures Time Forget.* London: Routledge.

Ingstad, B. 2001: Disability in the Developing World. In G. Albrecht, K. Seelman and M. Bury (eds), *Handbook of Disability Studies.* London: Sage.

Law, J. 1991: *A Sociology of Monsters: essays on power, technology and domination.* London: Routledge.

Morris, J. (ed) 1996: *Encounters With Strangers: Feminism and Disability.* London: The Women's Press.

Oliver, M. 1990: *The Politics of Disablement.* Basingstoke: Macmillan.

Oliver, M. 1996: *Understanding Disability.* Basingstoke: Macmillan.

Oliver, M. and Barnes, C. 1998: *From Exclusion to Inclusion: Social Policy and Disabled People.* London: Longman.

Pilger, J. 2002: *The New Rulers of the World.* London: Verso.

Price, J. and Shildrick, M. 1998: Uncertain Thoughts on the Disabled Body. In M. Shildrick and J. Price (eds), *Vital Signs: Feminist Reconfigurations of the Biological Body.* Edinburgh: Edinburgh University Press.

Price, J. and Shildrick, M. 2002: Bodies Together: Touch, Ethics and Disability. In M. Corker and T. Shakespeare (eds), *Disability/Postmodernity: Embodying Disability Theory.* London: Continuum.

Priestley, M. 1995: Commonality and difference in the movement, *Disability and Society,* 10 (2), 157-169.

Priestley, M (ed.) 2001: *Disability and the Life Course: Global Perspectives.* Cambridge: Cambridge University Press.

Priestley, M. 2003: *Disability: A Life Course Approach.* Cambridge: Polity Press.

Reeve, D. 2002: Negotiating Psycho-emotional Dimensions of Disability and their Influence on Identity Constructions. *Disability and Society,* 17 (5), 493–508.

Ritzer, G. 1995: *The McDonaldization Thesis: Explorations and Extensions.* London: Sage.

Roulstone, A. 1998: *Enabling Technology: disabled people, work and new technology.* Buckingham: Open University Press.

Roulstone, A. 2002: Disabling Pasts, Enabling Futures? How Does the Changing Nature of Capitalism Impact on the Disabled Worker and Jobseeker? *Disability and Society,* 17 (6), 627–42.

Sapey, B. 2000: Disablement in the Informational Age. *Disability and Society,* 15 (4), 619–636.

Shakespeare, T. 1996: Disability, Identity, Difference. In C. Barnes and G. Mercer (eds), *Exploring the Divide: Illness and Disability.* Leeds: The Disability Press.

Shakespeare, T. 1997: Cultural Representation of Disabled People: dustbins of disavowal? In L. Barton and M. Oliver (eds), *Disability Studies: Past, Present and Future.* Leeds: The Disability Press.

Shakespeare, T. 1999: Losing the Plot? Medical and activist discourses of contemporary genetics and disability. *Sociology of Health and Illness,* 21 (5), 699–684.

Shakespeare, T. and Kerr, A. 2002: Genetic Politics. London: New Clarion Press.

Shakespeare, T., Gillespie-Sells, K., and Davies, D. 1996: *The Sexual Politics of Disability: Untold Desires.* London: Cassell.

Skeggs, B. (ed.) 1995: Feminist Cultural Theory: Process of Production. Manchester: Manchester University Press.

Stone, E. (ed.) 1999: *Disability and development: learning from action and research on disability in the majority world.* Leeds: The Disability Press.

Thomas, C. 1997: The baby and the bathwater: disabled women and motherhood in social context. *Sociology of Health and Illness,* 19 (5), 622–43.

Thomas, C. 1998: Parents and family: disabled women's stories about their childhood experiences. In C. Robinson and K. Stalker (eds), *Growing Up With Disability.* London: Jessica Kingsley.

Thomas, C. 1999: *Female Forms: experiencing and understanding disability.* Buckingham: Open University Press.

Thomas, Carol. 2001: Feminism and Disability: The Theoretical and Political Significance of the Personal and the Experiential. In L. Barton (ed.), *Disability, Politics and the Struggle for Change.* London: David Fulton Publications.

Thomas, C. 2002: Disability Theory: Key Ideas, Issues and Thinkers. In C. Barnes, M. Oliver and L. Barton (eds), *Disability Studies Today.* Cambridge: Polity Press.

Thomas, Caroline. 2001: *Global governance, development and human security: the challenge of poverty and inequality.* London: Pluto Press.

UPIAS 1976: *Fundamental Principles of Disability.* London: Union of the Physically Impaired Against Segregation.

Varcoe, I., McNeil, M. and Yearley, S. (eds) 1990: *Deciphering science and technology: the social relations of expertise.* London: Macmillan.

Wendell, S. 1996: *The Rejected Body. Feminist Philosophical Reflections on Disability.* London: Routledge.

Williams, G. 2001: Theorizing Disability. In G. Albrecht, K. Seelman and M. Bury (eds), *Handbook of Disability Studies.* London: Sage.

Williams, S. and Bendelow, G. 1998: *The Lived Body: Sociological Themes, Embodied Issues.* London: Routledge.

Williams, S. 2001: *Emotion and Social Theory.* London: Sage.

Zarb, G. (ed.) 1995: *Removing Disabling Barriers.* London: Policy Studies Institute.

CHAPTER 4

In Search of a Social Model of Disability: Marxism, normality and culture

Bill Armer

Introduction

As my title suggests I do not presume to present a fully-fledged scholarly discourse on social modelling, accompanied by a finished theory of the underlying processes that lead to disability. Primarily I seek here to provoke discussion rather than to prescribe specific societal therapy: ultimately I believe that the formulation of a comprehensive social theory of disability should by its nature be a collaborative and incremental task.

My involvement here arises from an interest in the motivational forces that underlie eugenics (which I use in its widest sense, to include present-day work on human genetics with its avowed aim, at least initially, of 'improving' humanity – to coin a phrase, '*eu*genetics'). For example, in the words of Sinsheimer:

the new eugenics would permit in principle the conversion of all
of the unfit to the highest genetic level (cited in Kevles 1992: 18).

In order to do any sort of justice to the topic, I have found myself drawn into a consideration of which theoretical approach may best explain this most fundamental form of disability discrimination. In the course of this musing I have come to the opinion that Marxist-inspired ideas of the 'oppression' and 'exploitation' of disabled people do not necessarily explain tendencies to use genetic knowledge to *eliminate* certain categories of impairment and, with them, people as yet unborn.

Materialist approaches

I take as my reference point here Finkelstein's paper *The Social Model Of Disability Repossessed* (2001), and in particular what I interpret as his stance that the original social model, that of Oliver (1983a) built upon the thinking of the Union of the Physically Impaired Against Segregation (UPIAS 1976), should stand unrevised in tribute to its authors and their particular 'insight' into the topic of disability. Finkelstein does not object to 'people devising and promoting new social models in their own name' (Finkelstein 2001: 3), but strongly resists what he sees as a revisionist tendency within disability studies. Ultimately he nails his colours firmly to the Marxist mast:

> disabled people must find ways of engaging in the class struggle
> where the historical direction of society is fought, won or lost
> (Finkelstein 2001: 5).

Finkelstein depicts a model as being the middle stage of a three-step process that begins with the 'interpretation' of a phenomenon and ends in the formulation of a theory to 'explain' the processes in train. For him,

> [t]he disability movement still awaits an explanation of the
> social laws that make…people with impairments into disabled
> people (Finkelstein 2001: 3).

However, his position is unclear when he calls for a social theory, or explanation of disability formation: is he referring specifically to an explanation of the insight provided by the UPIAS-inspired social model, or does he seek a broader treatment? If the former, does he not himself lay the theoretical foundations with his claim that,

> Our society is built on a competitive market foundation and
> it is this social system which disables us (Finkelstein 2001: 4).

If the latter, the tone of the paper indicates that Finkelstein will reject any attempt to apply non-Marxist theory to the existing UPIAS-inspired model. This would seem to render his call for a social theory of disability rhetorical.

It is doubtful that disability studies is as bereft of theoretical approaches as Finkelstein appears to suggest. After all, as Abberley has it:

> The first thing you need to do when talking about disability
> today is to clarify your terms, and this immediately gets you
> into the realm of theory… (Abberley 1999: 1).

Tregaskis (2002) and Priestley (1998) both argue that there are a number of perspectives which have been applied to social modelling by researchers and commentators from within disability studies, several of which are ostensibly non-materialist. These latter include psychoanalytic and cultural approaches (Tregaskis 2002), whilst Priestley (1998) contrasts materialism with idealism.

My aim is to reply to the Marxist-materialism of Finkelstein (2001) in a similar vein. This is not to deny 'culture' as a potential source of disablement, nor is it to eschew the effects of the human psyche in moderating social intercourse. Indeed, as I proceed, I will suggest that the concept of 'normality', which some may wish to appropriate for culture (Hughes 2002: 572), is itself a product of materialist forces. I will further suggest that the material world may affect the inner psychological lives of members of modern society.

Finkelstein is very clear about the UPIAS social interpretation of disability: it is 'a materialist approach' (2001: 4) which, with its talk of oppression, may appear to owe much to Marx and has been from the outset an 'angry' approach to disability - it emphasises the perceived inequity, indeed iniquity, of societal constructions of disability. The social model, or rather the UPIAS-derived one, is effectively a political manifesto and as such is consciously contentious and pugnacious. This approach speaks, then, of a state of conflict between a minority group of disabled people and a host society that is at best uncaring, at worst deliberately oppressive:

> Disability is something imposed on top of our impairments, by the way we are unnecessarily isolated and excluded from full participation in society. Disabled people are therefore an oppressed group in society (UPIAS 1976: 3-4).

Finkelstein, throughout his many writings on disability, has consistently employed Marxist analysis. Likewise Oliver, credited by Finkelstein as the author of 'the' social model of disability, is specific about his personal inspiration: 'My own theorizing on disability is located in Marxist political economy (Oliver 1994: 1). An equally clear acknowledgement of a debt to Marx is found in the work of Abberley who informs us that: 'Oppression is complementary to exploitation, extending Marxist analysis' (Abberley 1987: 8). He then discusses the role of capitalism in producing certain forms of impairment, and in acting upon these and other impairments to produce disability. Perhaps ironically, given his espousal of a mid-nineteenth century politico-economic doctrine, he ends with a call to explain disability by the use of 'the tools of today's social science, rather than those of the day before yesterday' (Abberley 1987: 18).

There is an inherent theoretical problem, in the social model context, with Marxist analysis that is immediately apparent. As Abberley points out, the pre-eminence accorded to work, either as an economic necessity of capitalism or as some metaphysical expression of human-ness in a Marxian Utopia, 'implies that impaired people are still deprived, by biology if not by society' (Abberley 1999: 9). Thus Abberley seems to acknowledge that Marxist theory, when taken to its Marxian conclusion, runs contrary to the fundamental precept of a social model: biology has the ultimate power to disable. The Marxian Utopia is fundamentally an able-bodied construction. This contradiction, of itself, is sufficient to raise serious questions about the applicability of Marxist analysis to the social modelling of disability.

Another important tenet of Marxist-inspired disability theory, as Oliver, Finkelstein and Abberley each make clear, is that certain specified groups within capitalist society are oppressed by a dominant elite, so that the,

> disadvantages [*experienced by disabled people*] are dialectically related to an ideology or group of ideologies which justify and perpetuate this situation. ... [*This idea*] involves the identification of some beneficiary of this state of affairs (Abberley 1987: 7).

Abberley at least is specific: the development of a Marxist analysis of disablement demands both the demonstration of active oppression and the identification of a beneficiary of such oppression - no oppression or no beneficiary, no Marxist explanation. It is not sufficient to merely adduce evidence that disabled people are badly situated in economic society. In short, this is a conspiracy theory: a detective story with identifiable culprit(s) and victim(s) and a plot centred on greed. Whilst this may well make for a gripping yarn we must, as disabled academics, ask ourselves just how convincing this account is as a faithful reflection of the real world which we inhabit.

There are others within disability studies who are uncomfortable with Marxist analysis, for example Shakespeare, who bluntly states that, 'mono-linear explanations, reducing everything to economic factors, are misguided' (Shakespeare 1994: 225). His point is that disability is a complex issue: one that is not readily addressed by reductionist analysis. This does not necessarily mean that he ignores material causes and effects, simply that he does not place economic activity at the forefront of his analysis. However, Shakespeare tends to champion cultural factors as a major part of his explanation of disability, whilst here I wish to concentrate upon more overtly materialist views.

In particular the Marxist construction of 'oppression' with its call to identify the winners and losers, or culprits and victims, may appear to be a blunt instrument rather than a surgeon's scalpel when used to delve beneath the surface layers of contemporary society in a search for the causative factors underlying disability. Speaking immediately of disability, but within a broader social policy context, the writers of a recent text conclude that:

> as a basis for developing a theory about differentiation and power, oppression is vague, too universal in its incidence within human interactions, and yet not comprehensive enough.... The concept of oppression cannot easily embrace or elucidate the variety of circumstances and distributional issues that need to be considered (Harrison with Davis 2001: 59).

Important additional concepts refer to 'structured selectivity' within contemporary society leading to the 'differential incorporation' of ideas and people within society. With an emphasis on the differential distribution

of goods and life chances within a structured social world-view, Harrison
with Davis (2001) operate within a materialist paradigm, but one that
deviates markedly from most Marxist-inspired writings on disability.

The underlying theme of the latter is that people with impairments are
considered expensive and inefficient workers and thus discarded from the
workforce (Ryan and Thomas 1980; Oliver 1989: 10; Finkelstein 1993: 12;
Davis 1997; Gleeson 1999: 102), and thence from a position of full socio-
economic inclusion, as a direct result of market forces. This to me is a rather
outmoded argument that is no longer sustainable. It ignores the pace of
technological innovation, and particularly the effects of IT/ICT. Given the
reported change in contemporary western society from an economy based
on manufacturing to one based on the supply of information (Hall *et al* 1992
ch4), there is no inherent economic, or 'market', bias against the employment
of people with impairments *per se*.

It is potentially more cost-efficient to provide a home PC and telephone
line than expensive inner-city office space (Handy 1990: 84); meanwhile,
the use of IT can help negate many alleged effects of physical or sensory impairment
in relation to employment. On a lower level of technology, the increasing
development of power tools and aids has progressively reduced the physical
demands of much economic activity. In many (but not all) cases people with
various impairments are able to compete in the labour market on equal terms:
that they are often not allowed to do so suggests to me that factors other
than market economics are in play. This point is acknowledged by UPIAS:

> in the last fifty years or so developments in modern technology
> have made it increasingly possible to employ even the most severely
> physically impaired people and to integrate us into the mainstream
> of social and economic activity (1976: 15).

The suggestion that market economic factors alone cannot fully explain
the socio-economic exclusion of people with impairment is not merely an
invention of mine; nor is it simply a product of the disability studies 'liberal
right' of Finkelstein (2001: 4). The argument for employing disabled people
at standard rates of pay has already been made, on solid economic grounds,
by that arch-capitalist Henry Ford:

> Charity becomes unnecessary as those who seem to be unable
> to earn livings are taken out of the non-productive class and put
> into the productive.... there are places which can be filled by
> the maimed, the halt, and the blind. Scientific industry need not
> be a monster devouring all who come near it (Ford 1923: 208).

Ford argues that it is to the advantage of capitalist society (by reducing
the call for 'charity' or, in a welfare state setting, 'benefits') to fully incorporate

people with impairments into the workforce *via* the open labour market. This account runs directly counter to Marxist-inspired theories current within disability studies that such people are excluded from the world of work precisely to bring economic advantage to capitalist society, by reducing employment costs or increasing worker efficiency. This is not to deny that such an argument may have had merit in the early days of industrialization, but it is to suggest that, as early as 1914, the nature of technology had already changed to the extent that very many people with impairments were not *necessarily* debarred, on purely economic grounds, from full participation in the labour market and hence in the wider social world (Ford 1923: 106). That they were, and continue to be, discriminated against in socio-economic terms I accept – it is the explanatory theory I question.

The UPIAS interpretation of disability concentrates on the special case of 'physically impaired people' (1976: 3), at a specific time, the 1960s and 1970s. Given that the practice of the day was often to confine these people within a closed environment subject to petty and restrictive rules (Hunt 1966), the appeal of ideas of their oppression is clear. However,

> it is clear that our social organisation does not discriminate equally against all physical impairments and hence there arises the appearance of degrees of exclusion…. Nevertheless, it is the same society which disables people whatever their type, or degree of physical impairment, and therefore there is a single cause within the organisation of society that is responsible for the creation of the disability of physically impaired people (UPIAS 1976: 14, 15).

What is not so clear is how a theory of oppression coupled with market exclusion, in the sense employed by Abberley (1987), is readily adapted to explain the differential experiences of people with non-locomotive impairment, for example facial disfigurement. Marxism may offer some form of market explanation in special instances of discrimination: of the 'would you employ this person to sell cosmetics?' line of argument. At least as promulgated within disability studies, Marxism does not explain why facial disfigurement should be considered socially repulsive, and hence socio-economically disadvantageous, in the first place.

What then of people with the label 'learning difficulties'? They are often able to play a full part in the world of work – there are still many jobs which, although they may require physical strength and mobility, are well within their capacity. Yet there is much evidence that where such impairment is readily apparent, either from behaviour or physical appearance, these people are subject to discrimination. Marxism cannot fully explain this, for there is no clear evidence of a benefit accruing to capitalist society. There are no doubt many other examples. My point is that whilst Marxist-inspired theory may appear to explain certain *special* cases of disablement, it fails to explain the *general* case.

The discourse of 'normality'

One potential general explanation here is the idea of 'normal', for it may be argued that people subject to, for example, physical or sensory impairment, facial disfigurement, learning difficulties or stature which deviates markedly from the statistical mean are, in some way, not 'normal'. I do not intend to analyse with, or appeal to, 'normalization theory', which relies on a specialist usage of the concept; rather I use the word 'normal' in the sense in which it is understood in everyday language.

Language may serve to obscure rather than enlighten, and Oliver is certainly aware of potential problems arising from confusion between the word 'normal' and the specific concept of 'normalization'. Nonetheless, he remains adamant that,

> the social structures of late capitalist societies cannot be discussed
> in a discourse of normality/abnormality (Oliver 1994: unpaged).

This statement appears to represent a clear divorce between Marxist political economy and any idea of the 'normal'.

Whilst (disability studies) Marxism, then, eschews 'normality' as an aid to analysis, the concept of 'the normal' itself has a central place in contemporary society. It is, so to speak, normal to talk of normality, and this hegemony, to use a term of Gramsci's, may be seen as a product of industrial society, despite Oliver's comments. The idea of normality, I suggest, has an important place in a (non-Marxist) materialist analysis of disability.

For Davis (1997: 9-11) the words 'norm', 'normal', and 'normalcy' did not enter the English language until around 1840, at least in their current meaning as something approximating to 'average' or 'common'. Although Davis notes that it had its roots not in industrial processes but in French medicine (in its inception, Davis informs us, 'normality' was an attempt to define a physiologically average person), there are good grounds to suppose that the concept of normality was readily assimilated within the ethos of industrialisation. For Finkelstein the move to factory work, an integral part of modern society,

> raised the importance of 'normality' ... Being normal... became
> a dominant criterion for employment in industrial societies
> (Finkelstein 1993: 12).

Hughes goes further, relating modernity, which he describes as a 'normalising culture', directly to the adoption of:

> narrow norms of human authenticity [*which*] have played havoc with the lives of those who have been marked with 'incidental variances' from the ideal (Hughes 2002: 572).

Thus, modernity creates disability *via* the medium of normality, a medium which modernity has at the least appropriated for itself, if not directly manufactured. Once the concept of 'normality' is established, 'abnormality' is a logical progression. Although in its origins abnormality simply implies a state different from the norm, which could be either above or below the datum, the generally understood meaning is one of inferiority or subnormality.

Davis (1997) makes the point that, before the rise of the concept of normal, the state towards which people might have aspired was an ideal, and hence unattainable. That being the case, although there was merit in approaching the ideal, there was little shame in failing to match it. In contrast, to fail to match the new industrial norm led to a categorisation as inferior to most other people - an important change in thinking and, as a product of modernity, one with distinct materialist antecedents.

There is, I suggest, a further outcome of the application of ideas of normal within modern society: by providing a means of differentiating between people other than by the cultural distinctions between one tribe or caste and another, normal arguably facilitated the rise of 'heterophobia' (Bauman 1989), (relating to 'different'), as a divisive social process operating alongside an earlier notion of *xenophobia* (relating to 'alien').

It is relatively easy to trace the development of inter-group divisions, of the type referred to here as xenophobic, and such divisions appear firmly based on material considerations. The clearest examples of such an us/them dichotomy are to be found in inter-group conflict. There is archaeological evidence of the existence of human warfare between small hunter/gatherer groups at least 50,000 years ago, but it may be that technological advances were the key to the successful domination and subsequent enslavement of one group by another (Lenski et al 1991). History seems to suggest that, whatever the 'diplomatic' reasons advanced, a prime cause of warfare is the search for material advantage, be it in terms of slaves, treasure, *'Lebensraum'* or oil. Be that as it may, the coming of warfare as a human activity marks the clear establishment of a xenophobic division between 'us' and 'them'. If one is to have enemies one must be able to identify them.

Another form of inter-group division that leads to xenophobic ideas is found in religious observances. Perhaps the most famous is the Old Testament appointment of the Tribes of Israel as 'God's Chosen'. However, this quickly gave rise to intra-group, heterophobic, divisions based upon non-compliance with religious rites seen as having potentially dangerous material effects upon the larger society (Exodus: 32, 33). In turn, heterophobic notions of ritual uncleanness sprang from ideas of the need to strictly observe religious rites (Leviticus).

Material influences are not always immediately obvious in religious matters, but as the Old Testament unfolds the Israelites alternately sought material advantage – the Promised Land of Exodus (3:17) – from their special status on the one hand, or excused their lack of progress by reference to a failure to strictly observe their religious obligations on the other. Similar ideas of the material consequences of the observance or non-observance of religious rites are to be found in pre-modern or non-western societies (perhaps the most famous being the Native American Rain Dance rites used to avert drought).

The sub-division of complex societies into more or less discrete strata or socio-economic groups, such as status groups, classes, or castes (Weber 1999: ch.5), is explored in detail in the sociological literature. Likewise rivalry and exploitation between such groups is, most famously, dealt with in depth by Marx throughout much of his life's work. There is, then, little novelty (although much interpretation) attaching to the sociological topic of inter-group relationships. The situation of intra-group heterophobic divisions is more problematic.

Although direct evidence of the status of individuals in very early human society is absent, some have sought to extrapolate from studies of contemporary non-modern societies and apply those lessons to early pre-modern ones. Lenski (1966) suggests that a non-differentiated state of social equality was the standard within hunter-gatherer groups. Against this, however, must be set reports of the abandonment, by at least some of these groups, of weak young or old tribal members at times of famine. Such 'elimination of the unproductive members' (Lenski 1966: 104) has clear material origins, but also indicates that social differentiation is practised even in relatively homogeneous societies. It is, indeed, an extreme example of the 'structured selectivity' and accompanying 'differential incorporation' referred to by Harrison with Davis (2001). Similarly, the fatal exposure of 'imperfect' infants to the elements practised by at least some of the Classical Greek city-states, and Sparta in particular may be seen as having materialistic roots, in this case arising from the militaristic nature of Spartan society and its need for armed defenders (Barnes 1996). This also represents a division of male neonatals into 'acceptable' and 'non-acceptable' proto-citizens.

This materialistic differentiation between otherwise equals marks the beginnings of the 'normal/abnormal' dichotomy: in a hunter-gatherer society it is normal to provide first for one's own needs, then for the group in general (Lenski 1966), in Classical Sparta it was 'normal' for young male citizens to perform military duty in defence of the city-state. In either case, and especially at times of austerity, the evidence is that deviance from these norms may have fatal consequences.

Thus people with a shared cultural heritage (or social class) may still be differentiated by means of heterophobia from what is considered 'normal' for their peer grouping. This has an important consequence for Marxist approaches to disability production, for these explicitly seek to establish the transnational homogeneity of, for example, proletariat and bourgeoisie. Without class struggle there is no hope of changing, or indeed explaining, the social world. It is perhaps clearer now why it is necessary for Marxist disability analysts to avoid 'the normal/abnormal dichotomy' (Oliver 1994: unpaged).

As noted above, Harrison with Davis make use within a materialist analysis of the concept of 'structured selectivity' (2001: 73, 191) to explain, in part, the differential value assigned by society to particular discourses. Although the actual process is not fully analysed there, the consequences are frequently manifested in material terms; in enhanced or damaged life chances and in other socio-economic outcomes. I suggest that socially perceived deviance from some norm provides a plausible trigger point for such a differentiating social process.

The value of structured selectivity in this context is that it allows the clearly less eligible position of disabled people within contemporary society to be analysed without recourse to either oppression or exploitation. On the one hand it obviates the burden of identifying some specific beneficiary of a particular state of affairs, whilst on the other hand it moves the discussion beyond Marxist analysis. This facilitates a less emotive, or more objective approach to the topic area. On this basis, disabled people most certainly remain disadvantaged but are not necessarily oppressed.

In contrast, I suggest that disabled people are socially dislocated. I derive 'dislocation' from criminology, where it has been used to refer to 'both [the] physical and psychological distance from home' (Devlin 1998: 75) of prisoners. I propose that the concept may be applied fruitfully to disabled people and their enforced material, social and psychological distance from the mainstream of modern socio-economic life. It may appear particularly apt that Devlin refers specifically to incarcerated women, whilst UPIAS was originally founded to combat the incarceration of disabled people.

I have rather blithely introduced the psychological here, and this requires further explanation if I am to contend that modernity may influence human psychology. My starting point is the tendency of modernity, noted by several commentators from both within and without disability studies and with very different world-views, to reify 'normality' (Ryan and Thomas 1980; Bauman 1989; Finkelstein 1993; Davis 1997). Thus, I suggest, to be normal in modern society implies a safe and secure identity, one which automatically confers full societal membership - indeed only the normal are able to claim full social status. As a direct result we (including many disabled people) become socialized to respect and value the norm whilst vilifying deviance from it. This has important effects.

Psychologically we all have a need to be accepted as part of our peer group. This was demonstrated empirically fifty years ago by the psychologist Asch (1952), who devised a deceptively simple experiment ostensibly centred on the ability of a group to perceive straightforward differences in straight-line images. In practice, all but one of the group was briefed to give a manifestly wrong answer in concert, with the single naive subject left to disagree. As predicted in the research hypothesis, the naive subjects (over a series of experiments several different dupes were introduced) experienced feelings of extreme discomfort, self-doubt and rejection. However, there was also an unpredicted group reaction. The knowing actors reported feelings of anger and animosity towards the non-conformers, despite the knowledge that they were reporting honestly: the majority felt that the dupes were distancing themselves socially. Meanwhile the dupes began to feel ostracised - in both subjective and objective terms they experienced social dislocation.

The inference is not only that deviance from some norm, even an artificially imposed trivial one, has psychological effects on all parties, but also that there is a two-way interaction between psychological and sociological effects with the deviant becoming distanced from the 'mainstream' both internally and externally. Deviance from the norm, whether inadvertent or deliberate, is both uncomfortable and potentially dangerous.

Ideas of the 'abnormality' of non-productive members of society found their echo in early-modern times with the writings of Malthus, and in particular in his warnings of societal collapse should an allegedly under-productive labouring group be allowed to become non-self-supporting. As explained by Max Weber: the development of modern capitalism depends, in part, upon the availability of free labour. An important consequence of this is that 'the costs of reproduction and of bringing up children fall entirely on the labourer' (Weber 1999: 236).

In other words, it is a 'norm' of modern society that workers are not only to be self-sufficient, but are also to provide for their dependants: they must be capable of fulfilling a duty of care towards the greater society. This compares directly with the Spartan obligation on young males to be fit to perform military duty, and with the expectation within hunter-gatherer societies (at least at times of austerity) that individuals will feed themselves or starve. To fail to perform these roles is to be regarded as deviant or abnormal.

The growth of such ideas in the modern era is charted by Stone (1984) who notes the origin of a 'disability category' consisting of people granted, in her word, a 'privileged' position as non-workers. With her talk of the distribution of goods outside of the primary (work-linked) market, Stone envisages both the disability category and the 'privileging' of disabled people in material terms. However, 'privileged' or not, such a status differs markedly from the norm of a self-supporting worker. However, Bauman (1989) demonstrates that modernity shows a great reverence for normality in the abstract – it is a conservative force seeking to preserve social structures. In this way, norms that sprang from purely material sources may acquire a cultural meaning – as noted earlier, 'Modernity is a normalising culture' (Hughes 2002: 572).

Another major danger is that societal reverence of normality within modernity can give rise to:

> a garden culture. It defines itself as the design for an ideal life
> and a perfect arrangement of human conditions… there are weeds
> wherever there is a garden. And weeds are to be exterminated.
> Weeding out is a creative, not a destructive activity (Bauman
> 1989: 92).

It is easy to find correspondences between the urge to reinforce normality on the one hand, and to remove unwanted 'weeds' which may detract from the balanced composition of a modern 'garden society' on the other.

What emerges, is a picture of disabled people forcibly estranged – dislocated – from their host society. As a result, they experience socio-economic (and often psychological) disadvantage within modern society. The causative factors which I propose within this materialist analysis differ sharply from the disability studies 'orthodoxy', at least as defined by Finkelstein, Oliver and Abberley. Where a Marxist approach seems to look for something which may have the appearance of a malevolent collective consciousness (capital) deliberately seeking to oppress disabled people for its own benefit and ends, I stress a social world (modernity) thoroughly imbued with ideas of 'normality' and demonstrating a consequent abhorrence of deviation. Rather than an economic process of oppression grounded in capitalist ideology and driven by the search for profit, I see a social process rooted in normality and leading to social dislocation, as the primary cause of disability.

'Abnormality' and culture

In this way, the abnormality of disabled people has progressed from an edifice constructed on material foundations to a societal concept that now has a very large cultural component. Although Ford (1923: 208) and UPIAS (1976: 15) both argue that there are few, if any, remaining material reasons for the large majority of disabled people to be removed from the mainstream of contemporary society, they continue to be excluded in socio-economic terms. For me, this continuing exclusion is no longer due primarily to material forces – it has become encapsulated within culture.

On this alternative analysis the modern obsession with normality gives rise to a notion of the 'otherness of the abnormal'. This differs both from xenophobic ideas of differentiation along cultural or caste lines, and from Marxist ideas of societal fracture lines associated with class boundaries. It serves to distinguish one member of an otherwise peer group from another: it is an intra-, not inter-, group process. A material manifestation of this process may be seen in the form of structured selectivity, wherein the interests of some (the normal) are institutionally preferred over those of others (the abnormal). As a direct result of this selectivity, disabled people experience a social dislocation which isolates them in material, social and psychological ways from mainstream, normal, society.

The point raised by UPIAS (1976: 16) regarding the 'appearance of degrees of exclusion' may now be addressed. Since the normal is a fixed reference point, an individual's degree of deviation from it may, in principle, be measured. (This is the basis of I.Q. testing.). Put simply, a person who walks with the aid of sticks is more nearly normal than a wheelchair user: someone whose visual impairment is corrected by spectacles is more nearly normal than another with no sight. In terms of social dislocation, the distance from the 'normal' centre varies in direct relationship to the apparent degree of impairment.

However, there is evidence (Caplan 1992) that in the case of genetic testing of foetuses a 'non-standard' genetic endowment, of itself and without reference to degree of variation from the norm, may well lead to a diagnosis of genetic disease with a consequent recommendation to the mother to abort. According to Bauman (1989: 92), genetic abnormality places a foetus at risk of being 'weeded-out' from the carefully tended garden of modernity.

Initially, my alternative materialist analysis leads to a conclusion which is not markedly different to that of Marxism: at least some socially produced differences should be eliminated, and corrective action must take place at the societal, not individual, level. The means by which change may be achieved is, however, very different. In Marxism this is to be gained by the elimination of the bourgeoisie, by extinction or amalgamation within an expanded proletariat. Hence, in order to overthrow disablement, disabled people must find ways of engaging in the class struggle (Finkelstein 2001: 5). However, this does not indicate whether or not they should become subsumed within one or another class. Marx did not allow for a third party to engage with the essentially bipartisan class struggle, and it is doubtful that disabled people could demonstrate sufficient coherence to become a class in and of themselves.

For Marx emancipation from oppression will only be achieved once the proletariat is awakened from a state of false consciousness, becoming fully aware of itself as a class with shared interests, characteristics and socio-economic position - by becoming aware of its essential homogeneity. However,

> there is a great deal of variety within the disabled population
> as a whole - differences in social class, age, sex, family
> circumstances and clinical conditions (Oliver 1983b: unpaged).

In other words there is an essential lack of homogeneity within the community of disabled people. This represents another theoretical problem for disability studies Marxism.

I do not personally think in terms of revolutionary social upheaval, preferring to seek more incremental change: pragmatic considerations suggest that the Marxist revolution may be a long time in coming, especially in the contemporary western world. I do not see capital as the primary enemy, rather this role is filled for me by the concept of normality. In my world-view normality is a product of modern society, despite Oliver's refusal to incorporate it into a Marxist analysis. This being the case, a manufactured item may be modified. Not an easy task, but not inherently impossible. Indeed society has already begun to move in this direction, largely at the behest of disabled people themselves, with moves on the one hand to educate society into a revision of its norms, and legislation to enforce some degree of change on the other. Both need to be taken further and faster, but this relatively unexciting approach, for me, holds out more hope of success within a reasonable timescale than does the road of revolutionary Marxism.

Conclusion

The model of disability which Finkelstein guards so jealously, and which rests so firmly upon Marxist thought, has shed much light on the modern condition known as disability. It has brought about a distinct and perhaps epochal shift in attitudes both about and among disabled people – but is this sufficient cause to seek to fix it into something resembling the fossilised remains of a dinosaur, fit only for exhibition in some museum tableau of mid- to late- twentieth century disability politics? Surely, and despite Finkelstein's assertions to the contrary, a model, any model, makes implicit theoretical assumptions. To freeze such a model at any particular stage of its development is to deny the possibility of any future evolution in its theoretical underpinning. Dinosaurs may well tell us something of the consequences of arrested evolution.

I believe that it is a mistake to extrapolate from the position and experiences of a single small group of people with a narrowly defined and specific range of impairments and life experiences and attempt to impose their (UPIAS) ideology, in a 'one size fits all' manner, on the much broader and disparate constituency of disabled people. The UPIAS model has generated considerable insights into the reality of disability production. However, its value as a basis for a social theory of disability is much less clear. Ultimately we should ask whether we seek a theory to explain an economic model of disability, or a social one – the two are potentially very different.

Bibliography

Abberley, P. 1987: The Concept of Oppression and the Development of a Social Theory of Disability. *Disability, Handicap and Society,* 2 (1), 5–19.

Abberley, P. 1999: The Significance of Work for the Citizenship of Disabled People. Paper presented at University College Dublin, April 15th 1999.

Asch, S. E. 1952: *Social Psychology.* New York: Prentice-Hall.

Barnes, C. 1996: Theories of disability and the origins of the oppression of disabled people in western society. In L. Barton (ed.), *Disability and Society: Emerging Issues and Insights.* Harlow: Addison Wesley Longman.

Bauman, Z. 1989: *Modernity and the Holocaust.* Cambridge: Polity Press.

Caplan, A.L. 1992: *If Gene Therapy Is The Cure, What Is The Disease?* http://www.med.upenn.edu/~bioethic/genetics/articles/1.caplan.gene.therapy.html (accessed 15/7/98).

Davis, L.J. 1997: Constructing Normalcy. In L. J. Davis (ed.), *The Disability Studies Reader.* London: Routledge.

Devlin, A. 1998: *Invisible Women.* Winchester: Waterside Press.

Finkelstein, V. 1993: The Commonality of Disability. In J. Swain, V. Finkelstein, S. French and M. Oliver (eds), *Disabling Barriers – Enabling Environments.* London: Sage and Open University Press.

Finkelstein, V. 2001: The Social Model of Disability Repossessed. Manchester; Manchester Coalition of Disabled People. Accessed at http://www.leeds.ac.uk/disability-studies/ archiveuk/archframe.htm (1/8/2).

Ford, H. 1923: *My Life and Work.* London: William Heinemann Ltd.

Gleeson, B. 1999: *Geographies of Disability.* London: Routledge.

Hall, S., Held, D. and McGrew, T. 1992: *Modernity and its Futures.* Cambridge: Polity Press in association with Blackwell Publishers and the Open University.

Handy, C. 1990: *The Age of Unreason.* London: Arrow.

Harrison, M. with Davis, C. 2001: *Housing, Social Policy and Difference.* Bristol: The Policy Press.

Hughes, B. 2002: Bauman's Strangers: impairment and the invalidation of disabled people in modern and post-modern cultures. *Disability and Society,* 17 (5), 571-584.

Hunt, P. 1966a: A Critical Condition. In P. Hunt (ed.), *Stigma: The Experience of Disability.* London: Geoffrey Chapman.

Kevles, D. J. 1992: Out of Eugenics: The Historical Politics of the Human Genome. In D. J. Kevles and L. Hood (eds), *The Code of Codes.* Cambridge, Mass.: Harvard University Press.

Lenski, G. 1966: *Power and Privilege.* New York: McGraw-Hill.

Lenski, G., Lenski, J. and Nolan, P. 1991: *Human Societies. 6th edn.* New York: McGraw-Hill.

Oliver, M. 1983a: *Social Work with Disabled People.* Basingstoke: Macmillan.

Oliver, M. 1983b: *The Politics of Disability.* April 15, 1983. Accessed at: http://www.leeds.ac.uk/disability-studies/archiveuk/archframe.htm (9/9/02).

Oliver, M. 1989: *Disability and Dependency: A Creation of Industrial Societies*. In L. Barton (ed.), *Disability and Dependency.* London: Falmer Press.

Oliver, M. 1994: *Capitalism, Disability and Ideology: A Materialist Critique of the Normalization Principle.* Accessed at: http://www.leeds.ac.uk/ disability studies/archiveuk/archframe.htm (28/9/2).

Priestley, M. 1998: Constructions and Creations: idealism, materialism and disability theory. *Disability and Society,* 13 (1), 75-94.

Ryan, J. and Thomas, F. 1980: The Politics of Mental Handicap. Harmondsworth: Penguin.

Shakespeare, T. 1994: Cultural Representations of Disabled People: dustbins for disavowal? In L. Barton and M. Oliver (eds), Disability Studies: Past, Present and Future. Leeds: The Disability Press.

Stone, D. 1984: *The Disabled State.* Philadelphia: Temple University Press.

Tregaskis, C. 2002: Social Model Theory: the story so far. *Disability and Society,* 17 (4), 457–470.

Union of the Physically Impaired Against Segregation. 1976: *Fundamental Principles of Disability.* London: UPIAS and The Disability Alliance.

Weber, M. 1999: *Essays in Economic Sociology,* (editor R. Swedberg). Princeton, NJ: Princeton University Press.

CHAPTER 5

Social Model Theories and Non-Disabled People: some possibilities for connection

Claire Tregaskis

Introduction

Social model theories explaining the oppression of disabled people in Britain today are one in a long line of socially concerned responses to the effects of the rise of capitalism and the industrialisation which accompanied, and was a principal expression of, its development. It may be argued that one of the motivating factors behind the development of social model theories – along with the oppression theories of feminists and anti-racists - has been the need to challenge previous theoretical assumptions about the one-dimensional class-based nature of power relations. Hence, disabled people from across all social classes face oppression and exclusion by a capitalist society that does not take their needs into account (Finkelstein 1980; Oliver 1990; Barnes 1991; Thomas 1999). Although individual people with impairments may be protected from particular instances of oppression because of their class, gender, ethnicity or sexuality (Appleby 1993, 1994; Corbett, 1994; Vernon 1999; Humphrey 2000), it is equally the case that in many other situations impairment is used as the primary excuse for mainstream oppressive practices.

Given the ongoing oppression of disabled people, the further development of social model theories to support disabled people in their everyday struggles against social exclusion is essential. The question is perhaps how best this may be achieved in today's political and social climate. However, there are hopeful signposts of a better future. Most important are the examples of disabled people's resistance to oppression, starting from the development of social model theories. Responsibility for their social exclusion has been rightly placed at the door of a normalising society which has rigidly developed and maintained structures designed to create a docile workforce (Foucault 1991; Douard 1995), and to reward those who most closely conform to socially prescribed ideal models of appearance and behaviour.

Activism has also played a crucial role in challenging existing oppressive power relations, ranging from the increasing involvement of disabled people in policy-making on disability issues at both local and national level (Campbell and Oliver 1996), through to the work of the Disability Direct Action Network (DAN) in directly challenging oppressive practice and bringing disabled people's exclusion to the attention of wider society. Equally important has been disabled people's increasing visibility in everyday life, and the active celebration of the disabled identity through factors such as the growth of the disability arts movement (Swain and French 2000) and the increasingly high profile of disability sport. Thus parallel developments at the levels of theory, of activism, and of being, have been crucial in bringing us to where we are now.

Forming alliances for change with non-disabled people: opportunities and pitfalls

In seeking additional ways of furthering the agenda for inclusion, I want to explore whether some of our struggles against oppression may be facilitated by the formation of strategic alliances with non-disabled people. I take as my starting point Finkelstein's (1996: 11) suggestion that social change might best be achieved if disabled and non-disabled people started working together more systematically to tackle exclusion in all its forms. Thus, for example, disabled people's support alongside other local parents campaigning for the provision of safe crossing places outside schools might be reciprocated by those non-disabled people giving backing for struggles for more accessible public transport.

This argument is founded in a wider belief in social justice for all. Williams has explained the operation of stereotyping in capitalist societies as a means of dividing people against each other by concentrating on difference:

> There are in fact no masses; there are only ways of seeing people
> as masses. In an urban industrial society there are many
> opportunities for such ways of seeing' (Williams 1963: 289).

Williams was writing before the development of the disabled people's movement, and concentrates on class relations to the exclusion of other important forms of power relationship, including patriarchy. However, the process of 'othering' has been used as a tool of political, social and cultural oppression by non-disabled people against disabled people in Western capitalist societies

(Hevey 1992; Shakespeare 1994). Perhaps, in seeking to develop social model responses to these experiences of exclusion, we have done just the same thing with the non-disabled other, by viewing them in the mass as oppressors. Such a strategy has actually been essential in enabling disabled people to counter discrimination, not least through developing pride and self-worth as non-conformists to impossible social expectations.

However, whilst othering those engaged in oppressive practice is an appropriate political response in some situations, there are times and places in which engagement may be a necessary strategy to achieve change, such as where disabled and non-disabled people are co-participants on policy committees, or are seeking ways to improve physical and programme access to public venues. In such cases, finding ways of working with people who are not 'like us' may then enable us all to focus even more clearly on tackling the exclusionary structural barriers that divide us.

> To the degree that we find the formula inadequate for ourselves,
> we can wish to extend to others the courtesy of acknowledging
> the unknown (Williams 1963: 289).

We may concede that not all non-disabled people are oppressors of disabled people all the time, and indeed may be active allies in the push for change. The bigger problem, as theories of disability, patriarchy, ethnicity and heterosexism have demonstrated, lies in the structural barriers which differentially include and exclude particular groups in particular times and spaces, breeding additional socially-created divisions between individuals along the way (Foucault 1991). Hence, in seeking to develop appropriate situational alliances for change with non-disabled others, we may begin to challenge some of these wider socially-created barriers to inclusion.

The formation of 'unusual alliances' to tackle a range of exclusionary barriers may arise in many different areas, for example:

> we could link our struggles for women, for disabled people, working
> together for better social services, disability rights legislation, working
> for more equitable distribution of work within families, instead
> of seeing our interests as unalterably opposed (Finger 1991: 43).

Similarly, Phelan (1995: 341) has argued that lesbians may encounter particular problems about being 'out' in the community in poor neighbourhoods, but this also ties in with the wider problem of people on low incomes in getting decent housing. So, whilst acknowledging that there may be specific differences between the experiences of poor lesbians and poor straight people, it should be possible to establish a common agenda in struggling for better housing, without succumbing to the dangers of either essentialism or of over-generalisation.

I see the possibility of alliances between disabled and non-disabled people as only one thread in the development of disabled people's struggles against oppression. There will be times when disabled people need to organise alone, when the primacy of the disabled identity is of paramount importance and cannot risk dilution of energy and effort. Other dangers of a pluralist approach to bringing about change are also acknowledged. A strategy of multiple identification with people who are not 'like us' can lead to looking only at individuals (Young 1995: 195), thereby losing a sense of group identity and broad group political strategy, and also obscuring the individual's relative investments in particular identities (Rattansi 1995: 271). In campaigning for wider change, the risk also remains of disabled people's needs being overlooked or pushed to the end of the queue in favour of those with louder voices (Young 1995: 197). Hence, pluralism and coalitions as advocated by theorists and activists alike (Finger 1991; Appleby 1994; Corbett 1994; Phelan 1995; Humphrey 1999; Vernon 1999) are not unproblematic strategies.

Achieving change through consensus may also be harder, and may take longer, not least because it demands an understanding of 'the other' with whom the change is being negotiated. However, change achieved in this way is likely to be more effective and long-lasting. Given that many disabled people already routinely engage with non-disabled people, both as activists and at the more general level of being, it may be that social model theory is lagging behind real-world practice in not addressing some of the practical issues that arise during such necessary engagements between disabled and non-disabled people (Corker 1999; Germon 1999).

Engaging with non-disabled people: some sample strategies

My own interest in this area derives primarily from my fifteen years' work experience with mainstream countryside recreation and nature conservation organisations, in which I routinely utilised social model principles in negotiating improved physical and programme access for disabled people at countryside sites across England. The social model emphasis on tackling structural barriers was central to the success of such initiatives. For countryside staff previously influenced by individualised explanations of disability, the external barriers approach was new, but it made more sense to them, not least because it made their job easier. By adopting universal design principles they could easily develop access solutions that worked for all visitors – both those with and without impairments. This reduced their anxiety about the task, and made it more likely that they would implement the suggested changes. Thus a structural barriers approach was crucial to the success of access improvement initiatives, reinforcing the point that key aspects of social model theory already have significant practical application to 'real world' situations.

However, at a personal level, as an access advisor there were other areas of practice where I felt relatively unsupported by social model theory. This was particularly true in terms of the need to develop effective communication and negotiation skills to persuade non-disabled people of the need to improve access. Before working in this field I had never previously engaged as an equal with non-disabled people in the way that this work required, while most of the rangers with whom I had contact had never worked with a disabled person before. This meant that our early interactions were often something of an uphill struggle. In those situations it would have been helpful to have some analytical tools to help me understand and defend against the negative attitudes and potentially psycho-emotional impacts (Thomas 1999; Reeve 2002). Without such a frame of reference I often found myself absorbing non-disabled people's disablist views, and further internalising my own oppression.

Over time, however, I did develop survival strategies that enabled me both to begin to neutralise these personalised projections, and to engage in dialogue through difference with non-disabled others. These strategies are summarised below, and are offered as starting points for developing theory-level responses to the realities of engagement with non-disabled people.

a) Developing a shared agenda for change: the 'win-win situation'.

To start with a fairly obvious statement, access initiatives worked best where both parties could see that they were getting something they wanted from the project. In the difficult economic circumstances in which many countryside services were working in the 1980s and 1990s, it was unrealistic to expect that service providers would be keen to improve physical and programme access to sites without being persuaded of the benefits to them. However, in countryside settings improving access was almost never just a question of economics. Equally important was the need to recognise and make explicit the existence of a common bond between site staff and the disabled people pressing for improved access. As data from a networking workshop organised by one project showed (BT/The Fieldfare Trust 1997), the participants were united by their love of the countryside and the desire to conserve it for future generations.

However, one corollary was that disabled people wishing to introduce their family and friends to what the countryside had to offer them would only be able to do this if physical and programme access were improved. For highly-committed countryside staff who often accepted low wages as the necessary price they paid for the privilege of working as custodians of the natural environment, the recognition that disabled people were equally though differently committed to the same cause was the key to making them understand why improving access was so important, and to valuing disabled people as equal partners in this process. In turn, disabled people's initial perceptions of site staff as ignoring their rightful claims to improved access were changed by the realisation that many staff were doing the best they could with a limited knowledge of disability issues, and that they positively welcomed disabled people's constructive suggestions on access improvements. This commonality of purpose around conserving the environment was the key to the successful implementation of change.

b) The need to acknowledge and understand pressures faced by the other party

Not infrequently, I discovered that the rangers I was working with felt undervalued compared to other employees of their organisations, whom they perceived to be enjoying a higher status and to be more likely to have their views listened to and acted on. Sometimes, indeed, it emerged that my consultancy visit had been arranged by senior management without prior discussion and agreement with the staff I was due to meet. In these situations it was especially important to establish quickly a bond with those staff. Often the most effective way of doing this was to start by asking them to talk me through what the site had to offer to visitors, in much the same way as Freire (1997) has recommended starting from what people already know in beginning the process of change, so that you are more likely to carry them with you as the discussion develops. Almost invariably, this invitation led to what I came privately to term 'the half hour rant', during which they proceeded to provide me with a detailed account of why, although they would like nothing more than to improve access for disabled people, it wasn't really achievable for the following hundred reasons. Whilst I often found these renditions tedious in their similarity, I soon discovered that it was fruitless to interrupt the speaker or to try to engage in debate. Instead I came to recognise that this initial half-hour was a necessary space in which they were actually expressing (without always realising it) a range of negative responses to the consultancy process. These included a fear of having to engage with me as the outsider/access 'expert'/disabled person; their embarrassment that the site was not more accessible; and their concern that they personally did not have the skills needed to improve access in the ways they thought I would demand.

Faced with this situation I needed simultaneously to engage in active listening – to reassure them that I was hearing what they were saying – whilst also privately defending against internalising the negative attitudes they were expressing. This was often really hard to do, and I could only stay with the negotiation process because I knew I was getting paid to be there. This economic factor acted as a vital distancing tool by enabling me to contain these negative projections within the sphere of work-based relationships, so that I could hear their comments without letting them invade my private space and identity as a disabled person. But it was still dangerous work, and I couldn't always succeed in keeping the public and the private separate in this way.

However, at the end of the half-hour session, I would deliberately ignore the negatives in what they had told me, and instead emphasise the positives. This meant firmly re-stating my faith in their site management skills as an engine for change, and then suggesting that we go and look around the site together. This strategy almost invariably worked, because having been given permission to air their concerns at the outset it generally cleared the air for the rangers to engage seriously with the access issues under discussion. The development of access improvement strategies then became a joint effort, combining their knowledge of the site with my understanding of wider access standards and guidelines. This enabled us to develop site-specific solutions. Unsurprisingly, access solutions developed in this way were those most likely to be successfully implemented. However, the negotiation process was often personally demanding in a way that was difficult to maintain, or even to justify at times. Also, my professional identity as a consultant made it impossible to utilise strategies such as direct action to achieve change. Instead, my role had to be one of negotiating change through dialogue and consensus. This, is one area I believe social model theory could address, by developing strategies to support disabled people in their attempts to negotiate for change with non-disabled others, and hence to reduce the problems of fatigue and burn-out that affect too many members of social movements.

c) Sharing skills and knowledge to speed up achieving change

Access initiatives were easier to develop and implement when all parties pooled their resources. I initially found this strategy the hardest one to implement because it meant putting trust in non-disabled people to act in ways that would support disabled people. From my previous experience I doubted whether they were capable of doing so without acting in a patronising way or trying to hijack projects for their own ends. However, once the common bond of conservation had been established, the process of pooling skills and knowledge became much easier. This sometimes enabled the provision of new services that disabled people would not have achieved alone. For example, in one project disabled people wanted an accessible public transport service so they could travel independently from the city into the surrounding countryside at weekends (BT/The Fieldfare Trust 1997). The introduction of this pilot service was only possible with the backing and technical expertise of local authority public transport managers, and the provision of an accessible bus by the local bus company.

Still, it would be naïve to suggest that working together was unproblematic in all projects. Unequal power relations were always implicated in our interactions, and at times this resulted in the need for a facilitator's intervention in debates between countryside staff and disabled people. This was because the rangers were quite simply unaware of the enormity of the barriers facing disabled people, and so made real blunders in the negotiation process. For example, one ranger was enthusiastically listing all the sites he hoped the local access group would come and audit. It proved necessary to interrupt him to explain that if he wanted this to happen, he would need to fund disabled people's participation in terms of meeting their time, transport, personal support and childcare costs for the work. He was visibly taken aback, not because he did not want to pay up, but because he really had no idea of how hard it was for disabled people to get out and effect change. Thus, dialogue could only proceed through the pragmatic recognition of difference. The rangers had to be educated about disabled people's support needs, and disabled people had to realise this. On the positive side, with honesty and a willingness to learn, such discussions were an enormously powerful tool in educating non-disabled people about the reality of our lives, and hence gaining support in bringing about change.

Issues around linking theory and practice

I will now explore possible ways of developing theory in response to the activist strategies outlined above. A key finding has been that dialogue can only succeed through the pragmatic recognition of difference (Phillips 1999), and by acknowledging the reality of power relations that oppress disabled people. Even with goodwill on both sides, inadvertent mistakes and oppressive practice will still happen. In such cases disabled people will need to adopt defensive strategies to avoid internalising the oppression. Where it is not possible to come right out and explain to the non-disabled person why their behaviour is inappropriate, other self-protection defences may be utilised, ranging from mentally 'tuning out' of the discussion through to physical withdrawal and boycotting of services.

That said, where dialogue is mutually respectful, we can identify limited commonality of purpose with non-disabled people and utilise this in working together to achieve change. This finding may at first sight be hard to reconcile with implicit and explicit assumptions of an essentialist difference between disabled and non-disabled people. However, such essentialist accounts have also been pragmatic in their acknowledgement of the potential value of developing disability theory in partnership with some non-disabled theorists, notably in the field of medical sociology (Barnes, Mercer and Shakespeare 1999; Thomas 1999). Others have argued that areas of commonality do already exist between some disabled and non-disabled people, particularly in terms of their gender, race and sexual identities (Appleby 1993, 1994; Corbett 1994; Vernon 1999; Humphrey 2000). Such accounts have tended to concentrate primarily on the need to acknowledge the importance of a wider range of (minority group) identity politics than that associated with impairment alone.

At the level of theory, the debate has not previously been taken further to explore the possibilities that the development of situational alliances between disabled people and non-disabled members of the mainstream outside the academy might engender in promoting change. However, it may reasonably be argued that such alliances with members of the mainstream have already been important in struggles for inclusion, not only in relation to challenging barriers to countryside access or in pursuing academic engagement with non-disabled theorists, but also in other areas of social life such as education, as evidenced by dialogue and common action between disabled people, parents and teachers under the 'Inclusion Now!' banner.

In seeking to utilise examples of successful partnership-building from particular settings as wider exemplars of good practice, however, some difficulties must be acknowledged. For example, it is possible that targeted strategies for communication and negotiation with non-disabled people will be perceived as over-individualised and lacking a wider theoretical structure. Further, there is a danger that focussing on deliberation and dialogue in this way may take people's attention away from material inequality and conflict of interest, thus emphasising cultural issues at the expense of political ones (Phillips 1999: 119–20). It is therefore important to reiterate that such communication strategies are always intended to be utilised as part of a more general structural barriers approach to tackling oppression, and not as a substitute for a wider ethical and political strategy. Thus it is the combined application of both economic and cultural based social model principles to specific inclusion-related problems that is most likely to produce consensual and durable inclusive provision.

Secondly, there is the related difficulty that such strategies may be seen as solely individualised responses to atypical situations, and that as such they have no wider potential applicability. Certainly the specific way in which I interpreted and implemented the principles for collaboration discussed above in my own fieldwork will be different from the approaches adopted by other disabled people in working with non-disabled people, simply because everyone has their own ways of working and of developing such partnerships. However, alongside recognition of difference, there is a fundamental need to acknowledge the humanity of the individual non-disabled other, in those situations where we are aiming for dialogue and consensual change. Indeed, in seeking to engage with non-disabled people who had no prior experience of disability issues:

> Wherever we have started from, we need to listen to others who
> started from a different position (Williams 1963: 320).

Acknowledging other people's positionality in this way was sometimes personally difficult and demanding. However, I found that it was a necessary condition of engagement with those non-disabled people, just as they in turn were struggling to understand where I was coming from. This feeling of being on a journey of mutual discovery was a source of constant fear and delight throughout the negotiation process, because it required each of us to trust the other not to engage in exploitation by claiming that our own expertise was superior to theirs. Instead, it was the open sharing of skills, knowledge and experience for our mutual benefit that led to sustainable change.

Some theory-level starting points

In seeking to account for the possibility of relationships based on the mutual acceptance of difference at the level of theory, I suggest that we might usefully draw on literature from at least three areas of study. These are theories around inter-personal communication, multiple identity, and power relations.

i) Engaging in dialogue that acknowledges difference

Phillips (1999) and Taylor (1992) have both emphasised the dangers of dialogue that only sees the person with less cultural and economic power as being different from the more powerful other. Such an exclusionary approach merely reinforces existing inequalities, and may lead to the attempted cultural and political assimilation of the individual or minority group. Instead, dialogues that acknowledge and respect people's differences from each other, and which do not require the capitulation of one party to the other, are needed.

I have found the work of the medical sociologist Arthur Frank useful here. He writes as someone who has experienced serious illness, and who is thus under no illusions as to the exclusionary effects of the individual model of illness and impairment (Frank 1991a). He nonetheless propounds an ethical approach to dialogue with the non-disabled/non-ill other that seeks points of connection through the 'the communicative body'.

Its desire is for dyadic expression, not monadic consumption.
Whether it produces joy, sorrow, or anger, it uses itself to
express these. This expression takes the form of dyadic sharing.
In the further contingency of this sharing, the body has the potential
for more diffuse realization (Frank 1991b: 80).

Similarly, Taylor explores the 'fundamentally dialogical character' (1992: 32) of human life, and the way in which we work out who we are through dialogue and reflection with the people we share our lives with. As social beings, we do not develop our identities in isolation, but through our interactions with others. Frank's contribution is particularly important in directly relating this general philosophical approach to the particular experiences of illness and impairment. Although his argument is made primarily in relation to the ill/non-ill binary, he also elaborates his belief that the same process may be utilised by disabled people. Throughout his work (Frank 1991a, 1991b, 1995, 2000), he illustrates the importance of illness narratives as a means of reaching out to the other, a strategy that might also be of use in demonstrating the psycho-emotional effects of disabling attitudes to a non-disabled audience. Such dialogues are not easy, but may serve a deeper moral purpose:

Being alive is a dual responsibility: to our shared frailty, on the
one hand, and to all we can create, on the other. The mutual
responsibilities of the ill to express and the healthy to hear meet
in the recognition that our creativity depends on our frailty. Life
without illness would not just be incomplete, it would be
impossible (Frank 1991a: 128).

On the face of it, this is a profoundly optimistic assertion of the development, through communication, of an increased level of mutual understanding. It explicitly demands that members of the majority learn to listen to the voices of people with illnesses and impairments as a prerequisite for mutual growth and understanding. Such an explanation makes sense to me in the context of relationship-building with countryside staff.

Listening is hard, but it is also a fundamental moral act; to realize
the best potential in post-modern times requires an ethics of
listening... in listening for the other, we listen for ourselves.
The moment of witness in the story crystalizes a mutuality of
need, when each is for the other (Frank 1995: 25).

Developing such 'an ethics of listening' to support dialogues with the other that recognise difference, and that also acknowledge the reality of the differential effects of power relations on the various participants, would be of practical benefit to disabled people engaged in negotiating change. In the course of implementing such a strategy we might also begin to challenge the mechanism of stereotyping other people into 'masses' (Williams 1963), and thus develop new alliances for change. Frank's analysis of the communicative body is of potential value in explaining the power and possibilities of communication in our everyday lives. I believe, then, that this is one area where the further development of social model theory is desirable.

ii) Multiple identity as a means of engagement with non-disabled others
As already argued, some disability studies theorists have already elaborated areas of commonality between disabled people and members of other minority groups. Taking this argument further in terms of feminist debates, Mohanty (1995: 81) has called for members of social movements to look beyond their own experiences and explanations for oppression, and to acknowledge and utilise the intersections between the various expressions of identity politics as a means of developing future political strategy. Again, this may not be easy, even with members of other minority groups, because of the existence and interplay of cultural preferences and hierarchies in a wider context of shifting power relations. Bell-Hooks has discussed one way of overcoming such barriers in relation to her own experiences:

> We talked about the need to acknowledge that we all suffer in
> some way, but that we are not all oppressed or equally oppressed.
> Many of us feared that our experiences were irrelevant because
> they were not as oppressive or as exploited as the experiences
> of others. We discovered that we had a greater feeling of unity
> when people focused truthfully on their own experiences
> without comparing them with those of others in a competitive
> way (Bell Hooks 1984: 59).

Perhaps, it is only by attempting such engagements, and taking the risk that sometimes we will get it wrong, that areas of joint political action will be identified. Certainly, in seeking to map out the full extent of disabling oppression, social model theory has perhaps underplayed the existence of areas of common experience with some non-disabled people from the mainstream, and of jointly negotiating change.

In the limited circumstances of engagement with the non-disabled other, it is helpful to draw on Mouffe's (1995) post-structural approach to developing strategies for feminist action. She argues that the deconstruction of essentialist identities is necessary for an 'adequate understanding of the variety of social relations where the principles of liberty and equality should apply.' In practical terms, therefore, she argues that we need to lose the idea of a rational subject and of unified positions in order to 'theorize the multiplicity of relations of subordination', where the same person may be 'dominant in one relation while subordinated in another' (Mouffe 1995: 317-18).

Hence, it may be a mistake to assume that disabled people are always without power in their interactions with non-disabled others. For example, as a paid access consultant with expert knowledge, I sometimes had more situational power than the rangers with whom I was working. I was able to utilise this aspect of my identity in persuading them to adopt changes. Utilising the full multiplicity of our situational identities may also be a useful tool in deflecting further oppression. It enables us to attribute particular instances of oppressive behaviour to the other's response to us as parents, employees, consultants, consumers and so on, rather than always linking it to our identities as disabled people. Such deflective tactics do not deny oppression, but they may protect us from over-problematising our identity as disabled people, a trap that it can be too easy to fall into, especially for those disabled people who are isolated from the supportive networks of the disabled people's movement.

Thus, in the particular context of engaging with non-disabled people, I argue for the use of multiple identity as both a communicative and a political tool. First, it may enable us to identify limited areas of common ground with the non-disabled other from which a dialogue through difference may begin; whilst second, it may both deflect oppressive behaviour from our identities as disabled people, and enable us to challenge some aspects of oppressive power relations by highlighting areas where dialogue through difference enables disabled people's expertise to be recognised.

iii) Destabilising oppressive power relations

In addressing the issue of power relations, dialogue needs to proceed from the understanding that, in our identities as disabled and non-disabled people, we are different from each other (Taylor 1992; Phelan 1995; Phillips 1999). The big difficulty that disabled people face is in getting to this point of having our difference acknowledged in a non-judgmental way by members of a majority conditioned to see impairment as a personal tragedy (Oliver 1990). Indeed, most of the non-disabled writers cited here do not regard disability as a form of social oppression. Disabled people have adopted a range of strategies to bring their exclusion to the attention of the mainstream. Most dramatic of these have been the direct action tactics of DAN, but other developments such as the growth of the disability arts movement that celebrate the disabled identity (Swain and French 2000), and the increasing engagement of disabled people with non-disabled institutions to negotiate practical and inclusive changes to mainstream policy and practice (Campbell and Oliver 1996), are also slowly achieving recognition of disabled people as a political constituency that cannot be ignored. This heightened public visibility in turn has a crucial effect on the possibilities for future political change:

> the empowerment of the currently disadvantaged is often a prerequisite for, rather than a consequence of, more equitable social policies, for until people become active participants in the policy process, the policies adopted cannot be expected to reflect their needs (Phillips 1999: 31).

The enormity of the task still facing disabled people may be seen in legislative responses like the Disability Discrimination Act 1995 which, with its frequent use of qualifying phrases such as 'reasonable adjustment' and 'to the extent to which it is practicable', leaves us in no doubt that bringing about equality of provision for disabled people continues to be seen more as a gift conditionally bestowed by a paternalistic state onto 'those less fortunate' than an acknowledgement of our fundamental right to equality as citizens.

One option is to extend Oliver's (1996) analysis of disabled people's position in the citizenship debates. This is particularly important as the present government is prioritising disabled people's economic responsibilities as a condition of citizenship, expressed through initiatives such as 'Welfare to Work' and the 'New Deal for Disabled People'. These were designed to get disabled people off state benefits and into paid work, but there are considerable doubts that policy makers appreciate the full extent of disabled people's training and support needs in obtaining and retaining employment (Burchardt 2000; Roulstone 2000). In such circumstances:

> We need a more adequate understanding of political and civil equality that recognizes and respects our differences. It may be… that equality of citizenship requires different groups of people to have different kinds of rights (Phillips 1999: 27).

In terms of disabled people's experience, we could interpret such differential rights in a number of positive ways. For example, disabled people at work would benefit from a universal entitlement to the personal support they need to do their jobs, without that entitlement being restricted by the availability of 'Access to Work' funding; whilst those who are not able to work should have their right not to do so acknowledged and respected, rather than being made to feel like second-class citizens (Tregaskis 1998).

In pursuing this goal, action on a range of fronts would be beneficial. For example, disabled academics have a role to play in engaging with a wider range of equality issues than those around disability, so that in the future philosophical connections are routinely made between the experience and significance of disability and of other forms of social oppression such as class, race and ethnicity, gender and sexuality. Non-disabled people's ignorance of disabling barriers may also be challenged through the use of social model-based narrative accounts of the experience of disability, as a means of educating them about the realities of the oppression that they often unthinkingly perpetuate. The efforts of disabled people both inside and outside the academy who are already engaging with non-disabled people to influence the development of more inclusive policies and practices are also key to educating those non-disabled people. For the future, however, such individualised efforts need to be supported by wider structural changes, including a transition to a fully inclusive education system that enables all children to grow up learning to take each other's needs into account as a matter of course. In such ways might dialogue through difference become a practical everyday reality for disabled and non-disabled people.

Conclusion

I have explored some of the possibilities that exist for using social model theory as a means of making connections with non-disabled people. Whilst acknowledging that engaging with non-disabled people to bring about change is only one possible strand of political activity, I have argued that it is an area that has previously been under-theorised, with the result that disabled activists and practitioners have been left relatively unsupported in their attempts to bring about negotiated change in settings outside the academy. Having identified the centrality of issues around developing communication and negotiation skills, I have suggested that binary explanations of disability that place the disabled self in perpetual and unchanging opposition to the non-disabled other may be unhelpful in those situations where finding some common ground may be crucial to establishing a dialogue. This process helps recognise and acknowledge difference, but does not require assimilation of the minority to the majority point of view as the price to be paid for that engagement.

In attempting to develop social model theory in relation to disabled/non-disabled interactions we may need to draw on, and further elaborate, thinking on a range of issues. Here, theories of communication, of multiple identity, and of power relations have been utilised as starting points in trying to explain some of the dynamics implicated in such interactions, and to highlight ways in which such approaches might be used in conducting initiatives to bring about more inclusive practice. It is to be hoped that other relevant issues will be identified as theoretical debates around this area increase.

Bibliography

Appleby, Y. 1993: Disability and Compulsory Heterosexuality. In S. Wilkinson and C. Kitzinger (eds), *Heterosexuality: a feminism and psychology reader.* London: Sage.

Appleby, Y. 1994: Out in the Margins. *Disability and Society,* 9 (1), 19-32.

Barnes, C. 1991: *Disabled People in Britain and Discrimination: a case for anti-discrimination legislation,* London: Hurst and Co. in association with BCODP.

Barnes, C., Mercer, G., and Shakespeare, T. 1999: *Exploring Disability: a sociological introduction.* Cambridge: Polity Press.

Bell Hooks, 1984: *Feminist Theory: from margin to center.* Boston, MA: South End Press.

BT/The Fieldfare Trust. 1997: *BT Countryside for All Standards and Guidelines: a good practice guide to disabled people's access to the countryside.* Barnsley: Ledgard and Jepson.

Burchardt, T. 2000: *Enduring economic exclusion: disabled people, income and work.* York: Joseph Rowntree Foundation.

Campbell, J. and Oliver, M. 1996: *Disability Politics: understanding our past, changing our future.* London: Routledge.

Corbett, J. 1994: A Proud Label: exploring the relationship between disability politics and gay pride. *Disability and Society,* 9 (3), 343-357.

Corker, M. 1999: Differences, Conflations and Foundations: the limits to 'accurate' theoretical representation of disabled people's experience? *Disability and Society,* 14 (5), 627-642.

Douard, J.W. 1995: Disability and the persistence of the 'normal'. In S. Kay and D. Barnard (eds), *Chronic Illness: from experience to policy.* Indiana: Indiana University Press.

Finger, A. 1991: *Past Due: a story of disability, pregnancy and birth.* London: The Women's Press.

Finkelstein, V. 1980: *Attitudes and Disabled People: issues for discussion.* New York: World Rehabilitation Fund.

Finkelstein, V. 1996: The disability movement has run out of steam. *Disability Now,* February, 11.

Foucault, M. 1991: *Discipline and Punish: the birth of the prison.* Harmondsworth: Penguin.

Frank, A.W. 1991a: *At The Will Of The Body: reflections on illness.* Boston/New York: Houghton Mifflin Company.

Frank, A. 1991b: For a Sociology of the Body. In M. Featherstone, M. Hepworth, and B. S. Turner (eds), *The Body: social processes and cultural theory.* London: Sage.

Frank, A.W. 1995: *The Wounded Storyteller: body, illness and ethics.* Chicago: Chicago Press.

Frank, A. 2000: Illness and Autobiographical Work: dialogue as narrative destabilization. *Qualitative Sociology,* 23, Spring, 135-56.

Freire, P. 1997: *Pedagogy of Hope: reliving Pedagogy of the Oppressed.* New York: Continuum.

Germon, P. 1999: 'Purely Academic'? Exploring the relationship between theory and political activism. *Disability and Society,* 14 (5), 687-692.

Hevey, D. (ed.) 1992: *The Creatures Time Forgot: photography and disability imagery.* London: Routledge.

Humphrey, J.C. 1999: Disabled People and the Politics of Difference. *Disability and Society,* 14 (2), 173-188.

Humphrey, J.C. 2000: Researching Disability Politics, or, some problems with the social model in practice. *Disability and Society,* 15 (1), 63-85.

Mohanty, C.T. 1995: Feminist encounters: locating the politics of experience. In L. Nicholson and S. Seidman (eds), *Social Postmodernism: beyond identity politics.* New York: Cambridge University Press.

Mouffe, C. 1995: Feminism, Citizenship and Radical Democratic Politics. In L. Nicholson and S. Seidman (eds), *Social Postmodernism: beyond identity politics.* New York: Cambridge University Press.

Oliver, M. 1990: *The Politics of Disablement.* Basingstoke: Macmillan.

Oliver, M. 1996: *Understanding Disability: from theory to practice.* Basingstoke: Macmillan.

Phelan, S. 1995: The Space of Justice: lesbians and democratic politics. In L. Nicholson and S. Seidman (eds), *Social Postmodernism: beyond identity politics.* New York: Cambridge University Press.

Phillips, A. 1999: *Which Equalities Matter?* Oxford: Blackwell.

Rattansi, A. 1995: Just Framing: ethnicities and racism in a 'post-modern' framework. In L. Nicholson and S. Seidman (eds), *Social Postmodernism: beyond identity politics.* New York: Cambridge University Press.

Reeve, D. 2002: Negotiating Psycho-emotional Dimensions of Disability and their Influence on Identity Constructions. *Disability and Society,* 17 (5), 493-508.

Roulstone, A. 2000: Disability, dependency and the New Deal for Disabled People. *Disability and Society,* 15 (3), 427-443.

Shakespeare, T. 1994: Cultural Representation of Disabled People: dustbins for disavowal? *Disability and Society,* 9 (3), 283-301.

Swain, J. and French, S. 2000: Towards an Affirmatory Model of Disability. *Disability and Society,* 15 (4), 569-582.

Taylor, C. 1992: *Multiculturalism and 'The Politics of Recognition'*. Princeton: Princeton University Press

Thomas, C. 1999: *Female Forms: experiencing and understanding disability.* Buckingham: Open University Press.

Tregaskis, C. 1998: *Life Beyond Paid Employment: disabled women's experiences of giving up work.* Unpublished dissertation in partial fulfilment of MA in Disability Studies, University of Sheffield.

Vernon, A. 1999: The Dialectics of Multiple Identities and the Disabled People's Movement. *Disability and Society,* 14 (3), 385-398.

Williams, R. 1963: *Culture and Society 1780-1950.* Harmondsworth: Penguin.

Young, I. M. 1995: Gender as Seriality: thinking about women as a social collective. In L. Nicholson and S. Seidman (eds), *Social Postmodernism: beyond identity politics.* New York: Cambridge University Press.

CHAPTER 6

Psycho-emotional Dimensions of Disability and the Social Model

Donna Reeve

Introduction

Within the disability world, many of the current debates centre on the nature of disability and on interpretations of the social model of disability, which posits disability as the externally imposed,

> disadvantage or restriction caused by a contemporary social
> organisation which takes little or no account of people who have
> … impairments and thus excludes them from the mainstream
> of social activities (Oliver and Barnes 1998: 18).

This social relational definition of disability extends the one created originally by the Union of the Physically Impaired Against Segregation (UPIAS 1976) to include all impairments rather than just physical impairments. In this relational model, disability is seen as a form of social oppression, like racism, homophobia and ageism, rather than as an individual problem caused by impairment (as in the individual or medical model of disability). Recasting disability in this light has been a vital part of the move towards the emancipation of disabled people within society and has been able to highlight and challenge the social and economic disadvantage faced by disabled people (Barnes 1991).

In this chapter, I discuss the benefits of adopting the extended social relational model of disability proposed by Thomas (1999), which builds on the definition quoted above, to include both structural and psycho-emotional dimensions of disability. In this model, disability is seen as a form of social oppression that operates at both the public and personal levels, affecting what people can *do* as well as who they can *be*. I provide some examples of psycho-emotional disablism and show how this dimension of disability can leave some disabled people feeling worthless and ashamed, whilst removing others from the social world as surely as structural barriers. In the light of current debates about disability and identity, consideration of both dimensions of disability has useful implications for who is seen, and who see themselves as disabled.

However, although this extended model of disability allows for a more sophisticated and complete analysis of the ways in which both structural and psycho-emotional dimensions of disability are evident in the lives of people with impairments, there are compromises associated with adopting a more complex definition of disability. Nonetheless, more work needs to be done in order to raise the profile of the psycho-emotional dimensions of disability within disability studies and the disabled people's movement.

The extended social relational model of disability

One of the main criticisms of the social model of disability, with its emphasis on socio-structural barriers, has been that it ignores the cultural and experiential dimensions of disability (Shakespeare, 1994). Consequently, the focus has been on the 'public' experiences of oppression such as social barriers, at the expense of the more 'personal' experiences of oppression which operate at the emotional level (Thomas, 1999). In her book, *Female Forms*, Thomas (1999) proposes an extended social relational definition of disability that attempts to address this criticism:

> Disability is a form of social oppression involving the social imposition of restrictions of activity on people with impairments *and the socially engendered undermining of their psycho-emotional well-being* (Thomas, 1999: 60; *emphasis added*).

This extended social model of disability takes account of the socio-structural barriers and restrictions that exclude and discriminate against disabled people in addition to the social processes and practices which place limits on the psycho-emotional well-being of people with impairments. In other words, this extended definition of disability which incorporates both structural and psycho-emotional dimensions of disability, includes the limits on what disabled people can both do and be – for many people, such as myself, it is this latter form of disablism which is the most restricting. The agents of this disablism can be close family members or individuals with whom disabled people have direct contact such as 'professionals', in addition to disablism experienced within society at large (Thomas 1999).

These psycho-emotional dimensions of disability can be considered to be the effects of psycho-emotional pathways of oppression which are sustained through imagery, cultural representations and interactions with others:

> Going out in public so often takes courage. How many of us find that we can't dredge up the strength to do it day after day, week after week, year after year, a lifetime of rejection and revulsion?

> It is not only physical limitations that restrict us to our homes
> and those whom we know. It is the knowledge that each entry
> into the public world will be dominated by stares, by condescension,
> by pity and by hostility (Morris 1991: 25).

Thus, the experience of structural and/or psycho-emotional dimensions of
disability can prevent people with impairments from participating within
mainstream society.

Psycho-emotional dimensions of disability

The psycho-emotional dimensions of disability can be manifested in many
different ways. However it is important to note that the experience of
psycho-emotional disablism is not inevitable or unchanging. Not all disabled
people will experience this form of disability and it will change in intensity
with time and place; whether or not it is more or less disabling than their
experience of structural disability will vary and sometimes the two dimensions
reinforce each other. I will now briefly describe three examples of this
dimension of disability.

Responses to experiences of structural disability

For people with physical and sensory impairments, the experience of being
excluded from physical environments reminds them that they are different
and can leave them feeling that they don't belong in public and private spaces.

> It tells us that we aren't wanted in the places that non-disabled
> people spend their lives – their homes, their schools and colleges,
> their workplaces, their leisure venues (Morris 1991: 26-27).

Fred, a research participant who used a wheelchair, talked to me about
the problems he faced visiting a counsellor in her inaccessible house - he
had to be carried in, and once inside she made a show of needing to move
furniture in order to accommodate him. As he said,

> Here I'm supposed to be being helped, and I am just being made
> to feel more in the way (Reeve 2000a).

The counsellor's grudging admittance of Fred to her house, especially
in the way that she failed to move furniture out of the way before Fred
and his wife turned up for each of their appointments, reinforced the message
that Fred was getting from society – that he was different and that he
was not wanted here, he was out of place. Slack (1999) writes about her
experiences as a wheelchair user and the anger and frustrations which arise
from living in an inaccessible environment. She feels that her friends do
not want her to make a scene when she is faced with physical barriers
and that they do not want to recognise her experiences of oppression.

Whilst the suggestion by others that she should 'write and complain' is all very well, like many other disabled people, she could spend her entire life and energy complaining rather then trying to socialise or earn a living.

An important difference between the experience of disabled people and those from other oppressed groups in society is that the doctrine of 'separate but equal' is enshrined in law (Olkin 1999). At the start of the 21st century it would be unthinkable to make people from ethnic minority groups access a building through a different entrance to other people, and yet this is what disabled people do every day – entering an art gallery through a back entrance, using a goods lift to access a first floor classroom, travelling in the guards van on a train. Being forced to move within public space in this manner reinforces the feeling that one is a second-class citizen who is being tolerated, but only just. This manifestation of psycho-emotional disablism describes the emotional costs of moving within these 'landscapes of exclusion' (Kitchin 1998: 351) which add to the oppressive nature of structural disability.

Social interaction with others

In addition to the daily battle with disabling physical barriers, disabled people also have to deal with the reactions of others within society. Many disabled people with visible impairments have to deal with the frank curiosity of other people.

> We often experience the fascination that non-disabled people have with 'just how do you *manage?*' They have a consuming curiosity about how we pee, how we shit, how we have sex (*do* we have sex?) … Our physical difference makes our bodies public property (Morris, 1991: 29; *emphasis in original*).

It has been suggested that non-disabled people may feel that they have the right to ask these kinds of personal questions because disabled people are occupying 'their' public space, and like children and elderly people, can be approached with less respect and reserve than the average adult (Chouinard 1997). There are also expectations about what disabled people 'look' like and this can cause difficulties for those disabled people who do not match the stereotypical image of being elderly and/or a wheelchair user, especially when using facilities set up for disabled people such as disabled parking spaces or accessible toilets.

Another aspect of interacting with others that is a potential source of psycho-emotional disablism, is the experience of being stared at by others. Whilst acknowledging that the ways in which disabled people respond to the gaze of others vary and are affected by personal biographies and experience, nonetheless the experience of being stared at can leave disabled people feeling ashamed, vulnerable and invalidated. This is exemplified by one woman's narrative about her sexual experiences:

> The look of revulsion on a man's face at the sight of my naked flesh does absolute wonders for my self-esteem. And then there are the 'freak show' types. Their motives range from mild curiosity to fully blown fetishism. It's great to hear, at the peak of an orgasm, 'I've never fucked a woman in a wheelchair before' (Ball 2002: 170).

This experience of being gazed on is obviously affected by what is visible to the observer and so the experience of this form of disablism is mediated by how apparent impairment and impairment effects are to others. Someone who is unable to hide their impairment is most likely to be seen as 'disabled' by others at the expense of any other personal attributes (French 1994a). Whilst someone with a hidden impairment is less likely to be stared at by others, there is always the risk that their disability status will be revealed and this fear forms the basis for 'the negative psycho-emotional aspects of concealment' (Thomas 1999: 55).

This discussion about the interaction between disabled people and others in society is not new to disability studies. Goffman's (1963) work on stigma provides a descriptive account of how disabled people interact with non-disabled people and has rightfully been criticised for failing to provide an account of the true nature of disabled people's oppression and for presenting such interactions as inevitable (Finkelstein 1980; Bogdan and Taylor 1989). Nonetheless, for many disabled people, it is the reactions of others which affect their psycho-emotional well-being and indirectly 'restrict activity'; therefore this should be considered as an important part of the disablism present in society that needs to be challenged (Thomas 1999). As it is forty years since Goffman published his social interactionist analysis of stigma, it may now be appropriate to revisit this concept using a more recent sociological perspective.

Internalised oppression

The final element of psycho-emotional disablism I want to describe is that of internalised oppression. This can happen when individuals within a marginalised group in society internalise the prejudices held by the dominant group – the acceptance and incorporation of '*their* values about *our* lives' (Morris 1991: 29; *emphasis in original*). This form of oppression is most effective when it is acting at the subconscious level, affecting the self-esteem of the individual in addition to shaping their thoughts and actions (Marks 1999). Disabled people are surrounded by myths and stereotypes which underpin prejudices experienced on a daily basis (Morris 1991); the dearth of positive disabled role models means that these myths are never challenged and remain in place supported by media and film images (Barnes 1994). Terms of abuse within everyday language use words related to impairment such as 'too blind to see', 'out of your mind', 'words falling on deaf ears', and 'haven't got a leg to stand on' which all support the notion that to be of value, one must be physically, psychologically and mentally fit (Thomas 1995). Therefore, it is not surprising that disabled people can feel devalued and disempowered:

> Somewhere deep inside us is the almost unbearable knowledge that the way the able-bodied world regards us is as much as we have the right to expect. We are not full members of that world, and the vast majority of us can never hope to be. If we think otherwise we are deluding ourselves (Battye 1966: 8–9).

In addition, internalised oppression maintains the negative stereotypes of disabled people that are prevalent within society. If disabled people accept the prejudices and assumptions held by non-disabled people, then they become what they have internalised and become the 'slave of their archetypes' (Fanon 1986: 35).

As mentioned earlier, the agents of psycho-emotional disablism can be family, friends, professionals or strangers. Disabled children may experience more acute internalised oppression because their less powerful position means that they are more vulnerable to the views of the wider society; in addition, their parents may be unwitting oppressors in the process, because their beliefs and expectations will be shaped by the professionals they defer to (French 1994b). This can result in children having low self-esteem, which in turn can render them more vulnerable to being abused. The negative social values placed on children with impairments creates a situation in which abusers can believe that it is all right to abuse a child who is 'worthless' and the child accepts the abuse because they believe that they are 'defective' (Kennedy 1996). For example, a young man with cerebral palsy who had been sexually abused commented, 'Why bugger up a normal child, I was defective already' (Kennedy 1996: 127). This abuse extends into adulthood with disabled men and women tolerating abusive relationships because of their low self-esteem about being disabled and hence unlovable (Gillespie-Sells et al. 1998).

Again, the experience of internalised oppression is not inevitable and is affected by an individual's biography. There is the phenomena of multiple/simultaneous oppression faced by disabled people who belong to more than one minority group, such as disabled women, disabled gay men, disabled Black people (Morley 1992; Vernon 1998). Also, whilst some people will resist and fight internalised oppression, others will be unable to do so, either because they are isolated or unaware, or maybe because the support they receive is conditional on them being compliant and continuing to play the 'disabled role' (Thomas 1995). Despite the prevalence of negative stereotypes of disability within every aspect of society and the damaging effects internalised oppression has on the everyday life and health of disabled people, this phenomenon remains a currently neglected area of discussion (Marks 1999).

I consider internalised oppression to be one of the most important manifestations of psycho-emotional disablism because of its unconscious and insidious effects on the psycho-emotional well-being of disabled people and because it has a direct impact in restricting who someone can 'be'.

The relevance of the psycho-emotional dimensions of disability for a contemporary social model of disability

Whilst consideration of internalised oppression and social interactions are not new to disability studies, the inclusion of these oppressive relationships with the self and others within a social model of disability is innovative. I will now illustrate the contribution that inclusion of the psycho-emotional dimensions of disability within an extended social relational model of disability can make towards providing a more comprehensive account of disability and the related issue of identity.

Providing a more inclusive account of disability

Sometimes I don't go into my local town centre because I cannot manage the steps on that day, other times I don't go shopping because I cannot deal with the stares of others. Both of these have the same effect of keeping me out of a public space, both are the result of oppressive social relationships which require changes in the socio-structural and socio-cultural fabric rather than my individual acceptance of disability. Like psycho-emotional disablism, the experience of structural disability is not identical to all people with impairments because its effects are mediated by other factors such as class, gender and ethnicity, in addition to impairment. For people with invisible impairments or those who can pass, structural disability may be present at some time in their lives; however, the experience of psycho-emotional disablism may exert a greater influence on their well-being (Thomas 1999). Therefore, as disabled people each experience their own different degrees of structural and psycho-emotional disablism, it would be more accurate for a model to include both dimensions of disability rather than focus on structural disability alone.

These two dimensions of disability can also interact to affect the economic disadvantage faced by disabled people. The existing UPIAS social relational definition of disability does take account of the many ways in which disabled people are excluded from participation in mainstream life because of the prejudicial attitudes of others - for example, there is ample evidence of institutional and direct discrimination against disabled people in the labour market (Barnes 1991). Whilst this discrimination is undoubtedly the greatest cause of unemployment and underemployment amongst disabled people, there will also be some disabled people who do not feel confident enough to apply for jobs for which they are eminently capable because they have internalised the negative value afforded disabled people in society – the end result is the same, no job with the associated poverty this brings. It is also possible that the experience of psycho-emotional disablism can further add to this level of poverty; for example, a disabled person who is feeling worthless and stressed because of the continual experience of being excluded from the built environment, may not have the emotional strength to then fight for the benefits to which they are entitled, and instead, attempts to manage without. Thus psycho-emotional dimensions of disability can operate in conjunction with the experience of structural disability, further increasing the level of exclusion and material disadvantage experienced by people with impairments.

Whilst the Disability Discrimination Act and Disability Rights Commission are slowly improving access for disabled people to mainstream life, even in the utopian dream of a world free from socio-structural barriers, psycho-emotional disablism would still be present within our society because of the longevity of prejudicial attitudes and stereotypes about disability. Unfortunately the improvement of social attitudes towards disabled people will be a slow process if the experiences of women and minority ethnic groups are anything to go by – these two groups of people have been protected by legislation outlawing discrimination for many years and yet negative attitudes towards the members of these groups are still endemic within society (Corker 1999).

Finally, I want to briefly consider the relationship between disabled people and the medical profession. Within disability studies, criticisms have been made of the manner in which medicine advocates the pursuit of a 'normal' body at all costs and the way in which this locates the cure for disability with the individual rather than society (Oliver 1990). The treatment of disabled people at the hands of the medical profession can also have adverse effects on their emotional well-being, leaving them feeling ashamed, vulnerable and objectified (Marks 1999; Thomas 2001). Therefore, the use of a social model of disability which recognises dimensions of disability operating at the structural and psycho-emotional level allows for a more complete identification of the ways in which the actions and attitudes of health professionals disable people with impairments, in extreme cases rendering them more vulnerable to subsequent abuse by repeated exposure to medical examinations and the experience of 'public stripping' (Marks 1999).

Extending the social model of disability in this manner enables a richer analysis of the ways in which structural and psycho-emotional dimensions of disability operate within the lives of people with impairments. I now want to consider the implications of this extended definition of disability for issues of identity.

Identity and disability

A recent study (Grewal et al. 2002) showed that just over half of the people with impairments who were surveyed did not identify as disabled. The reasons for this varied: some did not feel that they were ill or incapacitated enough to count as disabled, others felt that their health problems were part of illness or the process of ageing, rather than disability. The negative images associated with disability caused some participants to be too embarrassed to identify as disabled. This same study showed that disability was persistently believed to be connected with a physical impairment that typically affected mobility, was visible, led to dependency and incapacity and was a permanent condition. This image of disability was at variance with how many of the people questioned saw themselves and so they did not see themselves as disabled. For example, one woman did not see herself as disabled because although she had severe psoriasis, she was mobile and 'able to do things'.

During a recent Disability Equality training session I was running it turned out that two of the participants in the class both had the same impairment; only one of this pair felt that she was disabled and the reason given was that she received Disabled Living Allowance. This is not the first time I have come across people with impairments who feel that they are 'allowed' to count as disabled because they qualify for disability-related benefits or have a disabled parking badge. Also many people do not see themselves as disabled because having an impairment is 'normal' for them and so they do not see themselves as different (Watson 2002).

Therefore, whilst having an impairment is an essential characteristic for someone to be able to identify as disabled, the presence of the former does not always lead to the latter. Even when people do identify as disabled, is it not a common identity for all such people – it varies from being associated with what someone is unable to do ('I'm disabled because I'm not able-bodied'), through to the 'I'm disabled and proud' identity associated with the disabled people's movement. Consequently, as Watson (2002) points out, this lack of a collective identity for people with impairments has consequences for who is actually being represented by the disabled people's movement and the associated organisations of disabled people. The issue of which individuals identify themselves as disabled, or are seen as disabled by others is not simple and clear-cut.

The issue of 'passing' is particularly interesting in this respect. Disabled people with less visible impairments have the option of passing, choosing whether or not to identify as disabled. Whilst this eases the strain of social interaction, especially amongst strangers, it can cause difficulties for the individual who is always at risk of exposure as described earlier. Unfortunately disabled people who do pass can be seen as traitors by others within the disabled people's movement – passing,

> may defend an individual against the commonality of our oppression but it is dangerous in that it denies our very identity (Morris 1991: 37).

This assumes that passing involves the active rejection of a disabled identity without allowing for the possibility that someone is simply attempting to reduce their experience of psycho–emotional disablism in that time and place (Kanuha 1999). Given the current debates about disability and identity, the issues of why, how and where people pass is of particular relevance. Consideration of the psycho-emotional dimensions of disability could contribute to a better understanding of the phenomenon of passing and its relationship to issues of identity.

Even people who do not pass, but who have visible impairments, can still experience difficulties having their disability identity accepted by others. It has been suggested that collective self-organisation is one way of developing a positive disability identity (Shakespeare 1996). Unfortunately this does not always happen; for example, the disabled people's movement has been accused of under-representing young disabled people and marginalising people with learning difficulties (Campbell and Oliver 1996). I have also come across cases in my own research where being part of an organisation of disabled people has been quite oppressive for some of the disabled people involved because of a perceived 'hierarchy of impairment' within that organisation. One of my participants did not feel she was seen as a 'real' disabled person because she was not a wheelchair user and did not have one of 'the biggies' like cancer, arthritis, multiple sclerosis or visual impairment. Consequently her identity as a disabled person was challenged by other disabled people in the organisation. The presence of a 'hierarchy of impairment' in which people with certain impairments are seen as being more entitled to identify as disabled does nothing to promote the growth of an inclusive disabled people's movement. Whilst this hierarchy has its roots in the way that society has traditionally divided disabled people up by impairment group, it is also maintained by internalised oppression, a psycho-emotional dimension of disability (Shakespeare et al. 1996).

Charlton comments that a disabled people's movement,

> must recognise that the phenomenology of oppression is a totality of lived experiences – from poverty and isolation to cultural degradation and self-pity (Charlton 1998: 82).

Thus an extended social model of disability which includes pathways of oppression operating at both the public and personal level would appear to offer one way of meeting this challenge. Consequently, this broadens the definitions of what are considered to be legitimate disability experiences which changes who identifies as disabled in the political and personal sense. This could have particular relevance for people with invisible impairments (and who can therefore pass) or those for whom impairment does not restrict physical activity, such as facial disfigurement - whilst such people may experience structural disability at some point in their life, they are more likely to be affected by psycho-emotional disablism. For example, although the woman with psoriasis described earlier did not see herself as disabled because she could 'do' things, she might view her experiences differently if the disabling reactions of others towards someone with a visible skin condition were explicitly included within a definition of disability.

There are many different reasons why people with impairments may or may not choose to identify as disabled, or be considered by others to be disabled. People may identify as disabled in one setting but not in others; one of my participants described how she identifies as a 'disabled person' at work, but elsewhere in her family and social life, her identity is that of mother and woman – her impairment and disability are not part of her identity in these other settings. Thus the process of identification is not fixed in time or place; it is also influenced by the complex intertwining of impairment effects and disability, in addition to other social identities and personal biography (Thomas 1999). In addition, the manner in which disabled people choose to resist or challenge psycho-emotional disablism has relevance for the ways in which people identify (or not) as disabled and how they challenge the 'disabled role' defined by society (Reeve 2002).

Discussion

I have described some of the ways in which psycho-emotional dimensions of disability, the 'barriers in here' work alongside and in conjunction with structural dimensions of disability, the 'barriers out there'. Whilst the psycho-emotional dimensions of disability act at the emotional level, leaving some disabled people feeling devalued and stressed, the material and physical effects of this form of disablism can be similar to the experience of socio-structural barriers which lead to exclusion and discrimination. This chapter has shown that the extended social model of disability suggested by Thomas (1999) which includes both structural and psycho-emotional dimensions of disability could offer a more sophisticated tool with which to understand the breadth of experience of disability and the associated issues of disability identity.

A powerful counter-argument to extending the social model in this manner could be that it weakens the campaigning power of the social model to effect material and political changes within society. I acknowledge that the social model of disability formulated by UPIAS in 1976, has been crucial to the fight against disabling barriers and discrimination as a means to improving the material and social lives of disabled people. I would agree that aspects of structural disability are easier to identify, challenge, and change than psycho-emotional dimensions of disability which are more deeply rooted in both the societal and individual unconscious. Therefore I can see how explicitly including a dimension of disability which operates at the emotional rather than the structural level could be perceived as weakening the power of the social model of disability to improve the lives of disabled people. One of the strengths of the current social model definition of disability is that of its relative simplicity as a concept in helping disabled people see disability as a social, rather than individual construction. This simplicity could be compromised by adopting a more complex definition of disability which explicitly references both structural and psycho-emotional dimensions of disability.

Additionally it could be argued that one of the roles of a disability culture is precisely to challenge psycho-emotional disablism by providing alternative images of disability, a collective context in which to share ideas and feelings as well as a space in which to reflect on the experience of disability from the perspective of different groups of disabled people.

> Taking part in the arts should also be viewed as a tool for change as much as attending meetings about, say, orange badge provision … Introducing disabled people to the social role of artistic creativity and opening a debate about disability culture is a dynamic way of assisting disabled people to challenge their assumed dependency and place in mainstream society (Morrison and Finkelstein 1993: 126-127).

For people such as Finkelstein, the existing social model of disability already recognises both structural and psycho-emotional dimensions of disability as evidenced by the presence of both political activism and disability arts. On the other hand, other disability studies writers (such as Shakespeare 1996; Thomas 1999) would argue that whilst this might have been the intention behind the UPIAS social model of disability, the academic and political interest has been much more focussed on structural dimensions of disability, and consequently the psycho-emotional dimensions of disability have received far less attention.

Importantly, if the social model of disability sets out to define what disables people with impairments, then it has to take account of structural and psycho-emotional dimensions of disability, which both have their origins in oppressive social relations. The question is, how should this be done? Should the social model of disability be extended to explicitly include psycho-emotional dimensions of disability as a way of bringing attention to bear on this neglected form of disablism? Or is it more appropriate to retain the political strength of a simple definition of disability and apply the social model of disability in its existing UPIAS-based form to clarify and explore psycho-emotional dimensions of disability? Whilst the extension of the social model proposed by Thomas (1999) offers a very valuable contribution to the development of a social theory of disability, it is less useful for the purposes of campaigning and effecting social change. On the other hand, the disabled people's movement must engage with some of the darker sides of the experience of oppression (Shakespeare 1996) - issues of internalised oppression and the related hierarchy of impairment. My concern is that it is easier for groups of disabled people to continue to avoid tackling these painful areas if they are not explicitly included within a definition of disability. The question about whether or not the social model of disability *needs* extending is complex and there is no obvious answer.

As part of the ongoing debates about whether or not the social model of disability should acknowledge the role of impairment in restricting the activity of disabled people, Oliver suggested that the social model of disability,

> has been a pragmatic attempt to identify and address issues that can be changed through collective action rather than medical or other professional treatment (Oliver 1996: 48).

Although the psycho-emotional dimensions of disability operate at an emotional level I would not suggest that this form of disablism can be 'fixed' by a visit to a psychologist or counsellor; such professionals generally work within an individual model of disability and are more likely to add to, rather than help resolve issues associated with the psycho-emotional dimensions of disability (Reeve 2000a; Reeve 2000b). Adopting this 'treatment of the individual' approach also supports the notion that people who are unable to participate in mainstream life because of the effects of psycho-emotional disablism are not 'really disabled' in the same way that, for example, a wheelchair user who cannot access the built environment is. Consequently their experiences of exclusion become their 'personal trouble' to overcome rather than something to be recognised and worked with collectively.

Given that psycho-emotional dimensions of disability emerge from oppressive social relations and cultural myths, then they are open instead to challenge by collective action in two ways. Firstly, experience of the disabled people's movement and disability culture can be more effective than individual counselling at challenging this hidden form of disablism through the provision of positive role models and exposure of the pervasive nature of prejudices and myths about disability. However, as indicated previously, the issue of how people identify as disabled and the ever-present hierarchy of impairment mean that even in such a collective context, some disabled people still doubt their right to be considered as a 'real' disabled person. Secondly, as socio-structural barriers within society are broken down, then it is reasonable to expect that the increasing presence of disabled people within mainstream society will slowly break down some of the stereotypes within our culture, thereby reducing still further levels of psycho-emotional disablism.

Apart from providing a possible refinement to the existing social model of disability, explicitly recognising this psycho-emotional dimension of disability will also contribute to the continuing development of a social theory of disability. Finkelstein and French have previously advocated the construction of a new approach to a psychology of disability:

> With the growth of new (social) approaches to disability, there
> is a need to develop fresh insights into the way disabled people,
> and others, make sense of, cope with, manage and overcome disabling
> social and physical barriers (Finkelstein and French 1993: 32).

In other words, there is a need to take account of the personal effects of living with disability in a manner which differs from the psychological models of loss which are more typically associated with the disability experience. This psychology of disability (rather than impairment) focuses on the psychological anxiety and distress caused by the social relations of disability and is therefore very closely related to the psycho-emotional dimensions of disability.

Finally, within disability studies there is a growing body of literature offering post-structuralist and post-modernist perspectives on disability, impairment and identity (Corker and Shakespeare 2002). Recently Shakespeare and Watson (2002) suggested that a social theory of disability would need to include all dimensions of disabled people's experiences – bodily, psychological, cultural, social and political – in order to make sense of the complex and situated nature of disability. I believe that consideration of both the psycho-emotional and structural dimensions of disability and how they interact with each other can contribute to these post-structuralist debates; I have already used a post-structuralist approach to theorise the psycho-emotional dimensions of disability, and their interrelations with impairment and identity (Reeve 2002).

Summary

This chapter has illustrated how the extension of the social model of disability to include both structural and psycho-emotional dimensions of disability, as suggested by Thomas (1999), facilitates a sophisticated analysis of the manner in which people with impairments are disabled by oppressive social relations. I have shown how the experience of exclusion from mainstream life can have an adverse effect on the psycho-emotional well-being of a person with impairments, illustrating the complex manner in which structural and psycho-emotional dimensions of disability can be intertwined and/or mutually reinforcing. Internalised oppression or dealing with the reactions of others can exclude a disabled person as effectively as an inaccessible public space and therefore any discussion about barriers to participation in mainstream society needs to include reference to both dimensions of disability. The psycho-emotional dimensions of disability also have an important contribution to make in examining the different ways in which people with impairments see themselves (or not) as disabled people, because it operates along emotional pathways.

Whilst a focus on identifying and challenging structural disability has led to considerable improvements in the lives of disabled people, this emphasis on the barriers 'out there',

> has the rather ironic consequence of leaving aspects of social life
> and social oppression which are so keenly felt by many disabled
> people (to do with self-esteem, interpersonal relationships,
> sexuality, family life and so on) 'open season' to psychologists and
> others who would not hesitate to apply the individualistic/personal
> tragedy model to these issues (Thomas, 1999: 74).

For many disabled people, it is the barriers that operate 'in here', at the psycho-emotional level which have the most disabling effect on their lives. Therefore it is high time that this dimension of disablism, which operates along emotional and psychological pathways, is given proper attention within disability theory. Whether this should be done as part of an extended model of disability as Thomas suggests, or by working within the existing social model definition of disability remains to be seen.

Acknowledgements
This paper was written as part of my PhD which is supported by an ESRC
studentship (R42200034345).

Bibliography

Ball, K. F. 2002: Who'd fuck an ableist? *Disability Studies Quarterly*, 22 (4),
    166-171.

Barnes, C. 1991: *Disabled People in Britain and Discrimination: A Case
    for Anti-Discrimination Legislation.* London: Hurst and Co. and
    BCODP.

Barnes, C. 1994: Images of disability. In S. French (ed.), *On Equal Terms:
    Working with Disabled People.* Oxford: Butterworth-Heinemann.

Battye, L. 1966: The Chatterley syndrome. In P. Hunt (ed.), *Stigma: The
    Experience of Disability.* London: Geoffrey Chapman.

Bogdan, R. and Taylor, S. J. 1989: Relationships with severely disabled people:
    the social construction of humanness. *Social Problems,* 36 (2), 135-148.

Campbell, J. and Oliver, M. 1996: *Disability Politics: Understanding our
    past, changing our future.* London: Routledge.

Charlton, J.I. 1998: *Nothing about Us without US: Disability, Oppression
    and Empowerment.* Berkeley: University of California Press.

Chouinard, V. 1997: Making space for disabling differences: challenging
    ableist geographies. *Environment and Planning D: Society and Space,*
    15, 379-387.

Corker, M. 1999: Difference, conflations and foundations: the limits to 'accurate'
    theoretical representation of disabled people's experience? *Disability
    and Society,* 14 (5), 627-642.

Corker, M. and Shakespeare, T. (eds) 2002: *Disability/Postmodernity:
    Embodying Disability Theory.* London: Continuum.

Fanon, F. 1986: *Black Skin, White Masks.* London: Pluto Press.

Finkelstein, V. 1980: *Attitudes and Disabled People: Issues for Discussion.* New
    York: World Rehabilitation Fund.

Finkelstein, V. and French, S. 1993: Towards a psychology of disability. In
    J. Swain, V. Finkelstein, S. French and M. Oliver (eds), *Disabling Barriers
    – Enabling Environments.* London: Sage and Open University Press.

French, S. 1994a: Dimensions of disability and impairment. In S. French
    (ed.), *On Equal Terms: Working with Disabled People.* Oxford:
    Butterman-Heinemann Ltd.

French, S. 1994b: The disabled role. In S. French (ed.), *On Equal
    Terms:Working with Disabled People.* Oxford: Butterman-Heinemann
    Ltd.

Gillespie-Sells, K., Hill, M. and Robbins, B. 1998: *She Dances to Different Drums: Research into Disabled Women's Sexuality.* London: King's Fund.

Goffman, E. 1963: *Stigma: Notes on the Management of Spoiled Identity.* Englewood Cliffs, NJ: Prentice Hall; Harmondsworth: Penguin 1968.

Grewal, I., Joy, S., Lewis, J., Swales, K. and Woodfield, K. 2002: *Disabled for Life? Attitudes Towards, and Experiences of Disability in Britain.* Leeds: Corporate Document Services.

Kanuha, V. K. 1999: The Social process of 'passing' to manage stigma: Acts of internalized oppression or acts of resistance? *Journal of Sociology and Social Welfare,* 26 (4), 27-46.

Kennedy, M. 1996: Sexual abuse and disabled children. In J. Morris (ed.), *Encounters with Strangers: Feminism and Disability.* London: The Women's Press.

Kitchin, R. 1998: 'Out of place, knowing one's place': space, power and the exclusion of disabled people. *Disability and Society,* 13 (3), 343-356.

Marks, D. 1999: *Disability: controversial debates and psychosocial perspectives.* London: Routledge.

Morley, L. 1992: Women's Studies, Difference, and Internalised Oppression. *Women's Studies International Forum,* 15 (4), 517-525.

Morris, J. 1991: *Pride Against Prejudice: Transforming Attitudes to Disability.* London: The Women's Press.

Morrison, E. and Finkelstein, V. 1993: Broken arts and cultural repair: the role of culture in the empowerment of disabled people. In J. Swain, V. Finkelstein, S. French and M. Oliver (eds), *Disabling Barriers - Enabling Environments.* London: Sage and Open University Press.

Oliver, M. 1990: *The Politics of Disablement.* Basingstoke: Macmillan.

Oliver, M. 1996: Defining Impairment and Disability: issues at stake. In C. Barnes and G. Mercer (eds), *Exploring the Divide: Illness and Disability.* Leeds: The Disability Press.

Oliver, M. and Barnes, C. 1998: *Disabled People and Social Policy: From Exclusion to Inclusion.* Harlow: Addison Wesley Longman.

Olkin, R. 1999: *What Psychotherapists Should Know About Disability.* New York: The Guilford Press.

Reeve, D. 2000a: Negotiation of disability and impairment within counselling relationships: a critical evaluation from the perspective of clients with spinal cord injuries. Unpublished MA Thesis, Leeds: University of Leeds.

Reeve, D. 2000b: Oppression within the Counselling Room. *Disability and Society,* 15 (4), 669-682.

Reeve, D. 2002: Negotiating psycho-emotional dimensions of disability and
    their influence on identity constructions. *Disability and Society,* 17 (5),
    493–508.

Shakespeare, T. 1994: Cultural Representation of Disabled People: dustbins
    for disavowal? *Disability and Society,* 9 (3), 283–299.

Shakespeare, T. 1996: Disability, Identity, Difference. In C. Barnes and G.
    Mercer (eds), *Exploring the Divide: Illness and Disability.* Leeds: The
    Disability Press.

Shakespeare, T., Gillespie-Sells, K. and Davies, D. 1996: The Sexual Politics
    of Disability: Untold Desires. London: Cassell.

Shakespeare, T. and Watson, N. 2002: The social model of disability: an
    outdated ideology? *Research in Social Science and Disability,* 2, 9–28.

Slack, S. 1999: I am more than my wheels. In M. Corker and S. French
    (eds), *Disability Discourse.* Buckingham: Open University Press.

Thomas, C. 1999: *Female Forms: Experiencing and Understanding Disability.*
    Buckingham: Open University Press.

Thomas, C. 2001: Medicine, gender and disability: disabled women's health
    care encounters. *Health Care for Women International,* 22 (3), 245–
    262.

Thomas, P. 1995: Internalised oppression, *Coalition,* February, 5–7.

UPIAS. 1976: *Fundamental Principles of Disability.* London: Union of the
    Physically Impaired Against Segregation.

Vernon, A. 1998: Multiple oppression and the disabled people's movement.
    In T. Shakespeare (ed.), *The Disability Reader: Social Science Perspectives.*
    London: Cassell.

Watson, N. 2002: Well, I know this going to sound very strange to you,
    but I don't see myself as a disabled person: identity and disability.
    Disability and Society, 17 (5), 509–527.

CHAPTER 7

The Dialectics of Disability: a social model for the 21st Century?

Nick Watson

Introduction

This chapter will argue that the social model of disability has been a useful political tool for the mobilisation of a movement. It is, however, suggested that the social model is inadequate and that, unless it is modified, political action will continue to be based on an incomplete picture of disability. Central to this argument is the social model's rejection of experience. This runs the danger of continuing to exclude the experiences of various groups such as women, older people and people from different ethnic groupings.

The chapter starts by briefly exploring the social model as a concept and as an ideology/practice. It then moves on to explore the social model in research. The final section presents ideas towards a new political construction of disability based on the ideas of the German philosopher Axel Honneth.

The concept and ideology of the social model

The social model of disability has been highly influential in the development of disability politics and disability theory in the UK. Its effect has been powerful in both the actions of and the underlying philosophy of organisations of disabled people and in academic circles. Indeed, one writer has gone so far as to proclaim it as 'the big idea' of the British disability movement (Hasler 1993). The social model was developed in the 1970's by disabled activists from UPIAS. The core definition of the British social model comes in the document, *Fundamental Principles of Disability,* which states:

> In our view, it is society which disables physically impaired people. Disability is something imposed on top of our impairments, by the way we are unnecessarily isolated and excluded from full participation in society. Disabled people are therefore an oppressed group in society…. To understand this it is necessary

to grasp the distinction between the physical impairment and
the social situation, called 'disability', of people with such
impairment. Thus we define impairment as lacking part of or
all of a limb, or having a defective limb, organism or mechanism
of the body; and disability as the disadvantage or restriction of
activity caused by a contemporary social organisation which takes
little or no account of people who have physical impairments
and thus excludes them from participation in the mainstream
of social activities (UPIAS 1976: 3-4, 14).

The importance of the social model cannot be downplayed. It challenged
understandings of disability and sought to dislodge the association of disability
with mental or physical incapacity. It contains several key elements. Disabled
people are an oppressed social group. It distinguishes between the impairments
that people have, and the oppression which they experience. And most
importantly, it defines 'disability' as the social oppression, not the form of
impairment.

The work of Mike Oliver (1983, 1990, 1996) has been among the most
influential in the articulation and academic development of the social model.
Under his influence, together with that of other theorists such as Vic
Finkelstein (1980, 1981) and Colin Barnes (1991) the social model has
become the mainstay of disability studies in the UK. The social model has
become what Shakespeare and Watson (2001) have termed 'the litmus test
of disability politics': if the work draws on the social model then it is seen
as progressive, if it does not it is seen as deficient.

Writings and research in this paradigm focus on the disabling environment
– the physical and social barriers which exclude disabled people and render
them powerless and voiceless. It presents a materialist analysis. Colin Barnes
in his book *Disabled People in Britain and Discrimination* (1991) provided, perhaps,
the most comprehensive and cogent account till then of the discrimination
faced by disabled people in the UK. He documents the barriers to equal
participation and opportunity in education, health service provision,
employment, housing, transport, the built environment, leisure and social
activities. This work has been replicated in other studies. For example,
employment (Hyde 1996), parenthood (Thomas 1997), education (Barton
1995), housing (Harris et al. 1997), and ageing (Zarb and Oliver 1993).

All of this work presents evidence of the systematic discrimination against
disabled people. It is clear that disabled people are treated unequally in almost
all aspects of their lives. This discrimination spans both the public and private
spheres and challenges those who suggest that disability should be seen as
an individual experience arising as a consequence of unfortunate personal

circumstances; what Oliver terms 'the personal tragedy theory'. Their arguments are very compelling. It closely mirrors early second wave feminist arguments. Thus when feminism distinguishes sex and gender, disability studies separates impairment and disability, the former physical and the latter social and cultural (Shakespeare and Watson 1995). There is, however, a key distinction to be made between the sex/gender and impairment/disablement analysis. The former does not assume oppression instead gender is a social role or identity.

The relatively straightforward reconstruction of disability, from the individual to the social, has proved to be a powerful tool in the mobilisation of a movement, and in political campaigns for change. At a political level, the social model has enabled the discussion of disability issues within a discourse of rights and citizenship, rather than one of personal inadequacy and professional competence. Put simply, it is no longer the individual that has the 'problem'. Further, this social re-location of disability reflected the numerous attempts to create more enabling environments and for a more concerted political assault on disabling barriers (Barnes 1991). Through the social model, organisations of disabled people and disability studies have challenged the medicalised division of disabled people into professionally controlled impairment groups and offered a new sense of commonality in the shared experience of resisting oppression (Oliver 1990)

There is no doubting the political potency of the social model. The strength of the Disabled People's Movement in the UK is testimony to this. It is also rhetorically appealing but its exposure to extended debate and academic scrutiny has placed it under strain. These critiques have come from both within the disabled people's movement and from outside. Critics have argued that the sense of political commonality often associated with the social model has been contested as an over-simplification of the complexity and diversity in disabled people's lived experience. Bury (1996) and Pinder (1996) for example, accuse the social model of producing an 'over-socialised' conceptualisation of the processes involved in producing disability. It is, they argue, relativist and reductionist. By reifying disabling environments, the social model runs the danger of presenting only a partial picture of the experiences of disability. This partial picture is as potentially damaging as the focus on 'bodies-to-be-rehabilitated' found in the medical model. The social model represents only a 'part of a much more complex multi-layered picture' (Pinder 1996:137). What is required, they suggest, is a working definition of disability linked to impairment.

Attention has also been drawn to the less than effective manner which the social model reconciles dimensions of gender (Morris 1991, 1993), 'race' and ethnicity (Stuart 1992; Vernon 1996), class (Williams 1983), generation (Shakespeare and Watson 2001), identity (Shakespeare 1996), and sexuality (Shakespeare et al. 1996), within or alongside disability. It could be argued, following Shakespeare (1994), that the bracketing of impairment, a central tenet of the ideology of the social model, is the cause of the inability of the social model to provide explanations in many of these examples. It could also be argued that the social model's emphasis on the material at the expense of the relational and consequent rejection of experience has been central to these deficiencies in social model theorising. It is to the place of experience in disability theory that this chapter now turns.

Research and the social model

The advent of the social model of disability has also challenged the methods employed in academic research on disability (Abberley 1987, 1992). Disability theorists have pointed out the divide that exists between those who are researched, 'the subjects', and those who research, the researchers, and the power imbalance that this creates. Researchers are able to control the design, the implementation, the analysis and the dissemination of their work. Consequently disabled people have little control in the overall research process (Barnes and Mercer 1997). This serves to promote an epistemology that reasserts an essentialist divide between disabled and non-disabled people, between the researched and the researcher. Disability studies' claims echo those in feminist theory by, for example Haraway (1988), which argue that the researched are 'othered' or forced into a position of difference: 'are not allowed *not* to have a body' (p.575). Thus, Abberley (1987) shows how, throughout so much of the research, disabled people are presented as 'passive research subjects' (p.141).

In addition, the usefulness of research and the motives of academics have been questioned (Oliver 1992; Barnes and Mercer 1997). In a controversial and acerbic attack on research into disability, Oliver (1992) condemns previous mainstream research in the area as a 'rip off'. He argues that it has failed to address the social oppression faced by disabled people or to establish an alternative social policy that may bring about an improvement in the lives of disabled people. For Oliver:

> Disability research should not be seen as a set of technical objective procedures carried out by 'experts' but part of the struggle by disabled people to challenge the oppression they currently experience in their lives (Oliver 1992:102).

Drawing on the evolving 'critical social research' paradigm of feminist writers such as Lather (1987) and Ribbens (1990) he argues against both positivist and interpretivist approaches that disability research should become emancipatory:

The development of such a paradigm stems from the gradual rejection of the positivist view of social research as the pursuit of absolute knowledge through the scientific method and the gradual disillusionment with the interpretative view of such research as the generation of socially useful knowledge within particular historical and social contexts. The emancipatory paradigm, as the name implies, is about the facilitating of a politics of the possible by confronting social oppression at whatever level it occurs (Oliver 1992:110).

He contends that oppression cannot be addressed in an objective or scientific manner; it warrants an openly partisan and politically committed approach and following Becker (1963) should take the side of the oppressed. He calls for 'what has variously been called critical inquiry, praxis or emancipatory research' (1992:107). Research must confront disability and must be located in the social model of disability, rejecting impairment as the root cause of disabled people's problems.

Oliver (1997:25) has further argued that one cannot 'do' emancipatory research, but it is the role of that research that must be emancipatory. For social model theorists such as Finkelstein, Barnes and Oliver, Utopia, namely the removal of disability, can be created by changing consciousness, replacing individualistic models of disability with the social model. Theory, following Marx, becomes transformative: as disabled people adopt the social model, their understanding of themselves, of their position in society, of the institutions they access are altered; disabled people are thus transformed into political activists. Research must therefore seek to document discrimination, making disabled people aware that the problems they face are the outcome of the way that society is organised to exclude them. Barnes' *Disabled People in Britain and Discrimination* (1991) exemplifies this approach. The approach closely mirrors that of Freire, the knowledge generated by research aims to redefine disabled people as subjects, allowing them to transform and recreate their world:

> the 'pedagogy of the oppressed' [is] a pedagogy which must be forged *with*, not *for*, the oppressed (be they individuals or whole peoples) in the incessant struggle to regain their humanity. This pedagogy makes oppression and its causes objects of reflection by the oppressed, and from that reflection will come their necessary engagement in the struggle for their liberation (Freire 1972:25).

This is not to suggest that these writers have reached their position without documenting the experiences of disabled people. Indeed the work by Oliver et al (1988), Zarb and Oliver (1993), and Barnes (1990) explicitly draws on the experiences of disabled people. As Zarb and Oliver write in their report on ageing with a disability:

> it is impossible to develop appropriate policies and support services without an awareness of, and a sensitivity to people's subjective experiences of ageing with a disability (1993: 32).

However, Oliver (1997), whilst acknowledging that research into disablement must provide a description of the experience of disablement, argues that this experience must be presented in a manner that,

> redefines the problem of disability away from it being an individual or welfare one, transforming it into a political one (p. 21).

By rejecting individual accounts of impairment, the focus is directed at political action:

> If a person's physical pain is the reason they are unhappy then there is nothing the disability movement can do about it. All that BCODP can do is facilitate the politicisation of people around these issues. Of course this politicisation is fairly difficult to make practical progress with – much easier to achieve anti-discrimination legislation than a total review of how society regards death and dying I imagine. This might explain why these subjects haven't been made a priority but their day will come (Vasey 1992: 43).

Research into disability must therefore be seen as part of an attempt to foster a critical attitude by disabled people towards a disabling society. The social model is a means to provide the theory of change, contributing to the transformation of a mass of disabled people into a politicised grouping whose personal discontents will be translated into a public struggle.

The danger of this strategy is that it leaves social model theorists open to the charge that if disability is already defined by the social model, then it assumes what it is intended to uncover. Disability Studies, with its reliance on a theory that was posited in the 1970's and its resistance to adaptation to the changing nature of society runs the risk of becoming a theoretical dogma, forsaking its critical purpose. It is attached to a fixed body of ideas and research is positioned in such a way as to reinforce that attachment rather than challenge it. The social model, if it is to be representative of the experiences of disabled people, must have a commitment to ongoing social change. Its claims to validity must be attached to the historical juncture in which it arose. If the aim of disability studies is to provide a critical theory then it must continually engage in the process of reconstruction and reformulation.

The social model, by its very nature, rests on a fairly unreflexive acceptance of the disabled/non-disabled distinction. There is an essentialist and totalising understanding of disability as a category. The awareness that the current understanding of disability and disabled people are historically contingent appears to have few implications for the degree to which it is utilised in the social model, or for that matter in the interactionist accounts, as a stable descriptive classification. Disabled people are seen as those who identify as such (Oliver 1996) or who can be so identified. But Liggett argues:

> From an interpretative point of view the minority group approach is double edged because it means enlarging the discursive practices which participate in the constitution of disability.... in order to participate in their own management disabled people have had to participate as disabled. Even among the politically active, the price of being heard is understanding that it is the disabled who are speaking (1988: 271ff).

Liggett is following those post-structuralist authors who point out the costs to identity politics. To be an activist - whether as a gay person, or a woman, or a disabled person - is to make the label into a badge, to make the ghetto into an oppositional culture. Yet what about those who wish to be ordinary, not different? Ligget is, in effect, arguing for a collapse of social classification, even though many disabled people do not self identify as disabled (Watson 2002).

The social model could not be described as ahistorical, but it does presuppose that disability is a bounded category with a singular intrinsic meaning. Whilst the issues surrounding disability might change, the crucial essence stays the same. Disability is allocated the status of a signifier so that research addresses the problem of disability. Disability is taken as a given. Disabled people and disability are positioned within well-worn dichotomies (such as impaired/ non-impaired, body/ society, therapy/ emancipation, resistance/ conformity, domination/ subordination). This is underpinned by an understanding of power as global, coercively subordinating disabled people. Thus a powerful ruling class, or capitalism as Oliver (1990, 1996) depicts it, is positioned as dominating powerless disabled people. Disabled people are unable to reach their full potential due to the repressive effects of a non-disabled society.

The social model has much to recommend it as the onus for change is placed on society rather than on disabled people. Disabled people cease to be the object of intervention and are repositioned as subjects in their own lives (Shakespeare 1994). Disability is conceptualised as a form of social oppression, and disabled people become a distinct social group, in a similar fashion to the way black people, lesbians and gays have claimed through respective political movements. Consequently, it is not useful to separate various impairment groups - people with visual impairment, with physical impairment, with learning difficulties - as has been the practice of charities, schools and other agencies and organisations. This is an important insight into the collectivity of the disability experience. Organisations of disabled people have challenged traditional approaches to disability and a new and active socio-political movement has emerged, transforming disability into a major area of political concern.

However, this notion of a collectivity can obscure differences between disabled people, which may be about gender, ethnicity, sexuality, class, generation and impairment. It can also deny the individuality of disabled people, presenting disabled people as a homogenous group and presenting a notion of an essential unity of disabled people. It tells little of the actual experience of living with an impairment or of the personal experience of disablement, or of how disabled people feel about themselves. Consequently, a more structural, material analysis is favoured. There is little room to allow for the differences between disabled people, indeed to even acknowledge the presence of such differences could be seen as weakening the disability movement, which, in the UK, has its theoretical framework in the social model. There is a danger that disabled people cease to be seen as individuals, as the commonality of their experience is all-important.

These many strains on the social model suggest that a new approach is needed; one that incorporates the experience of disabled people but at the same time maintains a political element. Importantly, experience must not be limited to disablement, but must include some acknowledgement of impairment. The discussion now presents ideas on what such a model might look like.

Towards a new political construction of disability
What is needed is an analysis that provides an alternative to these customary views, one that rejects these simplistic dichotomies, rejecting the idea of disability or disabled people as a coherent 'fact in itself'. Mairian Corker's (1999) work has been among the first to apply such ideas to the field of disability. To achieve this shift, it is necessary to employ a more subtle and flexible understanding of power than is found in much of the social model theorising and to extricate disability from the binary oppositions in which it is usually located.

Corker (1999), drawing on Oliver's (1996: 52) assertion that the social model should not be seen as a social theory of disability but as one strand of it and that there is a danger in trying to take it further than it is meant to go, argues that what is needed is an approach rooted in discursive strategies to complement the structural analysis favoured by the social model. She writes that it is the relationship between 'the cultural/structural and the material/discursive' (Corker 1999: 639) that should form the basis of theorising. This is seen as important because:

the addition of this paradigm would... open up political
discourse to issues of language and difference and their relationship
to the unequal distribution of knowledge. It would also allow
us to address more fully the question of disabled people's social
agency, and the sticky issue of attitudes and discriminatory
language that cannot be explained within materialism alone (Corker
1999: 640).

Through such an analysis, disablement would emerge not as the collective
experience of oppression, as in the social model, but through the relationship
between impairment and oppression. It therefore follows that if either
oppression or impairment is removed from the equation, then disablement
itself goes. The notion of disability as a 'universality' is rejected, disabled people
are not an homogenous group. It also allows for the inclusion of other types
of oppression. If disablement alone is the focus of attention, all other kinds
of oppression can become marginalised, hidden or repressed. So, in such
an analysis the differences in disablement experienced between gender,
ethnic groupings sexual preferences and age can emerge.

However, much post-modernism renders any application of the concept
of social justice as problematic (Harvey 1993). If there are no universal truths,
there is no concept of universal justice. There are no normative standards
to distinguish between the progressive and the reactionary, indeed these latter
two terms cannot be employed. Social justice is itself situated, contingent,
the concept can be deconstructed. So Harvey writes:

There are only particular, competing, fragmented and heterogeneous
conceptions of and discourses about justice which arise out of
the particular situations of those involved (1993: 98-99).

There are no foundational appeals to the common good, as such concepts
are no longer seen as carrying rhetorical authority.

The discursive turn as suggested by Corker (1999) denies, through its rejection
of a universal disabling condition, an appeal to a universal social justice. Yet,
at the same time, she is attempting to promote resistance to the cultural conditions
which shape and cause disablement. These cultural conditions are, in the
main, general and systematic. Disabled people all face discrimination, and if
a strategy is to be developed to tackle this discrimination, then it can only
be successful if a normative sense of justice using universally valid systems
is employed (White 1991). Only through applying such a normative standard
is it possible to develop and work towards a desired end, namely the removal
of disabling barriers and attitudes. Post-modernist approaches cannot engage
with the meta-narratives that dominate the lives of disabled people. The
wider political and economic powers that are manifest throughout capitalist

systems go unchanged. As the old joke goes 'How many post-modernists does it take to change a light bulb?' Post-modernism changes nothing.

Oppression still exists. It is a 'reality' for disabled people and is routinised in their lives (Watson *forthcoming*). To turn this into a political strategy, then, requires a means by which this hurt engendered by private experiences of injury are channelled into political actions that accord with the political aspirations of the disabled people's movement. A language needs to be developed which allows for the forming of a model of disablement through which these feelings of hurt can be seen not as individual assaults, but as part of a systematic attack which can be shown to be typical for disabled people as a whole. The social model, with its denial of the importance of experience and its emphasis on material relations fails in this in many ways. Disablement is not, at an individual level, perceived to be an attack on material opportunities. Disabled people are not competing for scarce goods in a market place. Rather, disablement is felt as the outcome of the withholding of social and cultural recognition, and it is this that should form the basis of the social struggle.

The German philosopher Axel Honneth (1995) argues that it is important to reconcile the individual as well as the collective dimensions of political struggles. He argues that disrespect can be the starting point for politically motivated action, leading to what he terms a 'struggle for recognition'. Disrespect comprises humiliation, disenfranchisement, insult and physical abuse, all processes to which the informants report that they are subjected to, whilst recognition is seen as the ascription of a positive status. He continues:

> the negative emotion accompanying the experience of disrespect
> could represent precisely the affective motivational basis in
> which the struggled for recognition is anchored (Honneth
> 1995: 135).

For him, self-confidence, self-respect and self-esteem provide the possibility of identity formation. This works at three levels; relationships, legal rights and solidarity. In the later term, Honneth is not referring merely to solidarity within groups, but, importantly, between groups. Through relationships, self-confidence emerges; through rights, a sense of personal dignity emerges; and through solidarity, self esteem. Denial of relationships can result in a loss of physical integrity, denial of self-respect, social integrity, and denial of self-esteem can damage honour and dignity. It is a need for recognition that drives minority communities to mobilise for change and it is the negative emotional reactions that result from the experiences of being denied recognition that form the motivational basis for social struggle. He cites the work of the Marxist historian E. P. Thompson (1963) who suggests that social rebellion requires more than economic hardship. It requires a violation of the accepted moral consensus, a denial of what are felt to be the moral expectations of people within that community, that is recognition.

There is a material element to Honneth's work, in that he clearly recognises the need for legal protection and civil rights. However, rather than seeing this as an abstract, unconnected concept, Honneth shows how the impact of rights can have an interpersonal, subjective element:

> Since possessing rights means being able to raise socially accepted claims, they provide one with a legitimate way of making clear to oneself that one is respected by everyone else (1995: 120).

Through such an approach he manages to present a rights-based discourse at a personal level. Further, his arguments on solidarity articulate why such an approach is important, again at an inter-subjective level:

> The more successful social movements are at drawing the public's attention to the neglected significance of the traits and abilities which they collectively represent, the better their chances of raising the social worth, or indeed standing, of their members (1995: 127).

What is therefore needed then is a political activism that is founded on ethical rights and expectations. The disabled people's movement, at the same time as focussing on, for example, employment legislation and environmental access, should be placing emphasis on interpersonal relations as it is through such relations that people experience recognition as active, capable social agents or find such recognition denied. By focussing solely on the material, a distance is created between disabled people's experiences of disablement, which occur at the interpersonal, and the political response. Through a focus on both legal and interpersonal relations the possibilities are opened up for an historically situated transformation of the social relations of disabled people.

What then would be the practical elements of such an approach? First, disablement should be challenged at an interpersonal level. Impairment and disablement are not dichotomous; one cannot be ascribed to the biological or personal and the other to the social. They are both experienced at a societal level and become apparent through interaction (Hughes and Patterson 1997; Watson 2000). These structures are experienced not as facts, but as an outcome. Social structures do not exist outside of the sociological imagination. So Lemert writes:

> social structures are by their very nature re-constructions of reality *after the fact*. No one ever encounters the reality of structures as such – not markets, not states, not stratification systems. Real people, rather, encounter insufficient pay checks, impossibly excluding bureaucratic rules, and particular slights and injuries,

but not the structures themselves. The reality of social structures is always, unavoidably, composed in the sociological imagination (1997:74).

Structures are perceived as the product of discourse, they occur in language, and through social interaction. Social structures are contingent and invented, they do not rest on a solid foundation, but are open to change, to local reading, to reinvention. To discuss social structures without examining the language, the signs, the images through which structures emerge is to suggest that structures exist as some form of social reality, some tangible product that can be seen and felt. It is this interaction that should form the basis of any challenges to disablement. These relationships are constructed through impairment and disablement. In terms of impairment, the disabled people's movement should seek to challenge and overturn essentialist notions of normality. This is not a new idea (Zola 1989; Shakespeare and Watson 1995; Hughes and Patterson 1997), and also draws on the work of Sutherland:

> A more radical approach is needed: we must demolish the false dividing line between 'normal' and 'disabled' [meaning impaired] and attack the whole concept of physical normality. We have to recognise that disablement [impairment] is not merely the physical state of a small minority of people. *It is the normal condition of humanity* (Sutherland 1981: 18, *original emphasis*).

Second, meta-narratives need not be forsworn. Disabling social relations are everywhere and, as Fraser and Nicholson (1990: 34) argue in relation to sexism, disablism is deeply embedded in contemporary society. Disabling societal macro-structures need to be analysed and challenged. However, these theoretical responses must be situated in specific social, cultural and historical contexts. There is no unitary notion of either disabled people or a disabled person. Impairment and disablement are but strands of a complexly constructed social identity. Age, gender, ethnicity, class and sexuality, among many others, are all of equal important and can create differences between disabled people. Whilst the acknowledgement of such differences could be seen as a threat to the internal solidarity of the disability movement, without it, there will be difficulties in building alliances with other movements. Further, within this analysis, it is important to remember that there is no such thing as a barrier free environment; facilitating some people excludes others. Even in the absence of barriers, people with impairment may still be excluded. This material reality must be acknowledged if the relationship between impairment and disablement is to be fully explored (Abberley 1987).

Third, disability studies and the disabled people's movement should engage in more ethnographic and qualitative research so as to present a

THE DIALECTICS OF DISABILITY:
A SOCIAL MODEL FOR THE 21ST CENTURY?

113

picture of the 'realities' of being a disabled person in the early 21st Century. That is, through stories and narratives of and by disabled people, disabled people will be enabled to express the heterogeneity of their lives, the fluid, situated and contextual nature of both disablement and impairment and the meaning of disability and impairment and through this to develop a value system that represents the diversity of the disability experience. Examples of this sort of approach include the work of Shakespeare et al. (1996) on sexuality and disability which documents, for the first time, disabled people's own views on sex and their sexuality; and studies of disabled children (Shakespeare and Watson 1998). This work, by presenting disabled children's perspective on their own stories, makes possible new forms of distinctive identities which are not based on essentialist characteristics. Work in the popular media also comes into this category, so for example the BBC television series *The Disabled Century*, and Peter White's Radio 4 series *No Triumph, No Tragedy* present new images of disabled people that challenge cultural stereotypes. This work, as well as challenging disabling images, establishes disabled people as active agents, as subjects rather than objects and allows disabled people to see themselves as a member of a social group who can accomplish things and whose worth is recognised by all members of society.

This focus on ethnography can create problems. As Connell (1997) argues in respect to ethnographic work on sexuality, there is a danger that emphasis can be placed on what distinguishes one group of people from another, in this case disabled people from non-disabled people, rather than what links them. This can be avoided provided similarities are highlighted and that disabled people are included in other ethnographic studies focussing on, for example, sexuality, ethnicity, age or gender.

Through this tripartite approach a more comprehensive and inclusive social theory of disability can emerge. This approach mirrors that of Zola (1994), who, just before his death, argued for a plurality of approaches in the study of disability. Further, the adequacy of current theory to support the actions of the disabled people's movement can be ascertained, for if these campaigns are to be effective they must work with rather than against disabled people's beliefs. By the use of studies giving primacy to the views and experiences of disabled people an understanding of commonly held ideas about the nature of disablement and the experiences of having an impairment that are historically situated can emerge. The question of whether research is or is not emancipatory becomes redundant. It is replaced with two questions: is this work based on the views and experiences of disabled people and has it come from a perspective that rejects normative values on the impact of impairment and disability on people's lives? If the answers are 'yes', then the work is emancipatory in that it will provide further evidence for the creation of solidarities both within and between groups. Through such an analysis an understanding of disability can evolve which is grounded in the social and cultural context of living with an impairment. Disability will be seen not as either the product of an individual trait, the impairment, nor as simply a social product, but as a fluid multiplicity that is subject to complex structural and interactional factors.

Review

Disability should not be studied from either an exclusively political approach, as found in the social model, or an academic approach confined to anthropology and sociology. Both approaches are needed so as to allow an analysis of the oppression faced by disabled people and the social experiences of living with an impairment. What the proposal here is suggesting is just such a plurality, but importantly, one that is grounded in the experiences of disabled people and that disabled people can themselves connect with. It provides the possibility of moving beyond boundaries and reinventing disability politics as a democratic movement.

Bibliography

Abberley P. 1987: The concept of oppression and the development of a social theory of disability. *Disability, Handicap and Society,* 2 (1), 5-19.

Abberley, P. 1992: Counting us out: A discussion of the OPCS disability surveys. *Disability, Handicap and Society,* 7 (2), 139-155.

Barnes, C. 1990: *Cabbage Syndrome.* Lewes: Falmer Press.

Barnes, C. 1991: Disabled People in Britain and Discrimination: A Case for Anti-Discrimination Legislation. London: Hurst and Co. in associations with BCODP.

Barnes, C. and Mercer, G. (eds) 1997: *Doing Disability Research.* Leeds: The Disability Press.

Barton, L. 1995: Segregated Special Education: Some critical observations. In G. Zarb (ed.), *Removing Disabling Barriers.* London: Policy Studies Institute.

Becker, H. 1963: *Outsiders: Studies in the Sociology of Deviance.* New York: Free Press.

Bury, M. 1996: Defining and researching disability: Challenges and responses. In C. Barnes and G. Mercer (eds), *Exploring the Divide: Illness and Disability.* Leeds: The Disability Press.

Connell, R. 1997: Sexual Revolution. In L. Segal (ed.), *New sexual agendas*. Basingstoke: Macmillan.

Corker, M. 1999: Differences, Conflations and Foundations: The limits to 'accurate' theoretical representation of disabled people's experiences. *Disability and Society,* 14 (5), 627-642.

Finkelstein, V. 1980: *Attitudes and Disabled People: Issues for Discussion.* (Monograph number Five). New York: World Rehabilitation Fund.

Finkelstein, V. 1981: To deny or not to deny disability. In A. Brechin, P. Liddiard and J. Swain (eds), *Handicap in a Social World.* Milton Keynes: Hodder and Stoughton, in association with Open University Press.

Fraser, N. and Nicholson, L. 1990: Social criticism without philosophy: an encounter between feminism and postmodernism. In L. Nicholson (ed.), *Feminism/Postmodernism.* London: Routledge.

Friere, P. 1972: *The Pedagogy of the Oppressed.* Harmondsworth: Penguin.

Haraway, D. 1988: Situated Knowledge: The science question in feminism and the privilege of partial perspective. *Feminist Studies,* 14 (3), 575-599.

Harris, J., Sapey, B., and Stewart, J. 1997: *Wheelchair Housing and The Estimation of Need.* Preston: University of Central Lancashire.

Harvey, D. 1993: Class relations, social justice and the politics of difference. In J. Squires (ed.), Principled Positions: postmodernism and the rediscovery of value. London: Lawrence Wishart.

Hasler, F. 1993: Developments in the Disabled People's Movement. In J. Swain, V. Finkelstein, S. French and M. Oliver (eds), *Disabling Barriers – Enabling Environments.* London: Sage.

Honneth, A. 1995: *The Struggle for Recognition: The Moral Grammar of Social Conflicts.* Cambridge: Polity Press.

Hughes, B. and Paterson, K. 1997: The social model of disability and the disappearing body: Towards a sociology of impairment. *Disability and Society,* 12 (3), 325-340.

Hyde, M. 1996: Fifty Years of Failure: Employment Services for Disabled People in the UK. *Work, Employment and Society,* 10, 683-700.

Lather, P. 1987: Research as Praxis. *Harvard Educational Review,* 56 (3), 257-273.

Lemert, C. 1997: *Post modernism is not what you think.* Oxford: Blackwell.

Liggett, H. 1988: Stars are not born; an interpretive approach to the politics of disability. *Disability, Handicap and Society,* 3 (3), 263 – 276.

Morris, J. 1991: *Pride Against Prejudice.* London: The Women's Press.

Morris, J. 1993: Gender and Disability. In J. Swain, V. Finkelstein, S. French and M. Oliver (eds), *Disabling Barriers - Enabling Environments.* London: Sage.

Oliver, M. 1983: *Social Work with Disabled People.* Basingstoke: Macmillan.

Oliver, M. 1990: *The Politics of Disablement.* Basingstoke: Macmillan.

Oliver, M. 1992: Changing the social relations of research production. *Disability, Handicap and Society,* 7 (2), 101-115.

Oliver, M. 1996: *Understanding disability: From theory to practice.* Basingstoke: Macmillan.

Oliver, M. 1997: Emancipatory Research. In C. Barnes and G. Mercer (eds), *Doing Disability Research.* Leeds: The Disability Press.

Oliver, M., Zarb, G., Silver, J. and Moore, M. 1988: *Walking into darkness: The experience of spinal cord injury.* Basingstoke: Macmillan.

Pinder, R. 1996: Sick-but-fit or fit-but-sick? Ambiguity and identity at the workplace. In C. Barnes and G. Mercer (eds), *Exploring the Divide: Illness and disability.* Leeds: The Disability Press.

Ribbens, J. 1990: Interviewing - An unnatural situation. *Women's Studies International Forum,* 12 (6), 579-592.

Shakespeare, T. 1994: Cultural representation of disabled people: Dustbins for disavowal. *Disability, Handicap and Society,* 8 (3), 249-264.

Shakespeare, T. 1996: Disability, Identity and Difference. In C. Barnes and G. Mercer (eds), *Exploring the Divide: Illness and Disability.* Leeds: The Disability Press.

Shakespeare, T., Gillespie-Sells, K. and Davies, D. 1996: *The Sexual Politics of Disability: untold desires.* London: Cassell.

Shakespeare, T. and Watson, N. 1995: Habeamus corpus? Disability studies and the issue of impairment. Paper presented at Quincentennial Conference, University of Aberdeen.

Shakespeare, T. and Watson, N. 1998: Theoretical Perspectives on Disabled Childhood. In C. Robinson and K. Stalker (eds), *Growing Up With Disability.* London: Jessica Kingsley.

Shakespeare, T. and Watson, N. 2002: The Social Model of Disability: An outdated ideology? *Research in Social Science and Disability,* 2, 9-28.

Stuart, O. 1992: Race and Disability: Just a double oppression? *Disability, Handicap and Society,* 7 (2), 177-188.

Sutherland, A. 1981: *Disabled We Stand.* London: Souvenir Press.

Thomas, C. 1997: The Baby and the Bath Water: Disabled Women and Motherhood in Social Context. *Sociology of Health and Illness,* 19 (3), 622-643.

Thompson, E. P. 1963: *The Making of the English Working Class.* London: Gollancz.

Vasey, S. 1992: A response to Liz Crow. *Coalition*, September, 42-44.

Vernon, A. 1996: A stranger in many camps: the experience of disabled black and ethnic minority women. In J. Morris (ed.), *Encounters with strangers: feminism and disability.* London: The Women's Press.

Watson, N. 2000: *Impairment, Disablement and Identity.* Unpublished PhD Thesis. University of Edinburgh.

Watson, N. 2002: Well, I know this is going to sound very strange to you, but I don't see myself as a disabled person: Identity and disability. *Disability and Society,* 17 (5), 509-529.

Watson, N. (*forthcoming*) Daily Denials: The routinisation of oppression and resistance. In S. Riddell and N. Watson (eds), Disability, *Culture and Identity.* Harlow: Pearson.

White, S. 1991: *Political theory and Postmodernism.* Cambridge: Cambridge University Press.

Williams, G. 1983: The Movement for Independent Living: an evaluation and critique. *Social Science and Medicine,* 17 (15), 1003-1010.

Zarb, G. and Oliver, M. 1993: *What Do They Expect After All These Years? Ageing With a Disability.* London: University of Greenwich.

Zola, I. 1989: Toward the necessary universalising of a disability policy. *Milbank Memorial Fund Quarterly*, 67 (Supplement 2), 401-428.

Zola, I. 1994: Towards inclusion: The Role of People with Disabilities in Policy and research in the United States – a Historical and political Analysis. In M. Rioux and M. Bach (eds), *Disability is Not Measles. New Research Paradigms in Disability.* York, Ontario: Roeher Institute.

CHAPTER 8

From Critique to Practice: emancipatory disability research

Geof Mercer

Introduction

In Britain, the development of a social barriers/model approach to disability (UPIAS 1976; Oliver 1983) was later complemented by the promotion of an emancipatory research paradigm. After its formulation in the early 1990s (Oliver 1992), it quickly exerted a dominant influence in the disability literature. Yet just as the move from a social model to a social theory of disability proved contentious, so there was a gathering debate about how emancipatory ambitions should be translated into empirical field studies. These discussions drew on competing theoretical and social research perspectives, as well as different interpretations of the social model.

The central criticism of 'mainstream' social science by disability theorists was that it ignored or rejected analyses of disability as a form of domination and oppression. Traditional social research was now similarly castigated as disempowering and supportive of an individual model approach. In contrast, emancipatory disability research was not only allied to the social model, it also adopted a radical critique of traditional 'scientific' research claims such as its impartiality and objective processes for validating knowledge. Disability writers stressed instead the participation of disabled people throughout the research process and the significance of this engagement in their own politicisation and of their experiences in producing knowledge about disability (Barnes and Mercer 1997; Beresford and Evans 1999).

At the same time, the wider policy context was changing: service providers, traditional charities and organisations for disabled people began to proclaim their support for a social model approach, while the government backed measures to involve users in the planning and evaluation of services, including research. However, these initiatives represented a consumerist emphasis in health and social care policy that typically produced a diluted form of user participation. This left a clear divide between mainstream approaches and the user-led model demanded by emancipatory researchers. Disabled people, who followed the social model, considered it was their right to be involved in disability research but also that there were strong epistemological grounds for arguing that this enhanced the quality of research outcomes and service support.

> User involvement is not an end in itself but is instead a means
> of enabling people to assert choices and have control over
> their daily lives (Lindow and Morris: 1995: 5).

My intention in this chapter is: first, to outline the claims to distinctiveness made in the early 1990s for emancipatory disability research; and second, to explore key issues raised in transferring this blueprint into everyday research practice. I conclude that disability research should allow a more grounded interpretation of challenging social oppression or it will become an 'impossible dream' (Oliver 1997).

The emancipatory path

The most influential contributor to the emancipatory disability research literature in Britain has been Mike Oliver (1992, 1997, 2002). He emulated Jurgen Habermas (1974) in distinguishing three main paradigms in the history of research: positivist, interpretive and critical-emancipatory. These were aligned with distinctive ways of producing knowledge (instrumental/technical, practical and critical/emancipatory), as well as specific forms of policy-making (engineering/prediction, enlightenment, and struggle). Moreover, each paradigm was associated with a characteristic approach to disability - individual, social and political. The emergence of an emancipatory approach was a response to the perceived shortcomings of the positivist and interpretative paradigms in contesting the social exclusion of disabled people.

More recently, this 'paradigm wars' approach was challenged by social theorists who highlighted differences within, and links between, paradigms (Lincoln and Guba 2000). Additionally, new ways of theorising gained ground, notably postmodernism and poststructuralism. These encompassed novel 'ways of knowing', representation (in experience and text), and styles of research (including its 'quality' or authenticity).

Nevertheless, there remained a broad consensus among 'social modellists' that mainstream social research had 'failed' disabled people:

> Disabled people have come to see research as a violation of their
> experi-ence, as irrelevant to their needs and as failing to improve
> their material circumstances and quality of life (Oliver 1992:105).

This was bolstered by widespread agreement on the general aims and characteristics of emancipatory disability research (Oliver 1992; Zarb 1992; Stone
and Priestley 1996; Barnes 2003). These centred on:

- rejecting the individual model of disability and its replacement by a
  social model approach;
- following a partisan approach/ accountable to disabled people/their
  organisations in their political struggles/ empowerment;
- reversing the traditional researcher-researched hierarchy/ social
  relations of research production, and challenging the material relations
  of research production;
- accepting a plurality of research methodologies/methods.

However, criticisms of the early formulations of the social model have
been matched by disputes about the implementation of emancipatory
disability research in empirical projects.

Social model approach

The orthodoxy has been that the social model of disability provided 'the ontological
and epistemological basis for research production' (Priestley 1997: 91). It focused
on socially constructed barriers (social oppression).

> Emancipatory research is about the systematic demystification
> of the structures and processes which create disability (Barnes
> 1992: 122).

However, alternative interpretations of the social model pointed disability
research down different paths. Thus, it was claimed that the pre-occupation
with the basic divide between disability and impairment ensured that research
focused on the structural bases of oppression. Instead, there were calls to widen
the ontological gaze to incorporate the feminist maxim that the 'personal is
political' and include the experience of impairment (Morris 1992). In
response, Vic Finkelstein (1999) re-iterated the traditional UPIAS viewpoint
that any such trend would obscure the crucial distinction between disability
as a form of social oppression and individual concerns around impairment.
He equated social model research with a critical analysis of the 'inner
workings of the disabling society' (p. 861), and argued forcefully against it
being enmeshed in individual concerns as much as professional or service
provider agendas.

In addition, the assumption of a universal/unified standpoint among
disabled people was countered by studies of diversity and differences in the
experience of oppression, for example, of gender, ethnicity and social class,
as well as type of impairment. D/deaf people, people with learning difficulties

and mental health system users/survivors all questioned the inclusiveness of the social model. As the notion of a homogeneous category of disabled people with a 'privileged' insight into disability gave way to competing experiences and discourses, the research spotlight shifted to marginalised discourses and hitherto 'silenced' voices (Corker 1999).

A further question mark was placed against the transferability of the social model to different national contexts and cultures. For example, Emma Stone (1997) reported considerable difficulties in conducting emancipatory disability research in China because the social model was viewed as an instrument of western imperialism and at odds with local circumstances.

Partisanship and commitment to political change

In the 1960s, critical theorists attacked mainstream social science for its defining obsession with objectivity such that entrenched political interests and ways of researching were uncontested. They drew particular inspiration from Paolo Freire (1972) who advocated partisan involvement in emancipatory struggles. Building a bridge between theory and practice was more likely where the researcher's participation in political struggles contributed to raising a social movement's *'capacity for historical action'* (Touraine 1981:145). Such 'conscious partiality' (Mies 1983) enabled a more flexible approach to theory-building grounded in empirical work that resonated with oppressed people's lived experience of an unequal society.

Hence, a stark choice was outlined for disability researchers: do they: wish to join with disabled people and use their expertise and skills in their struggles against oppression or do they wish to continue to use these skills and expertise in ways in which disabled people find oppressive? (Oliver 1992: 102).

This viewpoint rejected traditional criticism of a partisan approach in the social sciences because it risked a 'rampant subjectivity where one finds only what one is predisposed to look for' (Lather 1991: 52). Nevertheless, some disability writers argued that being partisan should not be equated with following the social model 'orthodoxy':

> By insisting on researchers adopting the social model, emancipatory
> research may restrict the intellectual freedom of the researcher,
> and their capacity to interpret the worlds and cultures of others
> (Davis 2000: 193).

A very different concern was that academic researchers worked within a range of personal, professional, and organisational constraints that often clashed with their commitment to challenge the social exclusion of disabled people (Goodley and Moore 2000; Oliver 2002).

Nonetheless, it was generally accepted that disability research should 'explore and identify appropriate avenues for change' (Finkelstein 1999: 862). More ambitiously, twin goals were specified: 'gain' and 'empowerment' (Oliver 1997). Accordingly, Mike Oliver downgraded earlier research in which he was involved – such as *Walking into Darkness* (Oliver et al. 1988) - because of its lack of tangible impact on service provision. However, the reasons why local and national policy makers accept, ignore or reject research findings and recommendations are rarely within the control of the researcher (Maynard 1994). Moreover, research may 'succeed' or 'fail' at several different levels, depending on the criteria employed, and the service location of the different 'stakeholders'.

Thus, 'emancipation' as a research outcome can be measured in very different ways, as the self-empowerment of disabled people might take several forms: documenting social barriers and oppression, re-evaluating perceptions of disability, and taking political action. Furthermore, empowerment rarely entails a sudden conversion on the road to Damascus, or even a simple progression to social inclusion or 'liberation'. Typically, it is more diffuse, uncertain, and drawn out. This leaves the unsatisfactory prospect that research is judged on its emancipatory effects only long 'after the event' (Oliver 1997: 25). In practice, separating out the impact of specific research projects from wider economic, political and social changes will be an extremely difficult and contentious exercise. A further possibility is that emancipatory research findings are used in unintended ways, perhaps to undermine disabled people's interests. Certainly, user involvement in research has been exploited to provide 'intelligence' for service providers and managers to 'manage' rather than 'empower' disabled people.

This research 'balance sheet' has been largely couched in terms of a stark polarisation between oppressors and oppressed. Nonetheless, in everyday social life, it has sometimes been difficult to agree on this calculation. Oppressors and oppressed were not always easily distinguished, nor were these stable categories across social contexts. Participants did not always agree about their key interests. How should disabled lives be represented, and by whom, when disabled people's voices diverge, or where lay knowledge and analysis is antagonistic to a social model assumption that people with impairments are 'oppressed'? What benefits one group of disabled people might be rejected by others just as disabled people might be implicated in the oppression of other social groups.

In an attempt to demonstrate and reinforce the partisan dimension to disability research, while bracketing evidence of a demonstrable gain, social modellists stressed the importance of making researchers formally accountable to disabled people (Barnes 2003). The most widely cited exemplar has been the project sponsored by the (then) British Council of Organisations of Disabled People into the social exclusion of disabled people in Britain (Barnes 1991). Its emancipatory credentials rested on its commitment to a social model approach, with control of the project vested in a small advisory group of representatives from organisations of disabled people. However, this was largely based on re-interpreting existing data rather than designing and conducting a 'field study' (Stone and Priestley 1996: 706). Accountability was further highlighted in the importance attached to the dissemination of research findings, particularly in accessible publication formats for disabled people, and more generally to influence policy makers and service providers (Barnes 2003).

Despite these formal checks on partisanship, considerable suspicion endured among disabled people about the 'political loyalties' of non-disabled and sometimes disabled researchers. This echoed Paul Hunt's (1981) denunciation of the 'parasite people'. Undoubtedly, researchers often benefited professionally and materially from their activities (as have those teaching and writing about disability studies). Indeed, it became routine to hear even disabled researchers 'confess' that they were the chief beneficiaries of their work - what Finkelstein (1999: 863) aptly called 'Oliver's gibe'.

Social relations of research production

Early statements on emancipatory disability research stressed the significance of how researchers positioned themselves with respect to the social and material relations of research production (Oliver 1992; Zarb 1992). Thus, the transformative potential of disability research became dependent on disabled people being 'actively involved in determining the aims, methods and uses of the research' (Zarb 1997: 52). This required a reversal of the social relations of research production so that researchers:

> learn how to put their knowledge and skills at the disposal of their research subjects, for them to use in whatever way they choose (Oliver 1992: 111).

However, full-blown user-control awaited the dismantling of the 'material relations of research production' and ending the restrictions imposed by external funding bodies, service providers and organisations that undertake research, such as universities (Zarb 1992; Oliver 1997). With that proviso, the extent of any transfer of power depended on answers to the following questions:

(i)   Who controls what the research will be about and how it will be carried out?
(ii) How far have we come in involving disabled people in the research process?
(iii) What opportunities exist for disabled people to criticise the research and influence future directions?

(iv) What happens to the products of the research? (Zarb 1992: 128).

As an elaboration of this theme, the Wiltshire and Swindon Users' Network suggested a continuum of user involvement in the research process from information provision, consultation, participation, and veto up to (full) control (Evans and Fisher 1999: 108). User-control entailed management of the whole project, including funding, and perhaps acting as researchers as well. Instances of disabled participants assuming full control were rare, but this has been claimed by some groups of mental health survivors (Chamberlain 1988).

In other writings, the aim of 'reversibility' was replaced by a positive collaboration between 'co-researchers and co-subjects' (Reason 1988: 1), with neither 'side' dominating the other (Lloyd et al. 1996). In this process the research was typified by reflective dialogue, and moving towards jointly agreed understandings, through continuous negotiation – akin to 'communicative action' (Habermas 1974).

However, the orthodox tendency in disability studies dismissed participatory research on the grounds that it presumed less than full control by disabled people – even if it was the more realistic option in the current political climate (Zarb 1997). Oliver (1992) simply equated it with playing by the rules of the system and improving organisational efficiency rather than challenging established values or structures. This ignored the several branches to participatory (action) research, and underestimated the,

> vital link between knowledge generation, education, collective action and the empowerment of oppressed people (Cocks and Cockram 1995: 31).

Thus, the more radical variants of participatory research included many instructive attempts to explore the processes of 'collaborative learning' (Reason 1988; Kemmis and McTaggart 2000). These emphasised that researchers should not monopolise knowledge production and that the process of participation was potentially empowering. Attention focused on how lay and academic concepts and theories were integrated, and how researchers responded when 'lay' and 'academic' accounts differed. In contrast, advocates of emancipatory research too often skated over the processes of analysing and theorising research data and how individual experience was 'collectivised' in the face of contrary views or negative audience reactions during the dissemination process (Humphries 1997). A similar 'oversight' has been the ways in which power hierarchies within a research team were 'managed'.

One disciplinary group that embraced 'participatory' research was critical ethnography. From this perspective, John Davis (2000) explored the significance of reflexive participation (or exchange of interpretations) in enabling respondents' ideas to shape research design. This entailed practising 'non-authoritarian techniques' (p. 201), with meaningful dialogue between researchers and participants dependent on the researcher bracketing his/her own theoretical preferences, and recognising that disabled participants were 'experts in their own lives' (p. 202). This also required that different perspectives among research participants were properly acknowledged, given concerns about:

> The danger of colonization and a silencing of the independent,
> challenging user voice is ever present (Evans and Fisher 1999: 106).

Not that all disabled people have the time or inclination to take over control of the research production. John Swain (1995) offered a graphic illustration of the difficulties in involving 14–18 year olds at a newly opened college for students with 'special educational needs' in disability research. His experience suggested a readiness to defer to 'research experts', and has been replicated in research with disabled service users:

> there was much resistance to the idea that emancipatory research
> should involve a *reversal* of the social relations of research
> production (Priestley 1997: 104).

Furthermore, the presumed 'independence' of the researcher might be exploited by the disabled people's organisation to enhance the credibility of its study, most often with service providers. In some instances, this underscored a research relationship built on a 'working partnership towards mutually beneficial outcomes' (Priestley 1997: 104-105).

In Britain, participatory research was boosted by the support of the Joseph Rowntree Foundation (JRF), a major funder of disability research. It insisted that projects must be located within a social model of disability, include significant and appropriate user involvement, and have a clear potential to improve disabled people's lives. Notable examples have included Jenny Morris' (1993) study of community support for disabled people, and a series of studies of direct payments building on Gerry Zarb and Pamela Nadash's (1994) influential work.

The commitment to user-control raised specific issues for research undertaken with people with learning difficulties (Chappell 2000; Walmsley 2001), but this has produced some of the most imaginative attempts to develop collaborative approaches.

> The separation of literature of the social model and literature
> associated with learning difficulties has created distinct ways of
> doing research (Chappell et al. 2001: 47).

People with learning difficulties have acted as research advisers, interviewers and life historians, as well as leading their own research with some 'external' support (People First 1994; Sample 1996; March et al. 1997; Ward 1997; Ward and Simons 1998; Rodgers 1999; Goodley and Moore 2000; Knox et al. 2000). In these ways, research with people with learning difficulties has moved a considerable distance over the last decade towards their recognition as reliable informants who were the 'best authority on their own lives, experiences, feelings and views' (Stalker 1998: 5).

Nonetheless, some doubts remained (Stalker 1998). Thus, concerns were expressed, even by 'sympathetic' researchers, whether all participants fully understood and agreed with the 'rules of engagement' in disability research:

> current models of the consultation and involvement of people
> with learning difficulties in issues affecting their lives suggest that
> the pulls either to the trivial or to the professionally stage-
> managed are hard to resist (Riddell et al. 1998: 81-2).

The dilemma was how to ensure meaningful participation by people with learning difficulties who have been conditioned into a spectator role by the attitudes of service providers and wider public.

Jan Walmsley (2001) has suggested that participatory research was easier to achieve where the research focus was on improving services rather than data analysis or theory generation. A related issue was the accessibility of the research process and discussions. In the case of people with learning difficulties this entailed being as clear as possible in the use of language, while participants generally might resist theorising lay experience and knowledge. However, these research support issues have received surprisingly little attention.

Greater concern has been expressed at the shortage of disabled researchers (Oliver and Barnes 1997; Zarb 1997). Many barriers must be overcome, particularly the under-representation of disabled people in higher education. In addition, the organisation of disability research has been less than accommodating to individual support needs. The uncertain trajectory of some impairments provided another challenge to project management. A frequent criticism of funding bodies was that they did not recognise that disability research often needed extra time and resources. For example, communication barriers and an inaccessible built environment and transport system often acted as constraints on fieldwork.

The resulting spread of opinion on the role of the researcher in emancipatory research may be illustrated by two very contrasting standpoints. Tom Shakespeare (1997) argued that, 'I don't really care' whether my work is rated as 'emancipatory research'. He followed his own 'individual and ethical standards, rather than trying to conform to an orthodoxy' (p. 185). While welcoming 'advice and feedback', he did not want 'to be accountable to anyone other than my publisher and my conscience' (p. 186). The roles of activist and academic were clearly separated. In contrast, Vic Finkelstein (1999) warned that, unless radical changes in the social relations of research production were carried through, a new breed of disability research 'expert' would merge that assumed the traditional mantle of 'disabling' professionals.

Methodologies and methods

The early elaboration of emancipatory disability research often conflated 'methodology' (the general approach to research) with 'methods' (specific techniques for data collection, such as surveys or participant observation, processing and analysis). It also treated these as technical or subsidiary matters. Largely because of its determination to ensure that disability research was 'onside' politically, relatively little significance was attached to the choice of methodology in designing disability research (Barnes and Mercer 1997).

Disability researchers have given more attention to the advantages and disadvantages of quantitative and qualitative approaches. They have mostly followed the emerging qualitative preference in recent social (and particularly feminist) research. This accompanied a dismissal of the quantifying method as positivist, 'pseudo-scientific' and exploitative, that owed much to its use in the widely criticised OPCS disability surveys. Their reliance on postal questionnaires and structured interviews reinforced the expert/lay disabled person divide (Abberley 1992). However, disability researchers have largely ignored debates in 'mainstream' social research about the merits of the qualitative/quantitative dichotomy.

In fact, quantitative research underpinned the 'demonstration' of disabling barriers in Britain and elsewhere (Barnes 1991, 1992). Moreover, quantitative studies, at least until very recently, have been far more influential than experiential research in persuading policy makers of the social exclusion of disabled people (Barnes and Mercer 1997), just as had been the case with women's oppression (Oakley 2000). Notwithstanding these constraints, few researchers attempted to devise structured interviews and surveys that were 'participant-centred' or encouraged resistance to disabling barriers and attitudes (Kelly et al. 1994; Maynard 1994).

Most often, the qualitative approach was equated with the 'face-to-face' semi-structured interview, or an equivalent focus group, on the grounds that these were located in non-hierarchical relationships and promoted inter-subjectivity. However, there has been little discussion how individual and group interviews compared in the information collected or changed participant understandings. There was an associated emphasis on participant validation, mostly by taking interview data back to respondents for verification of what they said. It was also widely assumed that the friendly relations built up with participants corroborated the quality of interview data.

Attempts to go further and collectivise data analysis (even in a small advisory group) were rare. For example, only two of the thirty key activists who provided in-depth interviews for Campbell and Oliver's (1996) study of disability politics took up the offer to 'validate' interview transcripts or read the draft manuscript. It was candidly admitted that 'we neither had the time, energy or money to make it a wholly collective production' (Oliver 1997: 19). Again, few studies have examined how meanings and interpretations were agreed or how researchers 're-presented' lay participant's views (Shakespeare *et al.* 1996; Vernon 1997; Moore et al. 1998). This contrasts with a considerable feminist literature arguing that choice of methodology really does matter:

> We who do empirical research in the name of emancipatory
> politics must discover ways to connect our research methodology
> to our theoretical concerns and political commitments (Lather
> 1991: 172).

One sign of a changing perspective in recent disability debates has been the developing interest in 'socially situated' knowledge, and the importance of exploring the differences between 'partial knowledges'. Even so, very different views were expressed over claims about the 'privileged' knowledge(s) or experience(s) of disabled people (Corker 1999; Barnes 2003). The notion of different knowledge and experience among disabled people cuts across the distinction between knowledge based on direct experience and more abstract, theoretical formulations (Evans and Fisher 1999). This resonated with a widespread tendency to marginalise lay knowledge in comparison to that of experts or professionals.

> The knowledge of disabled people has been dismissed on the
> basis of their perceived incapacity; that of survivors because of
> their assumed unreliability and irrationality of their perceptions
> and understandings and those of people with learning difficulties
> on the basis of their perceived intellectual deficiencies (Beresford
> 2000: 495).

In practice, researchers, participants, funding bodies and policy makers prioritised different forms of knowledge, each with its own ontological, episte-mological, technical and ethical characteristics and preferences. Hence the significance of asking:

> By what means are competing knowledge claims adjudicated
> and by whom? How are knowledge and mere opinion
> distinguished? Who is seen to possess knowledge? Who are the
> gatekeepers in knowledge production and distribution processes?
> (Stanley 1997).

Traditionally, the criteria for evaluating disability research diverged across paradigms. In the quantifying approach, the following aspects have been emphasised:

> internal validity (isomorphism of findings with reality), external validity (generalisability), reliability (in the sense of stability), and objectivity (distanced and neutral observer)... (while those within the interpretive paradigm stress)... the trustworthiness criteria of credibility (paralleling internal validity), transferability (paralleling external validity), dependability (paralleling reliability), and confirmability (paralleling objectivity) (Guba and Lincoln 1994: 114).

These indicated different ways of seeking transparency (for both participants and a wider audience) in how the research process unfolded, from design through data collection, analysis and dissemination (Stanley and Wise 1993; Maynard 1994). Despite this, the application of formal tests of 'quality control' promoted by mainstream research rarely allowed for the specific circumstances of doing research with disabled people, such as supporting communication or confirming shared understandings (Sample 1996; Stalker 1998).

More generally, disability researchers demonstrated little sensitivity to how they might directly and indirectly influence the research process, and if participants deferred to researcher expertise (Lloyd et al. 1996; Davis 2000). The main exception was a presumption about the impact of employing a disabled (rather than non-disabled) person, as researcher. This was illustrated by claims that disabled user interviewers obtained more frank and detailed responses in studies evaluating service provision than professional interviewers (Nicholls 2001; Faulkner and Thomas 2002), and more widely, that:

> if a researcher is to empathise with those being researched
> then it follows that their life history must be as near as possible
> to that of the people being studied (Barnes 1992: 117).

While a preference for disabled over non-disabled researchers was identified, there was considerable reluctance to extend the matching process, beyond perhaps gender, to include potential influences such as impairment, age, sexuality, ethnicity and social class (Vernon 1997).

The general view has been to ascribe a liminal status to the non-disabled researcher: sometime 'partisan or parasite, partner or oppressor, participant or voyeur' (Humphrey 2000: 77). Nevertheless, some have accepted that non-disabled researchers are capable of producing emancipatory disability research:

> I am not convinced that it is necessary to have an impairment in
> order to produce good qualitative research within the emancipatory
> model (Barnes 1992: 121).

That accepted, the contrary proposition that disability knowledge might be enhanced by involving a non-disabled researcher (albeit with a social model orientation) because taken-for-granted ideas and practices were more likely to be unpacked has won little support (Humphrey 2000).

Overall, the central message must be that disability researchers should devote more attention to methodological issues; in particular:

> how to strike a balance between empirical investigations of embodied and material differences, power relations and inequalities, and critical reflections on how knowledge is produced (Ramazanoglu and Holland 2002: 97).

Standpoints and stories

Emancipatory disability research started out by being grounded in an epistemology that assumed authoritative knowledge can be produced on the social oppression of people with impairments. The aim was to demonstrate the 'real oppression and discrimination that people experience in their everyday lives' (Oliver 2002: 13). Recent debates within the feminist literature exhibited a wider range of opinions. While feminist 'standpoint' theory offered some obvious similarities, postmodern/poststructuralist theorists, who were attracting growing interest among disability writers, denied that it was possible to agree general criteria for establishing 'truth claims', or even differentiate better or worse accounts of disability.

As an illustration, Sandra Harding (1993) explored ways in which a feminist standpoint epistemology might justify its knowledge claims. She rejected the standard criteria of 'malestream' social research and argued instead for 'strong objectivity'. This included: reflecting critically on the knowledge production process; building research agendas grounded in the experiences of subordinate groups; finding ways to judge some knowledge claims as better than others; acknowledging diversity and contradictions in subordinate groups; recognising that knowledge (about disability) was generated by a historically specific community; and espousing liberatory knowledge. This contrasted with denials from postmodernists (e.g. Lyotard and Baudrillard) and poststructuralists (e.g. Foucault and Derrida) that there were general rules for establishing a relationship between knowledge claims, experience, and social reality. The new theories analysed social research as an enterprise with its own history, norms and power relations (Ramazanoglu and Holland 2002). This aligned to a postmodern disdain for 'methodolatry', or rejection of general procedures for determining whether knowledge was valid and authoritative.

Foucault (1984) exerted a particular influence with his analyses of different forms of discourse (or ways of specifying what counts as knowledge/power) – rather than their 'truth'. This was exemplified by his study of the historical changes in discourse around 'madness'. The post-structuralist focus on the multiplicity of discourses ('truths' and 'knowledges'), and studies of the deconstruction of difference, re-invigorated studies of the power of language. Indeed, the postmodern interpretation of personal experience was that while 'real' to the individual concerned it was limited and partial rather than generalisable knowledge. This in turn raised the possibility of multiple readings and never-ending deconstructions. For some, explanations of the 'othering' of some groups were reduced to a choice between 'reality determinism' and 'discursive determinism' (Leonard 1997: 11). A more productive option stressed theorising and researching the interface between discourse and the material world (Corker 1999).

The editors of a recent volume on postmodernism and disability, Mairian Corker and Tom Shakespeare (2002), stressed the importance of:

> seeing and researching disabled lives as both constrained by social
> structures and as an active process of production which transforms
> social structures' (p. 15).

Post-modern writings claim distinctive theoretical, epistemological and political positions on social reality, the production of knowledge, how the 'knowing' disabled person is constituted. However, most of the contributors to their collection devoted little space to spelling out how postmodernism informed their (often very different) approaches to conducting disability research field studies or research discourses.

> If there are really no such things as 'facts' about the way people
> are treated, then there is no such thing as discrimination or
> oppression. Post-modernism is inherently political. It drives the
> enforced injustices of social inequality into the personal cupboard
> of privately experienced suffering (Oakley 2000: 298).

There has been a consensus among postmodernists/ poststructuralists that the social model orthodoxy threatened to become an overarching and totalising discourse (Corker and Shakespeare 2002). Yet, for their part, more 'orthodox' social modellists expressed considerable doubts whether a viable alternative was being offered to the methodological approach or political project underpinning emancipatory research.

Review

The emancipatory paradigm promised an innovative approach to doing disability research. This stemmed from its location in the social model of disability, a partisan commitment in challenging the social exclusion of disabled people and a broad accountability to disabled people and their organizations.

However, the bases of emancipatory research have attracted criticism from writers drawing on an increasingly diverse set of theoretical perspectives, while further issues are raised about translating its broad principles into research practice.

Reflecting on a decade's experience of disability research undertaken by, or accountable to, service users and their organisations, two of its early and most vocal exponents have produced contrasting conclusions. Mike Oliver re-iterated his earlier pessimism that it was proving more like an 'impossible dream' than a 'realistic goal' (Oliver 1997, 2002). The lack of policy movement towards promoting social inclusion was mirrored by the continuing pre-eminence of mainstream social research:

> From the fetishism on methodology that still haunts the ESRC to government obsession with scientific validity, the positivistic approach to social research continues to dominate its funding (Oliver 2002:3).

Yet from a similar social model vantage point, Colin Barnes elaborated a more positive case for continuing with emancipatory disability research:

> when directly linked to disabled people's ongoing struggle for change, doing emancipatory disability research can have a meaningful impact on their empowerment and the policies that affect their lives (Barnes 2003: 14).

This assessment concentrated on its political impact in mobilizing disabled people and challenging social exclusion. At the same time, emancipatory disability research cannot overturn social barriers by itself, although it should aim to contribute to these struggles. Equally, the emancipatory path raises many important methodological issues that should be addressed by disability researchers. In summary, emancipatory disability research must continue to explore disablist views of social reality, and contribute to debates about how this knowledge can be used to overturn the social exclusion of disabled people.

Bibliography

Abberley, P. 1992: Counting us out: a discussion of the OPCS disability surveys. *Disability, Handicap and Society,* 7 (2), 139-56.

Barnes, C. 1991: *Disabled People in Britain and Discrimination.* London: Hurst and Co., in association with the British Council of Organisations of Disabled People.

Barnes, C. 1992: Qualitative Research: valuable or irrelevant? *Disability, Handicap and Society,* 7 (2), 115-24.

Barnes, C. 2003: What a Difference a Decade Makes: reflections on doing 'emancipatory' disability research. *Disability and Society,* 18 (1), 3-17.

Barnes, C. and Mercer, G. (eds) 1997: *Doing Disability Research.* Leeds: The Disability Press.

Beresford, P. 2000: Service Users' Knowledge and Social Work Theory: Conflict or Collaboration? *British Journal of Social Work,* 30 (4), 489-503.

Beresford, P. and Evans, C. 1999: Research Note: Research and Empowerment. *British Journal of Social Work,* 29, 671-677.

Beresford, P. and Wallcraft, J. 1997: Psychiatric System Survivors and Emancipatory Research: Issues, overlaps and differences. In C. Barnes and G. Mercer (eds), *Doing Disability Research.* Leeds: The Disability Press, 67-87.

Campbell, J. and Oliver, M. 1996: *Disability Politics: Understanding Our Past, Changing Our Future.* London: Routledge.

Chamberlain, J. 1988: *On Our Own.* London: MIND.

Chappell, A. L. 2000: Emergence of participatory methodology in learning difficulty research: understanding the context. *British Journal of Learning Disabilities,* 28, 38-43.

Chappell, A. L., Goodley, D. and Lawthom, R. 2001: Emergence of participatory methodology in learning difficulty research: understanding the context. *British Journal of Learning Disabilities,* 28, 45-50.

Cocks, E. and Cockram, J. 1995: The participatory research paradigm and intellectual disability. *Mental Handicap Research,* 8, 25-37.

Corker, M. 1999: New disability discourse, the principle of optimisation and social change. In M. Corker and S. French (eds), *Disability Discourses.* Buckingham: Open University Press, 192-209.

Corker, M. and Shakespeare, T. 2002: Mapping the Terrain. In M.Corker and T. Shakespeare (eds), *Disability/ Postmodernity: Embodying Disability Theory.* London: Continuum, 1-17.

Davis, J.M. 2000: Disability Studies as Ethnographic Research and Text: research strategies and roles for promoting change? *Disability and Society,* 15 (2), 191- 206.

Evans, C. and Fisher, M. 1999: Collaborative evaluation with service users. In I.Shaw and J.Lishman (eds), *Evaluation and Social Work Practice.* London: Sage, 101-17.

Faulkner, A. and Thomas, P. 2002: User-led Research and Evidence-based Medicine. *British Journal of Psychiatry,* 180, 1-3.

Finkelstein, V. 1999: Doing disability research. *Disability and Society,* 14 (6), 859-67.

Foucault, M. 1984: *The Foucault Reader.* (P. Rabinow, ed.). Harmondsworth: Penguin.

Freire, P. 1972: *Pedagogy of the Oppressed.* Harmondsworth, Penguin

Goodley, D. and Moore, M. 2000: Doing Disability Research: activist lives and the academy. *Disability and Society,* 15 (6), 861-82.

Guba, E. G. and Lincoln, Y.S. 1994: Competing paradigms in qualitative research. In N. K. Denzin and Y. S. Lincoln (eds), *The Handbook of Qualitative Research.* Thousand Oaks, California: Sage, 105-117.

Habermas, J. 1974: *Theory and Practice.* (J. Viertel, Trans.), London: Heinemann.

Harding, S. 1993: Re-thinking standpoint epistemology: what is 'strong objectivity'? In L. Alcoff and E. Potter (eds), *Feminist Epistemologies.* London: Routledge, 49-82.

Humphrey, J.C. 2000: Researching Disability Politics, or Some Problems with the Social Model in Practice. *Disability and Society,* 15 (1), 63-85.

Humphries, B. 1997: From Critical Thought to Emancipatory Action: Contradictory Research Goals? *Sociological Research Online,* 2 (1). http://www.socresonline.org.uk/socresonline/2/1/3.html.

Hunt, P. 1981: Settling Accounts with the Parasite People: A Critique of 'A Life Apart' by E. J. Miller and G. V. Gwynne. *Disability Challenge,* 1 (May), 37-50.

Kelly, L., Burton, S. and Regan L. 1994: Researching Women's Lives or Studying Women's Oppression? Reflections on What Constitutes Feminist Research. In M. Maynard and J. Purvis (eds), *Researching Women's Lives from a Feminist Perspective.* London: Taylor and Francis, 27-48.

Kemmis, S. and McTaggart, T. 2000: Participatory Action Research. In N.K. Denzin and Y. S. Lincoln (eds), *Handbook of Qualitative Research,* 2nd ed. Thousand Oaks, California: Sage, 567-605.

Knox, M., Mok, M. and Parmenter, T.R. 2000: Working with the experts: collaborative research with people with an intellectual disability. *Disability and Society,* 15 (1), 49-61.

Lather, P. 1991: *Getting Smart: Feminist research and pedagogy with/in the postmodern.* New York: Routledge.

Leonard, P. 1997: *Postmodern Welfare.* London: Sage.

Lincoln, Y.S. and Guba, E. G. 2000: Paradigmatic Controversies, Contradictions, and Emerging Confluences. In N. K. Denzin and Y. S. Lincoln (eds), *The Handbook of Qualitative Research.* 2nd ed. Thousand Oaks, California: Sage, 163-188.

Lindow, V. amd Morris, J. 1995: *Service User Involvement: Synthesis of Findings and Experience in the Field of Community Care.* York: Joseph Rowntree Foundation.

Lloyd, M., Preston-Shoot, M., Temple, B. and Wuu, R. 1996: Whose project is it anyway? Sharing and shaping the research and development agenda. *Disability and Society,* 11 (3), 301-15.

March, J., Steingold, B., Justice, S. and Mitchell, P. 1997: Follow the Yellow Brick Road! People with Learning Difficulties as Co-Researchers. *British Journal of Learning Difficulties,* 25, 77-80.

Maynard, M. 1994: Methods, Practice and Epistemology: The Debate about Feminism and Research. In M. Maynard and J. Purvis (eds), *Researching Women's Lives from a Feminist Perspective.* London: Taylor and Francis, 10-26.

Mies, M. 1983: Towards a Methodology for Feminist Research. In G. Bowles and R. D. Klein (eds), *Theories of Women's Studies.* London: Routledge and Kegan Paul, 117-39.

Moore, M., Beazley, S. and Maelzer, J. 1998: *Researching Disability Issues.* Buckingham: Open University Press.

Morris, J. 1992: Personal and Political: a feminist perspective on researching physical disability. *Disability, Handicap and Society,* 7 (2), 157-66.

Morris, J. 1993: *Independent Lives? Community care and disabled people.* Basingstoke: Macmillan.

Nicholls, V. 2001: *Doing Research Ourselves.* London: Mental Health Foundation.

Oakley, A. 2000: *Experiments in Knowing. Gender and Method in the Social Sciences.* Cambridge: Polity Press.

Oliver, M. 1983: *Social Work with Disabled People.* Basingstoke: Macmillan.

Oliver, M. 1992: Changing the social relations of research production? *Disability, Handicap and Society,* 7 (2), 101-114.

Oliver, M. 1997: Emancipatory Research: Realistic Goal or Impossible Dream. In C. Barnes and G. Mercer (eds), *Doing Disability Research.* Leeds: The Disability Press, 15-31.

Oliver, M. 2002: *Emancipatory Research: A Methodology for Social Transformation.* Unpublished paper NDA conference 3rd Dec. http://www.leeds.ac.uk/disability-studies/archiveuk/index.html

Oliver, M. and Barnes, C. 1997: All We Are Saying Is Give Disabled Researchers A Chance. *Disability and Society,* 12 (5), 811-13.

Oliver, M. et al. 1988: *Walking into Darkness.* Basingstoke: Macmillan.

People First. 1994: *Outside not inside … yet.* London: People First London Boroughs.

Priestley, M. 1997: Who's research? A personal audit. In C.Barnes and G.Mercer (eds), *Doing Disability Research.* Leeds: The Disability Press, 88-107.

Ramazanoglu, C. and Holland, J. 2002: *Feminist Methodology: Challenges and Choices*. London: Sage.

Reason, P. (ed.) 1988: *Human Inquiry in Action: Developments in New Paradigm Research*. London, Sage.

Riddell, S., Wilkinson, H. and Baron, S. 1998: From emancipatory research to focus groups: people with learning difficulties and the research process. In P. Clough and L. Barton (eds), *Articulating with Difficulty: research voices in inclusive education*. London: Paul Chapman Publishing, 78-95.

Rodgers, J. 1999: Trying to get it right: undertaking research involving people with learning difficulties. *Disability and Society,* 14 (4), 421-33.

Sample, P. L. 1996: Beginnings: participatory action research and adults with developmental disabilities. *Disability and Society,* 11 (3), 317-22.

Shakespeare, T. 1997: Researching Disabled Sexuality. In C. Barnes and G.Mercer (eds), *Doing Disability Research*. Leeds: The Disability Press, 177-89.

Shakespeare, T., Gillespie-Sells, K. and Davies, D. 1996: *The Sexual Politics of Disability: Untold Desires*. London: Cassell.

Stalker, K. 1998: Some ethical and methodological issues in research with people with learning difficulties. *Disability and Society,* 13 (1), 5-19.

Stanley, L. 1997: Social transformation? Exploring issues in comparison, development and change. *Sociological Research Online,* 2 (4). <http://www.socresonline.org.uk/ socresonline/2/4editorial.html>

Stanley, L. and Wise, S. 1993: *Breaking Out Again: Feminist Ontology and Epistemology*. London: Routledge.

Stone, E. 1997: From the research notes of a foreign devil: disability research in China. In C.Barnes and G.Mercer (eds), *Doing Disability Research*. Leeds: The Disability Press, 207-27.

Stone, E. and Priestley, M. 1996: Parasites, pawns and partners: disability research and the role of non-disabled researchers. *British Journal of Sociology*, 47 (4), 699-716.

Swain, J. 1995: Constructing Participatory Research: In principle and in practice. In P. Clough and L. Barton (eds), *Making Difficulties. Research and the Construction of Special Educational Needs*. London: Paul Chapman Publishing Ltd, 75-93.

Touraine, A. 1981: *The Voice and The Eye. An Analysis of Social Movements*. Cambridge: Cambridge University Press.

UPIAS. 1976: *Fundamental Principles of Disability*. London: Union of the Physically Impaired Against Segregation.

Vernon, A. 1997: Reflexivity: The dilemmas of researching from the inside. In C.Barnes and G.Mercer (eds), *Doing Disability Research.* Leeds: The Disability Press, 158-176.

Walmsley, J. 2001: Normalisation, Emancipatory Research and Inclusive Research in Learning Disability. *Disability and Society,* 16 (2), 187-205.

Ward, L. 1997: Funding for change: translating emancipatory disability research from theory to practice. In C.Barnes and G.Mercer (eds), *Doing Disability Research.* Leeds: The Disability Press, 32-48.

Ward, L. and Simons, K. 1998: Practicing partnership: involving people with learning difficulties in research. *British Journal of Learning Disabilities,* 26 (4), 128-31.

Zarb, G. 1992: On the Road to Damascus: First steps towards changing the Relations of Research Production. *Disability, Handicap and Society,* 7 (2), 125-138.

Zarb, G. 1997: Researching Disabling Barriers. In C. Barnes and G. Mercer (eds), *Doing Disability Research,* Leeds: The Disability Press, 49-66.

Zarb, G. and Nadash, P. 1994: *Cashing in on independence.* Derby: British Council of Disabled People.

CHAPTER 9

Learning more from the Social Model: linking experience, participation and knowledge production

Katy Bailey

Introduction

This chapter suggests there is more to be learnt from the social model of disability through recognition of the context of its development, and that such a focus can be useful to the disabled people's movement and inform disability research.

The social model has often been used and viewed in a way that does not acknowledge its context of origin in, and continuing link to, disabled people's reflections on their experience of disability. I call this using a decontextualised social model. I will discuss the part played by this decontextualised social model in selected recent debates. I then examine the links that can be made between experience, knowledge production and participation by emphasising the process of the development of the social model, and suggest potentially useful directions for disability research.

The decontextualised social model

Many of us consider we know the social model rather than know about it. The recognition of our experience within the social model has been a transformative process for many disabled people and this recognition has often led to people becoming active within the movement. The social model has powerful resonance with disabled people's lived experience.

The written down social model also can and does stand alone as a piece of academic knowledge. The written down social model is a succinct communication and has been used, and continues to be discussed, as a tool (Oliver 2003). I suggest that the usefulness of the social model as a tool to communicate ideas has also been its major drawback; because it has become a 'thing' it is prone to being divorced from the context of the disabled people's movement's demands for the removal of disabling barriers. This is demonstrated in the almost unbelievable penetration of the language of the social model into institutional and organisational literature, often concurrently with continuing oppressive practice. This separation from the demands of the disabled people's movement can be seen as a neutralisation (Finkelstein 1999), or neutering, of the social model, and is arguably counterproductive for the emancipation of disabled people. Social model terminology can be adopted by anybody; but this adoption does not always involve a recognition of, or commitment to a relationship with, the social model's family of origin; the disabled people's movement. Proclamations of adherence to the social model of disability are now commonplace in mission statements of social services departments; traditional disability charities are queuing up to adopt it and it is *de rigueur* in the introduction to many research reports.

The context of the development of the social model

The defining of the social model by Mike Oliver (1990) was a late stage in its development. The earlier theorising, beginning with Paul Hunt (1966), largely took place within a group of disabled people in the Union of the Physically Impaired Against Segregation (UPIAS), who developed what was then called the social oppression theory of disability. UPIAS was passionately committed to a group-based (although not face-to-face) discussion, which was an analysis starting with experience but developing to theorising. The link with the disabled members' experience of disability was imperative, although within discussions that always moved on from any dwelling on descriptions of experience. UPIAS was not a support group; the discussions were intellectual and heated. However the connection with experiences of the members was retained, in fact it was required that the members were active in the community in order that they could reflect on their experiences in the real world in relation to the developing theory (Davis and Davis 2003; Finkelstein 2003). In this way the circular relationship between theorising and acting was emphasised, enabling the theorising to inform action and vice-versa. The group-based nature of the communication was important, while recognition of the shared aspects to experience supported the identification of the location of disability as external to the self.

Oliver's (1990) powerful definition of the social model is undoubtedly a major landmark in disability history; the ongoing theorising from the UPIAS was developed from work-in-progress to a model. The situation in the disability movement at the time was also significant: with the development of British Council of Organisations of Disabled People (BCODP) and

Disabled People's International (DPI) the time was right for a clear exposition of the recent thinking under which to gather and the social model was perfect. The production of a piece of decontextualised knowledge was not Oliver's intention when he named the social model (1996b, 1996c) but it became viewed as such and has been used in this way. However I suggest that the work-in-progress character was and is a continuing vital part of what became the social model, the defining of the content of theorising as a model can suggest a completed task. The delineation of a social model from the discussions did affect the status of the knowledge; there was a jump from realising the validity of the theorising within UPIAS to assumptions about the best way to use this theorising. The presentation of the content of the social model raises issues of the mechanisms through which knowledge supports emancipation.

Effects on debates

The use of a decontextualised social model has had an effect in recent debates in the field of disability. For example, the seeming completeness of the social model has meant that well intentioned ongoing theorising bumps into the edges of the defined social model, and thus appear as accusations and attacks (Crow 1996). This is a particular problem when apparent infighting plays into the hands of opponents of disabled people's emancipation who would like to see the social model discredited (Light 2001). Another example is how the social model, when seen as academic theorising separate from disabled people, entices academic attention and comparison with other academic theory. Whilst this can be interesting, as are most academic debates, the world is full of interesting things that can fill books and careers, and is 'interesting' enough? This is pertinent for disabled people, who have long been subjected to the gaze of the interested. A focus on the way the social model developed would support ongoing reflection on experience to develop theory and the importance of maintaining the link between theory and action. I will not develop these observations further in this chapter but will now concentrate on particular debates concerning the place of experience and the development of the emancipatory disability research paradigm.

Experience

The social model has been accused of rejecting experience (Watson 2003) or of not including enough about experience (Morris 1996; Crow 1996) and there are ongoing debates on the appropriate use of experience in disability research (Finkelstein 1996; Oliver 1996a; Barnes 2003).

In disability research a focus on studying experience or structural barriers has been presented as oppositional. The part played by the use of a decontextualised social model is that the lack of acknowledgement that experience of disability was the starting point for the recognition of structural barriers means that any discussion of structure seemed unconnected to experience. During the development of the social model the opposite was the case, theory developed through a discussion grounded in experience of disability. The importance of the experience connection in the social model was emphasised (Oliver 1996b, 1996c), as was the need for research based on discussions of shared experience (Finkelstein 1992), although unfortunately these arguments were not clearly separated from fierce debates that included conflation of the experience of disability and impairment and the rejection of both in the attempt to reject one (Oliver 1996a; Finkelstein 1996). There was and continues to be confusion on all sides (Thomas 1999), including the misunderstanding of the concept of the personal as political, or social (Oliver 1996a; Sheldon 1999) and issues of negotiating discussion of emancipation within the postmodern (Shakespeare 1997).

Whilst every disabled person has unique experiences, if disability is oppression (as all the above writers agree), there are mechanisms through which it operates that can be usefully explored through examining experience. I am unable to engage with the wider debate over the way experience is conceptualised and treated in research generally (Scott 1992; Maynard 1994; Humphries 1997), and am not suggesting that experience is an unproblematic representation of reality. However, situated experience includes 'a way in' to discussion of social reality. Recognising and valuing subjectivity does not preclude talking about shared experience or social processes or structure. People can explain their experiences and situated knowledge to a large degree (Dockery 2000). 'You can't feel what it's like to be me but I can tell you'. Crucially, the problems inherent in sticking at the level of relating experience should not lead to ignoring the place of experience in the development of thinking and theory. I disagree with Barnes, Oliver and Barton (2002) that the 'inside out' way of developing knowledge necessarily reduces things to the individual level. The large amount of research on experience that does lead to individualist explanations of experience (Oliver 1992; Goodley 1996; Oakley 2000) does not mean it is impossible to do it differently. The development of what became the social model illustrate that discussions that identify shared experience, especially group discussions, can indeed support the recognition of structural barriers, including attitudes, within discussion including analysis and theorising (Beresford and Turner 1997; Cunningham-Burley et al. 1999; Bailey 2002). The question of *who* interprets is important, in order to retain authorship and authenticity in the knowledge. Whilst oppressive analysis, much in the disability field, has been rightly deplored (Hunt 1981; Barnes and Mercer 1997; Humphries 1997), the problems associated with other people interpreting narratives should not lead to a wholesale rejection of interpretation, or meta-narrative. In fact, allowing people to tell only stories of equal worth with all other stories is disempowering when people are oppressed and share aspects of experience. The discussions in UPIAS show that people can build from a first line narrative of their own experience to produce shareable knowledge that retains a resonance with experience.

The particular power of resonant knowledge or theory lies in what the recognition does to people. The effects of recognition of structural barriers, discrimination or inequality in our experience should not be underestimated as a motivator for action. 'Experience draws you into a struggle' (Finkelstein 2003), and the recognition of social injustice in our experience is the motivator for action and a life of activism (Davis and Davis 2003).

Emancipatory disability research
The development of emancipatory disability research holds the social model centrally. I suggest that the use of a decontextualised social model has affected at least two aspects of the development of emancipatory disability research.

1. Knowledge production. Focusing on the content as the way in which the social model is powerful is paralleled in the continuing emphasis on formal research knowledge products as the mechanism through which research contributes to social change.

2. Methodology. The process of the development of the social model has not informed methodology; thus far methodology for emancipatory research in disability has not been developed in clear relation to the ontological and epistemological positions. This has contributed to practical problems in putting the emancipatory research paradigm into practice.

Knowledge and emancipation: the place of research.
Although the early debate about emancipatory disability research included discussion of the wider role of knowledge in emancipation (Oliver 1992) this has been insufficiently explored and at times a simple relationship between knowledge and social change has been relied upon, conflating knowledge with research knowledge and assuming the effectiveness of traditional mechanisms by which academic research persuades people, including

persuading disabled people. The traditional option is to aim research findings at powerful decision-makers, which can be effective at times, or not (Mercer 2002). The valuing of knowledge for its own sake is related to the emancipatory aims of enlightenment scientists, who believed that knowledge would be enough to produce change for the better (Humphries 1997). Without denying the positive policy responses to many advances in natural and social science; knowledge about society, including knowledge of oppression, has not proved enough to change the social conditions that produce and support oppression (Oliver 1992, 2003). In present times, emancipation is recognised as something that has to be done by oppressed people, not for them (Friere 1970; Lather 1991).

Definitions of emancipatory disability research and guidelines for practice emphasise control over the research process (Oliver 1992; Stone and Priestley 1996). However, an emphasis on the importance of the research product and lack of emphasis on the process of research can result in disabled people controlling research through commissioning traditional researcher-led research; buying in expertise, rather than controlling the process from within:

> critically formulated research (that with an emancipatory, political agenda) which adopts an expert model approach is paradoxically seeking change at one level (society), whilst at the same time reproducing unequal social relationships at another (within the research process) (Kitchen 2000: 26).

A common phrase is 'knowledge and skills at the disposal of disabled people', however changing the social relations of research to promote emancipation requires more than reversing control over a commodified research process (Stone and Priestley 1996).

The commissioning of professional research to support emancipatory aims is an option for organised groups of disabled people, however the concerns of unorganised disabled individuals or loose groups are rarely engaged with at their instigation. Demands for emancipation require a recognition of oppression. The process of the development of the social model illustrates that the discussion has to come first before experience of life with an impairment can be recognised as experience of disability/ oppression. Disabled people with a vague dissatisfaction (or burning anger) may not recognise this as a need for emancipation but research could still be a forum in which to explore issues and identify direction for action.

Another potential problem with following the expressed 'most pressing problem' of groups of disabled people is that the identified issues are often bound up with the complexities of current policy implementation, rather than calling for reappraisal of the whole system (Finkelstein 1999). For example, Oliver rejects, as inappropriate, research to 'develop bad policies'

(2003: 4). Whilst commissioning has produced some excellent research (Priestley 1999; Barnes et al. 2000), the most pressing problems are so caught up in the mechanisms of oppression that discussing them can avert focus from more basic problems, even seeing the issues as appropriate can inadvertently support the oppressive structures. This is the difference between what Friere (1970) calls 'problematizing', rather than 'problem solving'.

Emancipation requires action and is informed by knowledge. Useful knowledge for emancipation can include that produced by formal and informal research; however it is imperative that professional or expert researchers do not inhabit or claim the role of the only knowledge producers. Research means finding out about and understanding something and involvement of non-professional researchers in doing informal or formal research can bring benefits in terms of the quality of knowledge and the effects of the process of involvement. Demystifying the research process can assist in making overt how grassroots organisations and the disability movement have always used knowledge and can encourage viewing research as part of the ordinary process of deliberate action towards emancipation. This research can be about providing a forum for discussing the direction of a group and the social issues with which the group is concerned, making overt and developing the knowledge already in the group, identifying other research requirements and doing the fieldwork and analysis and theorising to produce useful knowledge and communicating it. However research can seem daunting, partly because it has been professionalised, and there arguably remains a role for those who know about and value research in encouraging research. Facilitating or supporting the doing of emancipatory research requires different skills to traditional social research and is unsatisfying for researchers who would rather be doing their own research or who have substantive agendas. Academic or professional researchers have to negotiate the practical concerns of academic esteem and/or making a living, which in many ways conflict with emancipatory aims.

Methodology

Although the choice of methods was not seen as the main issue in developing emancipatory disability research (Mercer 2002), the lack of emphasis on participation within the research process is surprising, considering the apparent influence of the writing of Freire (1970), Reason and Rowan (1981) among others and the use of concepts of praxis and critical enquiry (Oliver 1992; Cocks and Cockram 1995). More acknowledgement of the context of the development of the social model would support this emphasis on the significance of knowledge produced through disabled people's thinking. When Oliver drew on Friere's work he missed the central importance of participatory methods, especially the theorising of ordinary oppressed people. There was a lack of engagement with the mechanisms by which participatory research sought to achieve its emancipatory aims (Reason and Rowan 1981; Park 1999). Emancipatory disability research has not embraced participatory methodology or method (Oliver 1992, 1997) in the context of a general lack of attention to method:

> early elaboration of emancipatory disability research tended to conflate methods with methodology and treat both as ancillary, technical matters (Mercer 2002: 242).

Participatory methods continue to be rejected by some disability writers (Oliver 2003) although views vary (Zarb 1997; Barnes 2003).

> Participatory Research is an emancipatory approach which has already been developed, although it has been rarely used with the participation of persons with a disability (CILT 1995: 49).

The presentation paper by Finkelstein (1992), eloquently emphasising the importance of participation in research, especially the analysis stage, as more essential than the knowledge produced has unfortunately had less influence in the academic discussions about the development of emancipatory disability research. Debates in other areas including feminism have emphasised the importance of linking emancipation and participation (Humphries 1997; Lather 1986, 1991).

Problems in practice, interpreting data

The call for emancipatory disability research emphasises a social model explanation as the suggested interpretive theory (Stone and Priestley 1996). This again identifies the content of the social model as the only important part. The requirement for a social model interpretation is viewed by some researchers as inappropriate (Shakespeare 1997). The practical problems in fitting a social model interpretation to people's experience are discussed, especially when the disabled people may not recognise the social model (Stone and Priestley 1996). The social model, especially in an academic version, can seem alien to disabled people especially when the model is exported to other cultures (Stone 1997), and there are disabled people who disagree with a social model analysis. This is obviously a problem with any theory, as by definition theory concerns that which is not readily observable. The imposition of any external theory on people's experience can be oppressive and inappropriate, however liberating the theory (Lather 1991). Again an acknowledgement of the context of the development of the social model would remind us that the journey from experience to theory required a process of reflection. The social model can inform practice and methodology without imposing an interpretation. It can also be used to encourage disabled people to interpret their own experience. This use of research which embraces the social model to guide practice rather than impose theory is also more open to use in a cross cultural context.

Collectivising data

An identified method problem is the collectivising of data (Stone and Priestley 1996; Barnes 2003), and the maintenance of a social context when discussing experience (Vernon 1997; Barnes et al. 2002). The individualising tendency of specific methods including interviews was clearly described some time ago (Oliver 1992). Unfortunately, it was then used as an argument to reject interview methods and a focus on experience rather than being seen as an artefact of individual methods that could be improved by using group methods. The problem of collectivising data is lessened if data is not individualised in the first place.

Congruent methodology and methods in disability research

Whilst not all social research has emancipatory aims the use of the social model demands an emancipatory focus; the oppression of disabled people has not been theorised for descriptive purposes alone. There are increasing calls for social researchers to be clear about the connection between their choice of methods and methodology; and ontological, axiological and epistemological positions (Lather 1991). This means that researchers need to be choosing methods for a purpose and ensuring that their approach to a research subject fits with the way they view the social world, including their value system, and how they think the social world can be known. The content of the social model asserts an ontological position and acknowledgement of the significance of the process of the development of the social model requires consideration of epistemology, including the place of reflecting on experiencing in knowing about the social world.

In a context of the valuing of multiple methods, assertion of the suitability and unsuitability of methods for disability research is unfashionable. However, if disability is a social phenomenon then data should be looked for in a way that encourages a focus on social processes. Measurement of individual characteristics, whilst still common in medical research, has been rejected in social disability research (Abberley 1992; Zarb 1997). More controversially, I consider that despite being the 'gold standard' of qualitative research, the individual interview alone is often inappropriate for research, especially emancipatory research, because the one-to-one interaction supports explanation of experience on an individual level, and inhibits the recognition of social and structural factors, especially with a non–disabled interviewer (Vernon 1997). Group methods bring advantages at the level of the quality of data produced from 'bouncing ideas off each other and developing ideas' (Beresford and Turner 1997; Barbour and Kitzinger 1999; Cunningham-Burley et al. 1999). Group methods of data generation encourage a focus on the social context through the opportunity to recognise shared experience, with the accompanying challenge to initial perceptions and individualised explanations. Social processes in the small group can mirror those in wider society within an environment potentially safe enough for participants to discuss experience in the here-and-now (Mies 1983; Brydon-Miller 1995; Hill 1997; Bailey 2002). I am not suggesting that group discussions are unproblematic or that data from other sources is not useful but retaining some use of group discussion is fruitful and can be combined with other methods (Mies 1983; Aranda and Street 2001).

Potential of participatory research: linking experience, participation and knowledge production

Wholly (or paradigmatic) participatory research includes an overt aim of supporting emancipation (Reason and Rowan 1981; Park 1999). The difference (to emancipatory disability research) is that the process of the research aims to be emancipatory as well as the traditional knowledge product. This approach owes much to Friere's work on conscientization through critical reflection on social structure (1970). The acting towards emancipation or liberation requires power; a major part of Friere's argument is that critical reflection on the realities of life is accompanied by a recognition of power, albeit power unwielded up to that point. Recognising power is different to empowerment; for example, there are research projects using participatory methods that identify a main, or even the primary, aim as 'empowerment' of the participants, especially in practitioner research (Truman and Raine 2001; Gray et al. 2000). However as many researchers remind us (Lather 1991; Drake 1999; Dockery 2000), like emancipation,

> Empowerment is not something that can be given, but something
> that people must take for themselves (Zarb 1992: 128).

In order for a group in society to become empowered others must relinquish power. Humphries (1997) comments that the discourse on empowerment is located largely within the existing socially powerful groups. For research to produce an environment that supports empowerment or emancipation the researcher must share power, that is, give some up. Paradoxically, this is sometimes particularly difficult for passionate 'emancipatory' researchers, who already know what needs to be changed in the world, and requires a leap of faith in terms of faith in the participants' ability to know what is good for them too.

The ongoing problems of changing the social relations of disability research are assisted by using participatory methods. The call for emancipatory research can usefully link the use of social model content with a commitment to congruent participatory methods; this acts as a protection against the adoption of the jargon without changing the social relations of research. Researchers can adopt the terminology and methods of participatory research (in a way similar to the adoption of the terminology of the social model) without an ontological and epistemological position commensurate with participation, a major weakness of participatory research is what is done in its name (Hagey 1997). However an advantage of a participatory project is that participation, especially in the planning and analysis stages, cannot proceed successfully without the power shifting. There is a built-in check, doing participatory research with disabled people really unsettles researchers without the stomach for relinquishing power, and unresolved issues of participation and power show in the finished product.

I highlight the stage of analysis as particularly important. What happens in analysis and theorising in traditional social research is rarely opened up to scrutiny, even within an increasingly reflexive literature (Kelly et al. 1994; Truman and Raine 2001). The 'hygiene' in research has often bleached out the evidence of an oppressive analysis. Lack of transparency in traditional research was part of the motivation for the development of participatory research (Hagey 1997). Unfortunately this can be paralleled in the scarce attention to describing participation in the analysis, interpreting and theorising stages of research, (Stubbs 1999) even within otherwise participatory projects (Clear and Horsfall 1997):

> many have little to say about the process of data analysis, in particular
> the way in which a narrative emerged from the interview data
> (Riddel et al. 1998: 85).

Useful participation in the discussion stage has included the presentation of initial findings (albeit selected by the researcher) to groups or seminars including the participants and sometimes the wider disabled population (Rodgers 1999; Barnes, Mercer and Morgan 2002). The interest in these discussions suggests more potential to use the methods in analysis. Participation in analysis and concluding stages of research requires careful method choices, many studies have found that offers to check or comment on researcher analyses are insufficient to promote participation and are not taken up (Barnes and Mercer 1997; Beresford and Turner 1997). However, this is not the same as a real lack of interest, and should not be used as an excuse for not pursuing participation.

A notable exception is the work of the Citizens' Commission on the future of the Welfare State, in which:

> There was an important collaborative dimension to collation and analysis in the Commission. As far as we know this is the first time this has been done (Beresford and Turner 1997: 34).

Some useful strategies for participation in analysis and writing up are being developed (Brydon-Miller 1995; March et al. 1997; Bailey and Cowen 2003).

There is a great potential for analysis that is more participatory, to produce knowledge that retains a connection with participants' experience; that is resonant. Participation in the thinking stages of research are particularly important, for example in wholly participatory research, where participants' reflections on their experience of disability, in a group setting, can produce useful research products and also benefits from the effects supporting agency.

> Taking part in the research process is more important than ensuring a particular outcome will emerge. It is the involvement in the process of research, participating as a researcher, that can transform passive, dependent people into thinking decision-makers, whether or not 'good' solutions emerge (Finkelstein 1992: 3).

Researchers can learn from the process of the development of the social model by considering using group discussions, without requiring the content of the social model to be imposed on data. This practice represents a confidence in both the theorising abilities of disabled people and the potential of group discussion to support identifying structural barriers. Whatever my hunches about the likelihood of groups theorising social oppression this method does not require a social oppression or social model interpretation to arise and should not attempt to surreptitiously produce one. The validity of the process can support different and new theorising on disability that will retain a connection to the experience of disability; this knowledge will be likely to be resonant and useful to disabled people and the disability movement.

I do urge for the emancipatory aims of disability research to be achieved through participatory methods. I am not calling for only group discussion based participatory research projects, although I encourage this method. Participatory research has traditionally combined group discussion in planning with using a range of methods for data generation, including quantitative methods (Park 1999), which can be unbeatable in measuring disabling barriers (Stone and Priestley 1996; Oakley 2000). Participatory method in

the thinking stages also benefits research projects that are not wholly
participatory, for example in the planning of research questions and/or
analysis stages (for example, Priestley 1999; Fisher 2002). A reflection on experience
can usefully be used to produce research questions; this avoids the limitations
of using only issues that have emerged and allows disabled people outside
the disabled people's movement to be involved in directing research. The
use of reference or advisory groups can be expanded in the analysis and discussion
stages, including using and developing methods that encourage more active
contribution.

Conclusion

The unplanned emergence of a decontextualised version of the social model
has complicated discussions in the field of disability politics and research. I
have attempted to indicate some of these complexities and suggest the
importance of acknowledging the context of the development of what
became the social model within group based discussion and theorising with
a focus on the relationship between theory and action and a starting point
grounded in the experience of disability.

This chapter has discussed disability research that engages with the social
model, and therefore emancipation. It is important to be aware of the mass
of social science and medical research produced about disabled people or about
impairment in the fields of medicine, biological science, nursing and
psychology and numerous practitioner groups as well as governmental
research. Disability research of all kinds will continue to be carried out whether
or not disabled people see it as useful, although the option of refusing
participation in oppressive research is available to assert control over empirical
research (Oliver 1992). I think there should be some involvement of disabled
people in at least considering the appropriateness of disability research, and
there are attempts to encourage this (for example, Aspis 2002). This is a timely
debate for the disabled people's movement and other organisations concerned
with ethics and quality in social research. Disability research can have a place
in emancipation, when researchers are committed to social change and
when the 'purpose is to understand (disabled people's) oppression in order
that we might end it' (borrowing from Kelly et al. 1994). Truly emancipatory
research cannot be separated from the disabled people's movement and
researchers supporting emancipation need to be in a close relationship with
disabled people and the disabled people's movement, and committed to debate
beyond the confines of subscription journals.

Emancipatory disability research has suffered in its relating to a social model
that validates the content rather than the process of critical reflection on experience,

and this has contributed to a lack of recognition of the potential and centrality of participatory methods in research that aims to support emancipation. It is valuable to retain a link between knowledge and the experience of disabled people (without engaging in the apolitical practice of presenting only descriptions of experience). Good quality participatory research can produce knowledge with resonance.

The social model has been elevated into a thing in its own right, to be cherished, worshipped or vilified, and projected with the ability to empower or exclude. The social model, as an exposition of disabled people's oppression, has been important in the disabled people's movement in being a tangible banner, something to agree on and show people. It is amazing to see your realisations in print, but the power is not out there in the words. The power of the social model is its resonance as a naming of disabled people's experience of oppression, and as such it is transformative knowledge. Perhaps the clarity of a decontextualised social model, as words, has inhibited the ongoing process of recognising oppression; it can seem like repeating someone else's discovery to talk about how you have made sense of particular experiences, and ordinary disabled people cannot hope to describe it more eloquently. This belies the nature of the naming of oppression; each time the connection is made by an individual or group and they come to recognise aspects of their experience as oppression something happens, repeating the process is the whole idea. The social model is a naming of oppression; any disabled person can do this and thus create the same knowledge that is written down in the social model.

The disabled people's movement needs to ensure that people outside the movement, including academics, know that the social model is inextricably linked to disabled people's ongoing demands for the removal of barriers. We must act collectively to challenge those who appropriate social model language to come up with the necessary action and engage in an ongoing relationship with the disability movement. Disabled people and the disabled people's movement do and should feel they own the social model.

I hope to stimulate discussion within the disabled people's movement, including researchers committed to supporting emancipation. Mike Oliver (2003) was right to bemoan the amount of talk about the social model and call for more social change, but we cannot stop talking about the subject of the social model, our oppression, because the recognition of this is the motivation for action. The biggest resource for our emancipation is the ability of disabled people to get together and have ideas, including big ones, and act on them. The social model is brilliant, and there's more where that came from.

Bibliography

Aranda, S. and Street, A. 2001: From Individual to Group: use of narratives in a participatory research process. *Journal of Advanced Nursing,* 33 (6), 791-797.

Abberley, P. 1992: Counting us Out: a discussion of the OPCS disability surveys. *Disability, Handicap and Society,* 7 (2), 139-156.

Aspis, S. 2002: Community Living Campaign: How Valid is your Research Project? *Community Living,* 15 (4), 17-18.

Bailey, K. 2002: Disabled Parents Talking Together. Unpublished MA thesis, Department of Sociology and Social Policy, University of Leeds.

Bailey, K. and Cowen, S. 2003: Disabled Parents Talking Together, Disability Parenting and Pregnancy International.

Barbour, R. and Kitzinger, J. (eds) 1999: *Developing Focus Group Research: Politics, Theory and Practice.* London: Sage

Barnes, C. 2003: What a Difference a Decade Makes: Reflections on Doing 'Emancipatory' Disability Research. *Disability and Society,* 18 (1), 3-18.

Barnes, C. and Mercer, G. 1997: Breaking the Mould: an introduction to doing disability research. In C. Barnes and G. Mercer (eds), *Doing Disability Research.* Leeds: The Disability Press.

Barnes, C., Mercer, G. and Morgan, H. 2000: *Creating Independent Futures, Stage One Report.* Leeds: The Disability Press.

Barnes, C., Mercer, G. and Morgan, H. 2002: *Creating Independent Futures: Conference Report, Preliminary Findings and Policy Implications.* Leeds: The Disability Press.

Barnes, C., Oliver, M. and Barton, L. 2002: Disability and the Academy. In Barnes, C., Oliver, M. and Barton, L. (eds), *Disability Studies Today.* Cambridge: Polity Press.

Beresford, P. and Turner, M. 1997: It's Our Welfare: report of the citizens' commission on the future of the welfare state. London: National Institute for Social Work.

Brydon-Miller, M. 1995: Breaking Down Barriers: Accessibility Self-Advocacy in the Disabled Community. In P. Park et al. (eds), *Voices of Change: participatory research in the United States and Canada.* London: Sage.

CILT. 1995: *Independent Living and Participation in Research: a critical analysis.* Toronto: Centre for Independent Living.

Clear, M. and Horsfall, D. 1997: Research and Disability in a Local Community, *Disability and Society,* 12 (1), 119-132.

Cocks, E. and Cockram, J. 1995: The Participatory Research Paradigm and Intellectual Disability. *Mental Handicap Research,* 8 (1), 25-37.

Crow, L. 1996: Including all of our lives: renewing the social model of disability. In C. Barnes and G.Mercer (eds), *Exploring the Divide.* Leeds: The Disability Press.

Cunningham-Burley, S., Kerr, A. and Pavis, S. 1999: Theorizing subjects and subject matter in focus group research. In R. Barbour and J. Kitzinger (eds), *Developing Focus Group Research: Politics, Theory and Practice.* London: Sage.

Davis, K and Davis, M. 2003: Personal Communication.

Dockery, G. 2000: Participatory Research: whose roles, whose responsibilities? In C. Truman, D. Mertens and B. Humphries (eds), *Research and Inequality.* London: UCL Press.

Drake, R. 1999: *Understanding Disability Policies.* Basingstoke: Macmilan.

Finkelstein, V. 1992: Researching Disability: setting the agends for change, National Conference June. http://www.leeds.ac.uk/disability-studies/archiveuk/index.html

Finkelstein, V. 1996: Outside, 'inside out', *Coalition,* April, 30-36.

Finkelstein, V. 1999: Book Review of Barnes and Mercer: 'Doing Disability Research', *Disability and Society,* 14 (6), 859-878.

Finkelstein, V. 2003: Personal Communication.

Fisher, M. 2002: The role of service users in problem formulation and technical aspects of social research. *Social Work Education,* 21 (3), 305-12.

Friere, P. 1970: *Pedagogy of the Oppressed.* Harmondsworth: Penguin.

Goodley, D. 1996: Tales of Hidden Lives: a critical examination of life history research with people who have learning difficulties. *Disability and Society,* 11 (3), 333-348.

Gray, R., Fitch, M., Davis, C. and Phillips, C. 2000: Challenges of Participatory Research: reflections on a study with breast cancer self-help groups. *Health Expectations,* 3, 243-252.

Hagey, R. 1997: Guest Editorial: The Use and Abuse of Participatory Action Research. *Chronic Diseases in Canada,* 18 (1), 1-6. http://www.hc-sc.gc.ca/pphb-dgspsp/publicat/cdic-mcc/18-1/a_e.html

Hill, M. 1997: Participatory research with children: research review. *Child and Family Social Work,* 2, 171-183

Humphries, B. 1997: From Critical thought to Emancipatory Action: Contradictory Research Goals? *Sociological Research Online,* 2 (1) http://www.socresonline.org.uk/ socresonline/2/1/3.html

Hunt, P. 1966: A Critical Condition. In P. Hunt (ed.), *Stigma: the experience of disability.* London: Geoffrey Chapman.

Hunt, P. 1981: Settling Accounts with the Parasite People. *Disability Challenge,* 2, 37-50.

Kelly, L., Burton, S. and Regan, L. 1994: Researching Women's Lives or Studying Women's Oppression? Reflections on What Constitutes Feminist Research. In M. Maynard and J. Purvis (eds), *Researching Women's Lives from a Feminist Perspective.* London: Taylor & Francis.

Kitchen, R. 2000: The Researched opinions on Research: disabled people and disability research. Disability and Society, 15 (1), 25-47.

Lather, P. 1986: Research as Praxis. *Harvard Educational Review,* 53 (3), 257-277.

Lather, P. 1991: *Getting Smart: Feminist Research and Pedagogy with/in the Postmodern.* London: Routledge.

Light, R. 2001: Social Model or Unsociable Muddle? http://www.daa.org.uk/social-model.htm

March, J., Steingold, B., Justice, S. and Mitchell, P. 1997: Follow the Yellow Brick Road! People with Learning Difficulties as Co-Researchers. *British Journal of Learning Difficulties,* 25, 77-80.

Maynard, M. 1994: Methods, Practice and Epistemology: The Debate About Feminism and Research. In M. Maynard and J. Purvis (eds), *Researching Women's Lives from a Feminist Perspective.* London: Taylor & Francis.

Mercer, G. 2002: Emancipatory Disability Research. In C. Barnes, M. Oliver, and L. Barton (eds), *Disability Studies Today.* Cambridge: Polity Press.

Mies, M. 1983: Towards a Methodology for Feminist Research. In G. Bowles and R. Duelli Klein (eds), *Theories of Women's Studies.* London: Routledge & Kegan Paul.

Morris, J. 1996: *Encounters with Strangers: Feminism and Disability.* London: The Women's Press.

Oakley, A. 2000: Experiments in Knowing: Gender and Method in the Social Sciences. Cambridge: Polity Press.

Oliver, M. 1990: *The Politics of Disablement.* Basingstoke: Macmillan.

Oliver, M. 1992: Changing the Social Relations of Research Production? Disability, *Handicap and Society,* 7 (2), 101-14.

Oliver, M. 1996a: Defining impairment and Disability, issues at stake. In C. Barnes and G. Mercer (eds), *Exploring the Divide.* Leeds: The Disability Press.

Oliver, M. 1996b: *Understanding Disability.* Basingstoke: Macmillan.

Oliver, M. 1996c: A Sociology of Disability or a Disablist Sociology? In Barton (ed.), *Disability and Society, emerging issues and insights.* Harrow: Longman.

Oliver, M. 1997: Emancipatory Research: Realistic Goal or Impossible Dream? In C. Barnes and G.Mercer (eds), *Doing Disability Research.* Leeds: The Disability Press.

Oliver, M. 2003: *Emancipatory Research: A Methodology for Social Transformation,* paper presented to National Disability Authority, Dublin conference 3rd Dec.2002 http://www.leeds.ac.uk/disability-studies/archiveuk/index.html

Park, P. 1999: People, Knowledge and Change in Participatory Research. *Management Learning,* 30 (2), 141-157.

Priestley, M. 1999: *Disability Politics and Community Care.* London: Jessica Kingsley.

Reason, P. and Rowan, J. (eds) 1981: *Human Inquiry: a sourcebook for new paradigm research.* London: Wiley.

Riddell, S., Wilkinson, H. and Baron, S. 1998: From emancipatory research to focus group: people with learning difficulties and the research process. In P. Clough and L. Barton (eds), *Articulating with difficulty: research voices in Inclusive Education.* London: Sage.

Rodgers, S, J. 1999: Trying to Get it Right: undertaking research involving people with learning difficulties, *Disability and Society,* 14 (4), 421–434.

Scott, J. 1992: Experience. In J. Butler and J. Scott (eds), *Feminists Theorize the Political.* London: Routledge.

Shakespeare, T. 1997: Researching Disabled Sexuality. In C. Barnes and G.Mercer (eds), *Doing Disability Research.* Leeds: The Disability Press.

Sheldon, A. 1999: Personal and Perplexing: feminist disability politics evaluated. *Disability and Society,* 14 (5), 643-657.

Stone, E. 1997: From the Research Notes of a Foreign Devil: Disability Research in China. In C. Barnes and G.Mercer (eds), *Doing Disability Research.* Leeds: The Disability Press.

Stone, E. and Priestley, M. 1996: Parasites, pawns and partners: disability research and the role of non-disabled researchers. *British Journal of Sociology,* 47, 699–716.

Stubbs, S. 1999: Engaging with Difference: Soul-searching for a methodology in Disability and Development Research. In E. Stone (ed.), *Disability and Development.* Leeds: The Disability Press.

Thomas, C. 1999: Female Forms. Buckingham: Open University Press.

Truman, C. and Raine, P. 2001: Involving users in evaluation: the social relations of user participation in health research. *Critical Public Health,* 11 (3), 215-29.

Vernon, A. 1997: Reflexivity: the dilemma of researching from the inside. In C. Barnes and G.Mercer (eds), *Doing Disability Research.* Leeds: The Disability Press.

Watson, N. 2003: What's my Title? In C. Barnes and G. Mercer (eds), *Implementing the Social Model of Disability: Theory and Research.* Leeds: The Disability Press.

Zarb, G. 1992: On the Road to Damascus: First Steps towards Changing the Relations of Disability Research Production. *Disability, Handicap and Society,* 7 (2), 125–38.

Zarb, G. 1997: Researching Disabling Barriers. In C. Barnes and G.Mercer (eds), *Doing Disability Research.* Leeds: The Disability Press.

CHAPTER 10

Collectivising Experience and Rules of Engagement: close(d) encounters in disability research

Mairian Scott-Hill

Introduction

In the last decade, various authors have pointed to the existence of more than one social model of disability, each of which demonstrates different emphases (Priestley 1998). However, Colin Barnes (2003: 9) has recently suggested that 'in some respects, the social model has become the new orthodoxy'. Though he doesn't specify which social model, in the context of Barnes' work over the last two decades, it seems reasonable to assume that this 'orthodox' social model is that which emerged from The Fundamental Principles of Disability (UPIAS 1976). The structural and material emphasis of this document on status, rights and redistribution is clear, and is generally incorporated in 'orthodox' paradigms that guide emancipatory disability research. For example, these accounts commonly refer to the need to change 'the social relations of research production' (Oliver 1997: 18) – or, as Geof Mercer puts it, to reverse the:

> traditional researcher–researched hierarchy/social relations of research production, while also challenging the material relations of research production (Mercer 2002: 233).

Further, in a recent assessment of the state of disability research, Barnes suggests that:

> the social model of disability represents nothing more complicated than a focus on the economic, environmental and cultural barriers encountered by people viewed by others as having some form of impairment (Barnes 2003: 9).

At the same time, 'orthodox' accounts are littered with references to ongoing and largely unexamined difficulties faced by disability research. These difficulties include representation, the collectivisation of experience, teamwork

between disabled and non-disabled researchers, the rules of engagement in
the research process, and the issue of partisanship and research ethics (for example,
Campbell and Oliver 1996; Barnes and Mercer 1997; Mercer 2002). Further,
though there is a growing recognition that disability oppression is institutionalised, there is little serious attempt to address insidious, indirect forms
of oppression in the research context, in spite of the knowledge that they
can be just as injurious in their effects as more direct forms of oppression.
The common denominator in all of these issues is that they are to a very
large degree concerned *with social relationships between people*, relationships that
foreground issues of 'culture', 'language' and 'experience'. The question then
becomes this: Are 'orthodox' paradigms of disability research sufficiently alert
to and tolerant of the messiness of the social worlds of disabled people to
give social relations the kind of in-depth investigation that may go some way
towards resolving the difficulties they are perceived to pose?

If a paradigm, following Denzin and Lincoln (2000: 157), is defined as
'a basic set of beliefs that guide action', at first sight the answer to our question
seems to be 'no'. If we take the UPIAS social model as the driving paradigm
of 'orthodox' research, 'orthodox' social modellists insist that the social
model is *not* concerned with the analysis of experience or impairment
(Oliver 1996; Finkelstein 2002), while others argue that it should be (Morris
1992; Crow 1996; Thomas 1999). A similar conflict exists between orthodoxy
and those who are concerned with the analysis of 'cultural' and 'linguistic'
barriers and processes that are implicated in the social creation or construction
of disability (Corker 1998, 2001, 2003; Scott-Hill 2002, 2004). Nevertheless,
there is considerable evidence within disability research *at the paradigmatic
level*, to support orthodoxy's claims. That is, experience, impairment,
language and culture are important and legitimate projects for disability research,
but they cannot be properly or fully addressed using the 'orthodox' disability
research paradigm. However, as I will show below, my reasons for apparently
supporting orthodoxy are not the same as those that are commonly put forward
by proponents of these claims, because I believe these claims perpetuate the
discourse of individualism (Scott-Hill 2002).

It can further be argued that, for exactly the same reasons, if we uncritically
support mainly feminist counter claims, what we would be proposing is the
incorporation of experience, impairment, language and culture whilst leaving
the underlying assumptions of the 'orthodox' paradigm intact. So, for example,
while Mercer (2002: 235) suggests that 'subjective ... experiential studies too
often ignore power relations and wider contextual factors', it could equally
be the case that such studies do not aim to investigate these things from the
perspective of orthodoxy. In what follows, I want to examine how different

rules of engagement in research conversations approach the problem of collectivisation using two different disability research paradigms, which are summarised in Table 1. The first paradigm represents (how I perceive) 'orthodoxy' on the basis of the disability studies literature. The second paradigm represents my own 'take' on doing disability research, though it has much in common with research accounts that are lumped under the rather unfortunate umbrella of 'postmodernism'. These paradigms should not, however, be interpreted as yet another reiteration of the research 'typologies' that sociologists are so fond of. Rather, in applying them, I will focus on the view that research paradigms are showing an increasing tendency to 'interbreed' (Lincoln and Guba 2000), and attempt to examine the consequences of such interbreeding for collectivisation.

Closed encounters: collectivising experience the orthodox way

At a very basic level, the success of collectivisation is a product of how different perspectives function together in an intra-textual conversation. Alvesson (2002: 168) suggests that: 'a good conversation involves a combination of consensus, variation in views and dissensus. Too much of any of these elements means that the conversation becomes uninteresting; it becomes repetitive, it comes to consist of monologues or turns into a quarrel'. Ofelia Schutte (1998: 55) also notes that 'what we hold to be the nature of knowledge is not culture-free' but is determined by methodologies and data legitimated by the rational consensus – or what she calls the 'unstated norm'. She further suggests that we might:

> map the statements of the culturally different other according to three categories – readily understandable, difficult to understand, and truly incommensurable (Schutte 1998: 56).

When the degree of difficulty in understanding the position of someone who holds views that are incommensurable with our own is determined by the rational consensus, communication tends to reach closure very quickly.

Consider examples 1 and 2 below, both of which include challenges to particular positions taken by 'orthodoxy' ('truth', 'reality' and 'impairment'), though occurring at different stages in the research process.

Example 1, from the archives of the disability-research mailbase
<www.jiscmail.ac.uk/lists/disability-research.html>

Brad: 'Larry wrote: 'Reality is not fixed, it is relative' … wrong.'
Larry: '… Reality, as observed by any individual, is dependent upon the observers viewpoint, his/her sensory apparatus, cognitive framework, education, age, culture and so much else.'

Table 1: Contrasting disability research paradigms

KEY ISSUE	'Orthodox' disability research paradigm	'Communicative' disability research paradigm
Disability	A social relation of dominance.	A contingent social relation.
Impairment	Socially/institutionally constructed; perceived by others.	Ontology: impairment is experienced and lived by people in a structured and regulated world.
Society	Structured, ordered and patterned on the basis of social categories.	Messy, complex and sometimes chaotic.
Individual Culture	Passive, oppressed, pre-social. A reflection of socio-economic relations. A coherent pattern/uniform ethos.	(Potential) agentic, resourceful, social. The processes and resources involved in situated social practice.
Language	Language is either subordinate to or a distraction from structures of political and economic domination (determinism). It is viewed as a simple medium for the mirroring of objective reality through the passive transport of date (language represents 'reality').	Language is productive, interactive, creative, functional, situated and context-dependent. People make use of language to accomplish things.
Discourse	Institutional: broad institutionalised ideas or reasoning patterns with a material practice referent and with power to define and structure part of social reality. Language is divorced from action, and conversations are viewed as dialectic and inter-textual.	Institutional (regime of truth/knowledge) *and* local (what people do in dialogue with each other in specific social settings). Language *is* action, and conversations are viewed as dialogic and intra-textual.
Power	Top-down.	Dispersed, disciplinary.
Resistance	Collective resistance through the unity of oppressed groups.	Resistance through subversion of universals and grand narratives.
Politics	Consensus (internal); opposition (external). Challenging research as an	Relational (internal and external).
Research emphasis	apparatus of hegemony; reversing the traditional researcher/researched hierarchy through partisanship with the oppressed.	There is an analytical separation of talk (the language itself), practice (language in use) and meaning (production of research texts). The support of knowledge claims through empirical material based on care, awareness and insightful handling of production/ construction processes, and care in the interpretation of it.
Rules of engagement	Closure and a refusal of destabilising perspectives; focus on what is (assumed to be) present and readily understandable.	Openness, understanding, reflexivity, awareness of absence.
Collectivisation	Finding, constructing or imposing tendencies and patterns on 'reality' on the basis of predetermined assumptions about the nature of 'reality'.	Through dialogue between pattern and ambiguity; trends and variation; order and fragmentation; regularities and disorder.
Implications for social change	Focus on social transformation at the societal level. Research tends to result in the reinforcement of minority-majority relations, locational integration (tokenism), and/or social fragmentation.	The aim is to identify strategies for change that are both top-down and bottom-up. Research aims for social inclusion through critical awareness of complexity, whilst recognising that social change may not be immediately observable.

Brad: *'Reality depends on the superposition, or state, of the observation. We know
that superposition of possible outcomes must exist simultaneously at a microscopic
level because we can observe interference effects from these. [...] Indeterminacy
originally restricted to the atomic domain becomes transformed into
macroscopic indeterminacy, which can then be resolved by direct observation.
That prevents us from so naively accepting as valid a 'blurred model' for
representing reality.'*

Larry: *'I am afraid I simply do not understand what you are saying, I am not
sure that I ever will. Today's hard science becomes tomorrow's myth. My
apparatus for observing and processing that information is clearly different
from yours, don't impose yours on me.'*

Brad: *'I'm sorry to say the imposition is all yours. My thoughts are exactly that,
mine, and just another perspective.'*

Michael: *'I think this debate is getting out of hand so let's get back to, er, reality.
Q: Is Diarrhoea social? Or Cancer, or MS, or AIDS, or a broken spine?
Of course they're not. They're physical realities existing independently of
thought. The subjective experience of them may vary but that's not at all
the same thing as saying they in themselves are social...'*

Larry: *'At this point I shall step down from the podium of this virtual debating
chamber and leave space for greater minds than I to continue the debate.'*

In this conversation, there is too much emphasis on consensus, and so
the exchange has a dialectical flavour. As Bakhtin (1986: 147) writes:

> (t)ake dialogue and remove the voices ... remove the intonations
> ... carve out abstract concepts and judgements from living
> words and responses, cram everything into one abstract
> consciousness – and that's how you get dialectics.

Brad's position is clearly not 'just another perspective', because it is fairly
characteristic of accounts of 'truth' and 'reality' that are part of the 'orthodox'
paradigm. Moreover, it represents an 'unstated norm' because this is not transparent.
Instead, the 'norm' is disguised as an individual's 'thoughts' and dressed up
in academic jargon - a strategy that may be lost on those list members who
are not steeped in the list's history, aims and objectives, or who make other
'culturally different' interpretations of disability. It is also noticeable that Brad
doesn't invite Larry to explain his 'difficult to understand' difference further,
a closure that prompts Michael to further marginalise Larry's still unexamined
perspective. An in-depth analysis of the archive suggests that this kind of
conversation is fairly typical. The broad topic 'language', for example, has
occupied a great deal of time and space on the list over the years. However,
discussions tend to be reduced to matters of terminology, to revolve around

the multiple meanings of words, and to be closed prematurely by 'orthodox' interventions that invite participants to revisit the ('orthodox') history of the topic. This failure to acknowledge that social relationships do not hinge simply on the meaning of words creates social distance rather than mutuality, where the need to maintain the existing consensus overrides everything else, and is built on the marginalisation of dissenting voices. The processes of collectivisation employed simply reinforce orthodoxy along with its existing majority–minority relations.

Example 2: taken from Emanuel and Ackroyd (1996: 181)

'There were two groups of disabled people on the strategy group who could not agree with each other on terminology. While people from GMCDP (Greater Manchester Coalition of Disabled People) preferred to use the term 'impairment' ... the profoundly deaf (sic) members of the group felt the word 'impairment' has a negative meaning and should be rejected. They preferred to talk in terms of 'difference'. They emphasised cultural and language differences rather than the existence of impairment. However 'difference' was unacceptable to the GMCDP members because it was regarded as too general and did not classify the functional range which is the basis on which oppressive societal and individual attitudes are formed. As no consensus could be reached, it was agreed to use the word 'impairment' but to include a statement outlining the deaf member's perspective.'

Once a particular voice is enshrined as a 'minority viewpoint' within a particular orthodoxy, it will always be a minority viewpoint because orthodoxies tend to take the majority viewpoint as given. This is usually reflected at every stage of the research process, including the production of the final research text. For instance, it could be argued that the above extract is an example of what Potter and Wetherall (1987) call *selective interpretation*. On the basis of predetermined ideas ('orthodoxy'), the researcher structures an account in such a way that a potential multiplicity of meanings (e.g. 'difference') is neglected in favour of what is regarded as a 'primary' meaning ('impairment'). In the production of research texts, it may also mean that such a 'primary' meaning is read from the variety, ambiguity and inconsistency of the statements in the accounts in order to preserve the 'orthodoxy'. Selective interpretation therefore views the collectivisation of experience in terms of patterns of inclusion and exclusion that are predetermined by this 'primary' meaning. Far from 'breaking down barriers', one outcome of such an approach when used consistently is social fragmentation, often on the basis of competing social and political agendas. Again, the emphasis is on refusal of destabilising perspectives and on closure.

Close encounters: struggling for mutuality

The 'communicative' paradigm takes the view that social relations between people are notoriously messy and complex. Research that examines these issues – perhaps even all research because most research is conducted through and with people – must therefore show 'a tolerance for ambiguity, multiplicity, contradiction, and instability' (Wolf 1992: 129). At the heart of this paradigm is the belief that language must be taken seriously, but, as Table 1 shows, the way that language, discourse and culture are understood is very different from how they are understood within the 'orthodox' paradigm. There are three points that must be emphasised in this respect. First is the view that language *is* doing, and language practice has effects – there is no contrived divorce between speech and action. Second, the importance of *not* understanding is as critical as the importance of understanding. Therefore researchers need to be sufficiently reflexive and alert to what is not present and visible, and to note the contradictions that emerge in the research over time. Generally, though not always, this means more data rather than selective use of data, and a tight, qualitative and locally-oriented research focus. And third, it is not assumed that reaching understanding and mutuality will be easy because meaning is not always transparent and practice is context-dependent. But, as the following two examples show, these things have to be struggled for and struggle requires a great deal of time and reflexive energy. Both of these examples centre on the question of impairment. The first looks at how impairment operates in an example of teamwork between disabled and non-disabled researcher, and the second examines the consequences of not understanding the ontological character of impairment in the research context.

Example 3: taken from Corker and Davis (2003)

This discussion took place at the end of a day's research in a mainstream school, which had been particularly frustrating for both of us. It was our practice to record all our conversations with each other, as researchers, in addition to those that we had with the disabled young people we were working with, and those that the young people had with each other and with other adults in the different social contexts under investigation. This particular conversation began with each of us stating a position in relation to a situation that we had encountered that day:

John   .... Isobel [one of the 'specialist' teachers] ..... *wants us to sit in the base, next period, to stop the [other teacher] coming in.*

Mairian   *Well that's not our role.*

The conversation became focused on meanings of the word 'stop', which we had interpreted differently. This initially led to John's insistence that he didn't mean what Mairian thought he meant, which in turn resulted in the dialogue becoming more intense.

Mairian   I think you're dodging the issue. (laughs)

John   But I can just. I can justify. No, but I can justify doing it on an academic level. Yeah? Do you know what I mean? I can do anything.

Mairian   I don't think this is a …. I don't think that the issues arising are anything to do with academic or personal level. I said to you, you changed the language. What I meant was….

John   Yeah, but that's OK.

Mairian   What I mean was ….

John   Yeah, but you interrupted me when I was trying. You …

Mairian   When, when you first … when, when you first described what Isobel said to you, you said quite clearly that she had said, 'Would we stay in there, and stop the [other teacher] going in there?' Then when you referred …

John   That's what she said….

Mairian   …. to it again, a few minutes ago, you changed the language to make it seem as if Isobel wasn't being quite so … you know … insistent?

John   Yeah, because that's what we do. I say words. You make an interpretation I don't agree with, so I say it a new way. Do you know what I mean?

Mairian   No.

John   So the first time, when I say stop, I don't mean we physically, or verbally stop them. I mean that we are there. That was it. We were to be there.

Mairian   Right.

John   OK? If it stopped them, wasn't our choice. It was going to be the teacher's choice.

Mairian   Yes. So what does that tell you?

John   That tells me about the way that we hone something down so that we both agree, OK? I don't see it as bad that I change. I see it as good, because if I didn't change, you'd get what I consider to be the wrong perception of what, of what I'm saying. Do you know what I mean? If I don't change.

Mairian   No. No … what I'm saying. What I'm saying is that the two different languages actually convey to me two very different scenarios, right?

John   Yeah, but they don't to me.

Mairian   Now, hang on a minute….

John   They convey the same to me.

Mairian   What I'm saying is what does that tell you about, for example, our work with the deaf kids here?

John   Don't patronise me … I, I want to know what you think, and I'm getting angry now. OK?

Mairian   Why?

John	*Because I think that you are being evasive. OK? You tell me what you think, never mind the kids … what you think about me changing sentences.*
Mairian	*Yeah.*
John	*I mean, do you understand what I was saying? I don't know that you understand.*
Mairian	*Put it this way. The first time I understood one thing....*
John	*And that is?*
Mairian	*… the second time I understood something different.*
John	*Right, OK, OK. And I understand it, but what about now, what about now?*
Mairian	*Then the, what is eh. There are two things, one, you did say very clearly that using the word stop, you said that I'd made an assumption about the meaning of stop.*
John	*Well whatever, yeah.*
Mairian	*OK? Now, yes of course I would.*
John	*Yeah yeah. I'm not saying that's bad. I'm saying that's good.*
Mairian	*No, but …*
John	*… that's good.*
Mairian	*Relating that to the kids, ok?*
John	*Right.*
Mairian	*There's a lot of my way, my behaviour which is very similar to theirs and not being able immediately, to look beyond the concrete, the concreteness of the word stop. So I go for the most familiar meaning. Now that's why I understand, for example, the results in the science tests and the fact that they can answer the factual questions, but they can't answer the questions so easily which ask them to think*
John	*Right, right. Now, so yeah it's OK ….*
Mairian	*…. and answer.*
John	*Now … now I'm happy. I'm happy now, because we're talking about the same thing now and that's OK.*
Mairian	*Yeah.*
John	*But before I wasn't sure what, what you were. When you went off to the kids, I wasn't sure what …*
Mairian	*No well I was just …*
John	*… you were talking about ….*
Mairian	*… I was only trying to draw you out to see if you picked that up.*
John	*… know it differently. The way, the way I picked it up was more in a eh visitation sense. So that when we first came here, Callum [one of the deaf kids] would respond in one way and I would get a fixed idea about him. But each time I come back it's more nuanced.*
Mairian	*Mmm, mmm.*

John	*You know what I mean?*
Mairian	*Mmm.*
John	*But I think it's the same thing, because it, all the time I'm taking him on face value.*
Mairian	*Yeah.*
John	*But it's OK, because the next, the next time I'm willing to change that. You know what I mean? But I agree that it's something that I haven't really picked up.*

One of the biggest problems facing the collectivisation of disabled people's experience is the particular perceptions of impairment that are employed. Impairment is not generally subject to the same kind of analysis as race, gender and sexuality, for example, in spite of the fact that many disabled people clearly feel excluded both from society and from disability theory and politics on the basis of their impairment. In spite of the growing recognition that impairment is socially constructed, 'orthodox' disability studies consistently downplays the implications of this: namely that the impairment categories in question are not ontological categories. Impairment categories are perceived by 'orthodoxy' as operational categories that are based on 'expert' judgements about what constitutes a particular kind of divergence from 'normality'. At the same time, however, impairment is lived in and through relationships with others, and it has 'real' consequences for how the social world is perceived and for social practice. Those who argue that the presence of impairment is of little or no consequence to the ability to do 'good' disability research tend to take an acultural view of impairment, and to assume that the nature of knowledge is culture-free.

The above conversation initially bears many of the hallmarks of example 1, and there is a danger that it will have a similar outcome up to the point where John says 'don't patronise me'. But this doesn't happen because both of us invite each other to explain further, thus opening up the possibility for greater understanding, along with a collective consensus that was tolerant of our differences. Thus, in the second part of the dialogue, it becomes clear that John has been reading Mairian's responses from within his own, hearing world-view and that Mairian has been reading his responses from within her deaf world-view. What follows is a useful analysis of how this has impacted on the way that each of us was doing and interpreting research with deaf children. John's initial, unsuccessful attempts to engage with Mairian provide some insight into how impairment differences can be downplayed within the 'orthodox' paradigm – something that might have happened in example 1 if Brad and Michael had attempted to draw Larry out, and if Larry hadn't subsequently withdrawn from the debate. In this context, it is interesting that when an earlier version of the research from which example 3 is taken was sent out to journal referees in the discipline of sociology, it was read through the lens of 'orthodoxy'. The 'cause' of the communication breakdown was identified as 'gender differences' and the second part of the conversation was expressly ignored.

Example 4: taken from Corker (2001)

[Translation of video-taped interview with Linda, aged 15years, conducted in sign language]

Mairian: *So what do you think about disabled people?*

Linda: *About disabled people … I like them. It must be horrible to be disabled but there is nothing wrong in it. I certainly wouldn't think or say what Glenn Hoddle said. I wouldn't do that. It's horrible and the teasing, it's not nice.*

Mairian: *Do you think you're disabled?*

Linda: *No!*

Mairian: *No?*

Linda: *Someone did say to me that deaf is disabled, is that true or not?*

Mairian: *I'm asking you … what do you think?*

Linda: *No.*

Mairian: *You don't think so?*

Linda: *No … what about you?*

Mairian: *…. Um … disabled … has many meanings and maybe when I use the word disabled, I mean something different from you. But … I would say yes, I think I am disabled.*

Linda: *(laughs) Why, you don't look disabled. You can walk naturally. Disabled people have funny walks, you know - like Kevin. They have a funny walk and they are disabled and you are deaf and are not disabled. Other people have said that you are deaf so that means that you are disabled but I think I am deaf but I'm not disabled. If you have a funny walk then you are and I am not. If I was disabled that would really upset me I think I would always wish that I could walk properly. So not being able to walk or see is disability - not me.*

One area where 'orthodox' interpretivist accounts often lack explanatory power is in their failure to make explicit what is not said but which may hold the key to rendering something more readily understandable. In a visual-spatial world, looking and seeing are of central importance, but so too are the consequences of an education system that concentrates on the delivery of 'the facts' and does not value reflexivity. Deaf people are constantly juggling the apparent conflict between what they see (literally) and what they are told is 'true', but sometimes these worlds reinforce each other. Deaf studies, like 'orthodox' disability studies, often leaps to present a discussion like the one above as concrete empirical evidence that the experience of Deaf people and disabled people is so incommensurable that it cannot form a basis for collectivisation (Ladd 2003). However, if we fill in the absences in this conversation *by interpreting it from Linda's perspective*, cracks begin to appear in the concrete. Linda interprets 'disability' on the basis of what she can see – visible impairment – in spite of the knowledge that 'someone' has said to her that 'deaf is disabled'. Moreover, she appears to use the normative view that impairment is incapacity and therefore, for her, would be 'upsetting' and 'horrible' – something that being deaf is clearly not. Deaf and disabled are interpreted in terms of what she can do – see - and not in terms of what she can't do – hear – which seems logical and coherent only if the ontological character of deafness is made visible and allowed to enter this conversation.

As a researcher, even though I do not identify as Deaf, my own dependency on vision as a deaf person alerts me to this, and perhaps this gives me the advantage of lived experience over perceived experience. However, once in full view, and indeed it is referred to again and again in the Deaf studies literature, this knowledge is there for all to learn – if they choose to do so. It is interesting, therefore, that the only way that 'orthodox' disability studies can incorporate the experience of deafness is the easy way. It assumes the experience of deafness to be a bounded, coherent pattern or uniform ethos – as a thing rather than a process – and this renders it incommensurable. Correspondingly, it is difficult for partisans working in the research context to see that mainstreaming – as the educational 'reality' for most deaf children for the last 3-4 decades – might interact with impairment to produce very different ontological forms of deafness that seek a greater understanding of difference-in-dialogue. 'Difference' is, after all, what they live with.

Concluding remarks

Proponents of the 'orthodox' social model insist that it should be a conceptual tool or heuristic device that clarifies the meaning of disability and impairment, and:

> enables us to see something that we do not understand because in the model it can be seen from different viewpoints' (Finkelstein 2002: 13).

As such, the social model amounts to a 'multidimensional replica of reality that can trigger insights that we might not otherwise develop' (p.13). Finkelstein's reference to 'different viewpoints' suggests a degree of flexibility in how the model might be interpreted and used in practice, and, if this is indeed the case, then it seems a likely explanation of how the social model has come to mean different things to different people. But, set against this, there is the suggestion that there is one 'reality' than can be replicated, which arguably works against flexibility. In view of this, Finkelstein's vision seems to be at best limited, at worst, seriously compromised by the naive view of the actuality of social practice that is taken by 'orthodoxy', along with its focus on defining the content of oppression in an a priori fashion. These limitations make it difficult for 'orthodox' social model research to identify the mechanisms or relationships that generate a disability outcome, other than to propose that it takes the form of oppression.

Any attempt to gain critical enlightenment on these matters tends to be interpreted by 'orthodox' social modellists as threatening the unity of disabled people's political campaigns, and accused of promoting a relativistic world in which the 'fact' or 'reality' of disability can no longer be assured. The suggestion is that 'multiple definitions of different actions cannot be tolerated' if the fight for social change is to prevail (Altman 2001: 117). However, the refusal to privilege some types of accounts on epistemological grounds – relativism, as it is often called – need not be seen as a morally or politically vacuous stance, or as rhetorically ineffective. There is still the imperative to establish the claims of some versions over others. This struggle is certainly reinforced by the knowledge that normative discourse is not ephemeral but powerful in constituting social formations in ways that are oppressive for certain social groups. But the *process* of struggle can only be adequately researched, and appropriate intervention strategies formulated, where the commitment to studying disability is also a commitment to the critique of some positions, some of the ways in which power is exercised and some forms of social practice.

The 'communicative' paradigm, when applied sensitively, does not deny the existence of social structures and categories nor does it suggest that social relationships are never structured. What it does do is to urge researchers to develop an awareness of how far these structures can permeate, and to caution us that partisanship with the oppressed is not always an effective guarantee of anti-oppressive practice or social change. But this claim comes with a word of warning. Disability research needs to take the messy side of social life much more seriously and to hesitate before finding, constructing or imposing tendencies and patterns on reality. For this is what continues to happen when important differences between research paradigms are glossed over, and it results in their widespread mis-representation and abuse. The communicative paradigm represents a more careful and reflexive approach to research that will be more appropriate for the investigation of social relations across difference. It is capable of providing us with a deeper understanding of the processes of collectivisation and, as such, may yet prove to be a useful tool in examining the mechanisms of inclusive societies.

Bibliography

Altman, B. M. 2001: Disability definitions, models, classification schemes and applications. In G.L. Albrecht, K.D. Seelman and M. Bury (eds), *Handbook of Disability Studies.* Thousand Oaks, CA: Sage.

Alvesson, M. 2002: *Postmodernism and Social Research.* Buckingham: Open University Press.

Bakhtin, M.M. 1986: *Speech Genres and Other Late Essays.* C. Emerson and M. Holquist (eds), (V.W. McGee translator). Austin: University of Texas Press.

Barnes, C. 2003: What a difference a decade makes: reflections on doing 'emancipatory' research. *Disability and Society,* 18 (1), 3-18.

Barnes, C. and Mercer, G. (eds) 1997: *Doing Disability Research.* Leeds: The Disability Press.

Campbell, J. and Oliver, M. 1996: *Disability Politics.* London: Routledge

Corker, M. 1998: *Deaf and Disabled or Deafness Disabled?* Buckingham: Open University Press.

Corker, M. 2001: Sensing disability. *Hypatia* 16 (4), 34-52.

Corker, M. 2003: Deafness/Disability – problematising notions of identity, culture and structure. In S. Riddell and N. Watson (eds), *Disability, Culture and Identity.* London: Pearson.

Corker, M. and Davis, J.M. 2003: Shifting selves, shifting meanings, learning culture: Towards a reflexive dialogics in disability research. In D. Kasnitz and R. Shuttleworth (eds), *Engaging Anthropology and Disability Studies.*

Crow, L. 1996: Including all our lives: renewing the social model of disability. In C. Barnes and G. Mercer (eds), *Exploring the Divide: Illness and Disability.* Leeds: The Disability Press.

Denzin, N. K. and Lincoln, Y. S. (eds) 2000: *Handbook of Qualitative Research* (2nd edition), Thousand Oaks, CA: Sage.

Emanuel, J. and Ackroyd, D. 1996: Breaking down barriers. In: C. Barnes and G. Mercer (eds), *Exploring the Divide: Illness and Disability.* Leeds: The Disability Press.

Finkelstein, V. 2002: The social model of disability repossessed. *Coalition,* February, 10-16. Available on the Disability Archive: www.leeds.ac.uk/disability-studies/archiveuk/archframe.htm

Ladd, P. 2003: *Understanding Deaf Culture: In Search of Deafhood.* Cleveland: Multilingual Matters.

Lincoln, Y.S. and Guba, E.G. 2000: Paradigmatic controversies, contradictions and emerging confluences. In N. K. Denzin and Y. S. Lincoln (eds), *Handbook of Qualitative Research* (2nd edition), Thousand Oaks, CA: Sage.

Mercer, G. 2002: Emancipatory disability research. In C. Barnes, M. Oliver and L. Barton (eds), *Disability Studies Today.* Cambridge: Polity Press.

Morris, J. 1992: Personal and political: a feminist perspective on researching physical disability. *Disability, Handicap and Society,* 7 (2), 157-66.

Oliver, M. 1996: Defining impairment and disability: issues at stake. In C. Barnes and G. Mercer (eds), *Exploring the Divide: Illness and Disability.* Leeds: The Disability Press.

Oliver, M. 1997: Emancipatory research: realistic goal or impossible dream? In C. Barnes and G. Mercer (eds), *Doing Disability Research.* Leeds: The Disability Press.

Potter, J. and Wetherall, M. 1987: *Discourse and Social Psychology: Beyond Attitudes and Behaviour.* London: Sage

Priestley, M. 1998: Constructions and creations: idealism, materialism and disability theory. *Disability and Society,* 13 (1), 75-94.

Schutte, O. 1998: Cultural alterity: cross-cultural communication and feminist theory in North-South contexts. In U. Narayan and S. Harding (eds), *Decentering the Center: Philosophy for a Multicultural, Postcolonial and Feminist World.* Bloomington, IN: Indiana University Press.

Scott-Hill, M. 2002: Policy, politics and the silencing of voice. *Policy and Politics,* 30 (3), 397-409.

Scott-Hill, M. 2004 *forthcoming*: Impairment, difference and identity. In C. Barnes, S. French, J. Swain and C. Thomas (eds), *Disabling Barriers, Enabling Environments,* 2nd edition. London: Sage.

Thomas, C. 1999: Female Forms. Buckingham Open University Press.

UPIAS 1976: Fundamental Principles of Disability. London: Union of Physically Impaired Against Segregation. Available on the Disability Archive: www.leeds.ac.uk/disability-studies/archiveuk/archframe.htm

Wolf, M. 1992: *A Thrice-told Tale: Feminism, Postmodernism and Ethnographic Responsibility.* Stanford: Stanford University Press.

CHAPTER 11

Research with Children: ethnography, participation, disability, self-empowerment

John Davis and John Hogan

Introduction

This chapter discusses the use of participatory and emancipatory methods with children and young people. Initially, it discusses the theoretical basis of such work before critically reflecting on the practical benefits and limitations of such approaches. It specifically reports on the experiences of a participatory project carried out in Liverpool in 2001/2002 (Davis and Hogan 2002).

Children/young people and participation

A number of authors have argued that children in the UK are positioned within a welfare discourse that does not respect their abilities (De Winter 1997; Roche 1997; Cockburn 1998; Hogan 2002). That welfare policy focuses on making children into 'better' future adults rather than making children's lives better in the present (Cockburn 1998; Prout 2000). In schools, an elitist culture is reinforced by rigid control of the curriculum, inflexible processes of assessment and regular HMI (Her Majesty's Inspectors) evaluation (Hargreaves 1989). The focus on schools as a place where future workers are produced leads to exaggerated adult control of school and free time and results in children's own wishes becoming 'invisible' (Prout 2000).

The philosophical basis of the welfarist agenda is found in the idea of socialisation. This concept haunts both sociological writing on social capital and constructivist perspectives in psychology (Davis and Watson 2001; Davis 2002). In sociology, Parsonian perspectives on socialisation have resulted in the child being represented as a danger to society unless properly taught, trained and controlled by parents and professionals (Corsaro 1997).

In psychology, notions of development from Piaget and Vygotskia underpin the perception that adults must intervene in children's lives to ensure 'normal' development. Such intervention is required at the earliest age possible:

> Modern social policy starts from the perspective that children are weak, meek, poor, dependent, and needy. They require redemption by way of a technical rational child care that is privatised, universalised, has specific goals/outcomes and that can be scrutinised to establish its usefulness. (Moss and Petrie 2002: 84).

Welfare discourses have been challenged by a children's rights perspective, that aims to pave the way for childhood citizenship that is both empowering and inclusive (Hogan 2002). Examples ranging from the UN Convention On the Rights Of the Child, The Children Act 1989, to Quality Protects have helped to promote the idea that children are agents that can influence the policy agenda around them. This is particularly evident in the *Reggio Emilia* experience in Italy:

> Fascism taught them that people who conformed and obeyed were dangerous and therefore they wanted to encourage children to think and act for themselves. This requires the local policies to be discussed and scrutinised by children parents and practitioners. It also requires us to view the child (not as an isolated human being) as always in relationships with other children and adults, with the past, with society/cultures, etc. (Moss and Petrie 2002: 103).

Moss and Petrie (2002) believe that participatory approaches can shift us from viewing parents as the protectors of children to viewing them as the protectors of children's rights who ensure that they enable children to put forward their own views as 'social participants'. A similar separation occurs in disability studies where non-disabled people are encouraged to contribute to those processes that enable disabled people to achieve self-emancipation (Barnes 1992).

The children's rights perspective has led a number of writers to promote the idea that adults should develop partnerships with children as fellow citizens and equal members of communities (De Winter 1997; Hart 1997; Roche 1999; Tisdall and Davis 2003). They suggest that citizenship is not simply a formal legal status but is enacted through social processes (Davis and Watson 2001; Hogan 2002). The children's rights agenda has created a clamour to carry out participatory projects. These projects invariably aim to 'enable' children to exercise their rights, to make choices about things that influence their lives and/or to be consulted by policy makers.

Participation projects also have their own problems. On a practical note it is worth recognising that many participatory projects fail to achieve

tangible outcomes because they:
- take the form of consultation without action;
- are selective in the types of children they allow to participate;
- do not include children as organisers or in decision-making positions;
- do not create ongoing and sustained dialogue between policy makers and children (Davis 2002).

There is little evidence that children and young people have had an impact on policymaking (Kirby and Bryson 2002). Indeed, there is little practical evidence in childhood studies within the UK to support claims that participatory projects are a path to emancipation (Bailey 2004). On the contrary, in childhood studies participatory approaches have been labelled as tokenistic because the children and young people who take part very often receive no feedback on what happened to their ideas and do not discover if their views have stimulated policy change (Morrow 2000; Hill 2003; Tisdall and Davis 2003.

A classic example of token consultation occurs in relation to children's rights in schools. A number of children and young people have complained about the processes by which specific children are chosen to participate in school based forums and projects (Alderson 1999; Morrow 2000; Hill 2003). The suggestion is that some schools may create mechanisms for 'listening' but rather than contributing to the process of developing 'democratic communities', these mechanisms often act to reinforce traditional divisions (Alderson 2002). This means that though schools may inform children about 'rights' within their curriculum, they very often fail to demonstrate how children can exercise rights by example.

This criticism can also be found in the field of health promotion, where it is suggested that though schools teach children about healthy life styles they very often fail to set an example of what healthy living might be. For example, they have been criticised in relation to the standard of food provided in canteens and levels of hygiene particularly with regard to toilet facilities (Mayall 1994). In practice, young people's roles within participation projects are variable due to lack of time, confidence, interest and skills. Problems can arise: if young people are expected to be 'professional researchers'; if project organisers fail to identify young people's own skills; and if organisers fail to ask young people how they want to work in a participatory team (Kirby with Bryson 2002).

However, there are some participatory projects that overcome these hurdles. For example, a few have enabled children to be involved in processes of change. This has been achieved by developing policy in partnership with service providers and creating processes of dialogue that lead to agreed change rather than consultation that leads to nothing (Cairns 2001; Mitchell 2001). These examples suggest that the creation of useful participation projects is very much dependant on the types of organisations that control the development processes (Kirby with Bryson 2002). Indeed, there is very little evidence that university based research projects that claim to be participatory actually lead to tangible changes in the life experiences of those who participate (Morrow 2000; Tisdall and Davis 2003). This raises the question; what are participation projects that include children and young people really for?

Emancipatory research

In the interest of avoiding overlap with other chapters in this volume, we merely note that emancipatory projects are promoted by a number of key works in disability studies (Barnes 1992, 1996; Oliver 1992, 1996, 1999; Zarb 1992; Shakespeare 1996, 1997; Stone and Priestley 1996; Corker 1999). These works are underpinned by a number of key ideas:

- disabled people should take an active role in the projects that involve them;
- disabled people should lead projects themselves or work in equal partnership with those who lead projects;
- disabled people should be consulted about the planning of projects and that they should be able to alter the course of such projects;
- projects should not be done simply to improve the careers of non-disabled academics; disabled people should not be treated as guinea pigs in experiments; and projects should lead to real changes in the life conditions of disabled people;
- it is not possible to carry out value free projects and those that organise projects should state their emancipatory aims (e.g. their relationship to the social model) from the outset.

There is an underlying assumption in the early literature on emancipatory research that it is mostly carried out by academics in universities. This assumption can also be found in literature concerning research with children (Grieg and Taylor 1999). Traditionally the university bias meant that the lust for original research findings was put before any recognition of the importance of the educational processes available during research. That is, the participatory and emancipatory potential of research projects went unrecognised.

However, in recent years the division between the academy and disabled people has changed. Many academic projects have been designed and carried out by disabled people who are also academics. Their outputs

include a variety of forms of writing, for example: writing that contributes
to our knowledge of the structural barriers that disabled people encounter,
for example, a lack of support for transition to adult services (Morris 1999);
projects that illustrate the cultural processes that create disability, for example,
values held by educational professionals that lead to discrimination in schools
(Adams et al. 2000); writing that breaks down stereotypes about different
disabled people, for example, by explaining the diversity of experiences of
disabled People (Corker and Davis 2001); and texts that examine the
potential for collaboration between service users and providers that challenge
traditional power relations (Beresford 2004).

Many disabled academics aspire to carry out projects that are participatory
and emancipatory. Often they collaborate with academics that are not
disabled. We do not know the exact extent to which disabled academics
have contributed to the long-term self-emancipation of disabled people. Some
of their projects may have had immediate impacts, while others have
contributed less dramatically to the overall raising of awareness of the barriers
to inclusion that disabled people experience. Occasionally there is a clear
link between a research project and social change. For example, the ESRC
'Life as a Disabled Child' project that was designed and managed by a team
of academics (3 with impairments, one without) contributed to local processes
of dialogue between disabled young people and policy makers in both
Edinburgh and Leeds (Davis 2000). This type of contribution by university-
based projects is rare because the Research Assessment Exercise judges
researchers by their production of academic publications and because
academic researchers tend to look at the 'meaning' of phenomena (e.g. what
is a disabled child?) rather than the practical aspects of people's lives.

This means that though many academics aspire to carry out emancipatory
projects, the ideal may not always come to practical fruition. If we relate this
problem to the earlier criticism of participatory projects in childhood studies,
we can raise a number of questions:

- what criteria are used to chose/invite disabled people to take part in
  emancipatory projects?
- does participation in emancipatory projects actually involve sharing
  or gaining control of the project from the organisers?
- does choosing which side we are on (e.g. that of the social model)
  guarantee that projects contribute to the self-emancipation of disabled
  people?
- are researchers/academics/project organisers who have impairments
  just as careerist as the non–impaired academics who traditionally have
  used disabled people as a stepping stone on their career path?

- do emancipatory projects in the field of disability studies actually achieve changes in disabled people's lives, or are they an ideological utopia?

In looking for a vehicle by which to consider some of these questions we will discuss a participatory project carried out in Liverpool by John Davis (previously a university-based researcher who had become an independent research consultant and has since rejoined the ranks of academia), in collaboration with John Hogan (a senior project worker from a voluntary organisation with experience of working in community education/ with young people). The intention was to build on our complementary and contrasting skills and experience of developing participatory approaches. It was supported by a group of interested parties, including the assistant director of children's services, two senior managers in children's services, a number of disabled people employed in health and social services, the leader of a disabled people's arts forum, a group of disabled young adults, and a number of groups of disabled children/young people.

Diversity and difference: a case study from Liverpool
This project was first raised by Mike Jones, Director of the Liverpool Bureau for Children and Young People, in conversation with John Davis. He pointed out the lack of participatory work with disabled children in Liverpool. On returning to Liverpool, Mike Jones and John Hogan worked with Jackie O'Carroll and Peter Duxberry (Liverpool children's/social services) to identify funding for such a project. The aim was to improve on the current position whereby managers within children's and social services rarely consulted with disabled children and young people. The aim was to develop a process where children and young people were enabled to participate in ongoing and substantive service planning. We hoped to be able to support (on a long-term basis) disabled children and young people to influence decisions affecting their lives.

With this aim in mind we established the Diversity and Difference Group to oversee the project. Its aims and objectives were to:
- develop a range of mechanisms to enable children and young people who experienced a variety of social and attitudinal barriers to express their views and influence decision-making including forums, newsletters, website, IT, a variety of communication systems, and advocacy;
- develop agreed standards of practice across agencies for promoting the involvement and participation of disabled children and children with complex needs;

- develop a culture in which the participation of all children in the decision making process is promoted and valued;
- enable children to identify their own issues and agendas;
- consult with children on issues which affect them from a service agenda – including integrated services, transition, advocacy services, review processes;
- enable children to develop their own mechanisms of communicating their views collectively and individually;
- support children in developing ongoing mechanisms for participation;
- highlight models of good practice.

The aims and objectives of the 'Diversity and Difference Group' complemented a number of other initiatives that aimed to influence service delivery for children and young people in Liverpool. One example was Quality Protects Objectives 6 and 8 (which are used to audit the outcome of services delivered by local authorities in England and Wales) and the Liverpool Children's Fund Plan 'Realising Dreams and Ambitions' (June 2001).

Quality Protects objectives

• Objective 6
To ensure that children with specific social needs arising out of disability or a health condition are living in families or other appropriate settings in the community where their assessed needs are adequately met and reviewed.

• Objective 8
To actively involve users and carers in planning services and in tailoring individual packages of care and to ensure effective mechanisms are in place to handle complaints.

Liverpool Children's Fund Plan
This sets a number of aims with regards to disabled children:
- engage with disabled children to improve participation, inclusion and access to services;
- empower children as users of services and to increase their participation in service planning;
- support improved co-ordination of services and access to information;
- achieve a shift in the culture of play, youth and leisure services towards greater inclusion.

These policy initiatives provided us with a sound platform from which to encourage disabled people to support the Diversity and Difference Group. Principally, support was sought on the basis that the projects would lead to policy change that took account of children and young people's views.

Project details/methods

Approximately 40 children and young people aged 9-21 years took part in the consultation exercise. Focus groups and informal discussions were carried out with 16-21 year olds working as volunteers of a local voluntary organisation, 11-16 year olds who attended a mainstream school and 9-18 year olds who attended a Deaf youth club. The consultation process covered 2 stages. The first comprised an open discussion to enable the children and young people to raise their own issues. The second stage involved asking the children and young people to comment on the objectives of Quality Protects.

Many of the stage one comments involved descriptions of very negative experiences. These reflected the depth of discrimination that disabled children and young people experience on a daily basis. However, in an effort to move beyond a culture of complaint we asked the children and young people to tell us about the positive as well as the negative situations they had experienced. Where they complained about services we asked them how they would change the service if they were put in charge. Their responses enabled us to create a list of recommendations on what and how services should be improved. We also asked the children and young people to suggest specific projects (outlined later in the chapter) that they wanted to participate in to enable 'ongoing and sustained consultation and dialogue' with service providers.

What follows is not an exhaustive illustration of disabled children's lives in Liverpool. For example, very few children with learning difficulties took part in the project. However, this did act as a starting point from which to gather a broader range of views and experiences. The findings are separated into a number of sections that the children and young people developed in their discussions (Davis and Hogan 2002).

Social Services
The children and young people did not feel that social service staff fully consulted them about the services they received. Indeed, many of the older children had been involved in legal processes aimed at improving their service provision:

> Some staff treat you as stupid.
> The system creates an atmosphere of constant crisis in the family.

There are inequalities in service provision.

I'm not being funny but some people get loads of support because their parents have got big gobs and those that need it don't get any. There has got to be a fairer way.

Social Services are fighting in court not to give me a support worker and my mum says she is not going to do all the things she used to cause she is getting older. It's not just the kids that need help it's the parents too. My Mum's doing a placement with her work and she just can't look after me too. She needs her independence too. She has to be out to work at 8 am and social services don't care about that because they haven't got a budget to provide what we need.

Respite care

Most children who had experienced respite care were positive about this service. However issues of concern were raised with regards to ownership of the service:

Respite is designed more for parents, I mean I got on well at respite but it wasn't really like that I was consulted. It might have been better if I got a say in what the respite was. I'm a lot older now but my parents still make the choice of when I go to respite. It should be designed more for young people.

Education

The children and young people suggested that they experienced restriction of choice of which schools they attended; a lack of opportunities to be included structurally and culturally in mainstream schools; and a lack of disability equality awareness, mediation and advocacy.

I wasn't allowed to go to a mainstream school – just cos I can't do it physically it doesn't mean I can't do it mentally.

A lot of teachers are arrogant. At my first school three teachers sat down to discuss who was teaching me next year and the new teacher said I don't want her in my class. She doesn't have the qualities I like. So I was going to have to move classes but my Mum moved me school.

There is no one to complain to in the schools, even if we did have someone to complain to they would have to know how to communicate properly. Like you've brought a level 5 signer with you that's good we can understand them but in school there are not enough staff who can sign (to level 5). The stage 1-2 teachers are just crap, and there are just not enough BSL communicators.

Health care

Disabled children did not present themselves as people in need of continuous health care. It is worth noting that a number of university studies have indicated that children associate good health with good relationships rather than issues of health and illness (Backett-Milburn et al. 2000). Illness tends to be an event that gets in the way of everyday life (Christensen 1999). Most of the children who participated in the review had impairments that did not involve continuous ill health, though many made regular visits to hospitals. Those who did discuss issues relating to health services discussed issues such as the behaviour of staff, rather than whether they were receiving appropriate medical care.

> At hospital they tell your parents instead of you and you don't know what's going on.
> We should know what happens, it should be explained in a way we can understand.
> I think the Doctor should come and talk to the staff in schools. Here a nurse did come and speak to the teachers but not at my old school.

Clubs and leisure/play services

All of the children and young people felt that play and leisure services could be substantially improved.

> Blind kids need balls with bells and play schemes don't have them.
> At my church there is a boy who is autistic. They sang songs in maketon, taught people to sign and all kinds of ways of communicating. When he was aged three to six they used to take him in and he wasn't any different. When he got older they left him out and wouldn't include him.

Transition

The disabled young people who had experienced careers advice were scathing about the attitudes of staff. They felt:
- they were not offered the same opportunities as other young people;
- staff were prejudiced about their potential to gain full-time employment;
- staff attempted to coerce them into dead end jobs or benefits;

> I phoned the Disabled Advice Line at the job centre, it was an answering machine – useless – I hung up.
> I was on work placement and they went to health and safety and wouldn't let me, I wasn't allowed to type or be a receptionist even

> though I have level 3 and this was a major health authority. They
> didn't want me there at reception because I was disabled. I just gave
> up the placement I wasn't putting up with that.

Role models

Many children and young people were aware that job opportunities were
limited for disabled people:

> When I leave school I want to be a builder so that I can train
> other deaf people to be builders so that they get jobs.
> Why aren't there any deaf teachers?
> Where are the disabled social workers?
> Why are none of the support workers in schools disabled?

Unfortunately these observations are not that surprising but are in keeping
with the findings of other studies (Middleton 1999; Morris 1999). What
was different with this project was the steps taken after we had carried
out the consultation.

Recommendations

There is a list of recommendations that the young people suggested in the
full report (Davis and Hogan 2002). For example, the development of key
workers, disability equality training for all local authority staff, and an
increase in peer education, mediation and advocacy. However in this
chapter we want to concentrate on how the young people wanted to
influence service planning and delivery.

All the young people expressed a wish to be able to put their views across
to service providers and participate in projects that might challenge their experiences
of exclusion and discrimination. Their specific proposals were for:

- an Art and Drama project to highlight the issues that disabled children
  have identified as key to their everyday lives (e.g. inclusive education,
  play and leisure opportunities, school and home transition, transport);
- a peer education/counselling and disability equality training project
  to be run in schools to counteract stereotypes and bullying by staff
  and pupils;
- an independent advocacy project to provide support across different
  sites e.g. schools, hospitals, multi-agency meetings;
- a project to check local buildings compliance on accessibility and to
  evaluate the availability of support to aid access to cultural activities
  within buildings;
- an event to enable disabled children to meet service providers face-
  to-face to put forward their views on the development of services

These projects are under development. The Disability and Diversity Group are in negotiation with a number of organisations who are well placed to organise and/or fund the projects (e.g. local art groups, disability equality training providers, local planners, local advocacy projects, the children's fund). An action plan has been developed and many of the children and young people's recommendations have already been addressed. For example:

- the Diversity and Difference Group collaborated with North West Disability Arts Forum to submit a funding proposal to the Liverpool Children's Fund (and received a £150,000 grant to enable disabled artists to develop a number of creative projects involving both disabled and non-disabled children);
- some disabled young people now sit as equals on the Diversity and Difference Group and contribute to developing policies;
- disabled young people were involved in accessibility audits of summer play schemes and are working with support workers to develop an apprenticeship scheme for disabled young people to become access auditors;
- the Liverpool Children's Fund has funded two advocacy support workers posts to develop support across a range of services;
- the Liverpool Bureau for Children and Young People has run a number of conferences and day seminars to establish agreed standards of good practice for increasing children and young people's participation in decision making processes across services and within voluntary organisations in Liverpool.

Though we both worked from a social model perspective and were keen that the project should be emancipatory, it has thrown up problems:

- though we achieved our major aims, it remains to be seen, in the long term, if the Diversity and Difference Group will sustain itself;
- though our project was participatory and disabled young people moved into partnership roles, we wrote the final report, and the participants chose the style of cover and received copy of the report;
- had there been more time and money (we failed to receive funding from the Joseph Rowntree Foundation for a fuller evaluation), it may have been more participatory during the writing up stage, and we would have carried out a more rigorous evaluation. Indeed, this field is underdeveloped, there being very few cases of full scale research to assess children and young people's views of research projects and methods (Hill 2003);
- our evaluation took the form of checking the children and young people's views once we gave them the report. We assumed that participation

was a good thing. Subsequently, we realised that further dialogue is required to investigate participant's views over the longer term and to consider the effectiveness of the new projects.

This suggests that that even after deciding 'whose side are you on' (that of the social model/emancipatory practice), the researcher cannot guarantee that the emancipatory objectives will be met in full. Moreover, there is a danger that researchers and project organisers might impose their own view of the social model on participants, and so dis-empower them. Finkelstein (1999) has suggested that a new type of expert might emerge just as disablist as those associated with the medical model. It has been argued that many social model studies of childhood (disabled and non-disabled) are just as restricting as medical model perspectives because they reduce disabled children and young people to the status of passive social victims (Davis et al. 2003). Our feeling is that any dogma (social or medical) is dangerous because it encourages people to scrutinise, comment on and regulate each other's behaviour in ways that can suppress self-expression. In short, you cannot encourage self-empowerment at the same time as telling people how to think. This means that emancipatory projects should in a post-structural way recognise people's varied life experiences and opinions at the same time as asking people what material changes they require. If and when disabled people offer conflicting opinions we should not see this as a starting point for collective crisis, rather as an agenda for consultation, dialogue, negotiation and agreed action. We should also not deride participatory projects because they fail to challenge immediately the influence of national policy networks. We believe that emancipatory research can be judged successful where it supports disabled children and young people in challenging their local life conditions or where it enables children and young people to develop skills that will support them in later life.

An associated argument is that those running participatory projects need to use a mixture of methods to evaluate participant's (both service users and providers) experiences and the short/ long term benefits to participants/ service providers/ communities (Davis 2002). It is arrogant to assume that simply because a researcher chooses a specific philosophical stance that he/she has legitimacy. More efforts should be made in both disability and childhood studies to carry out long term post-project evaluation of participant's views on the extent to which participatory/ emancipatory projects actually meet participant's objectives.

A further concern is to represent the diversity of disabled people. Though the arts projects in Liverpool will mean that a greater range of disabled young people will have the opportunity to put forward their views, the original focus groups were not representative of a wide range of disabled children and young people. A great deal of money is required if participatory projects are to achieve this representative target.

Discussion

What is emancipation and participation? We had an idea that we would build a process in Liverpool that began to reconstitute power relationships between adults and children. The children and young people in our study engaged with this perspective and they suggested that they wanted:

- to work with policy makers on a face to face basis;
- to access resources to plan and carryout their own projects;
- to work in partnership with adults;
- to have time to meaningfully develop their ideas.

These findings challenge the stereotypical representation of disabled childhood as static, vulnerable and dependent, and disabled children as lacking agency, imagination and creativity (Shakespeare and Watson 1998). It requires that adults who provide services stop treating disabled children as objects of service delivery and start engaging with disabled children as subjects who can work together with adults to plan and deliver services (Davis et al. 2003).

The Diversity and Difference Group were able to initiate a participatory process that required policy makers and service providers to listen to disabled children and young people and act on their ideas. We were also able to begin to develop self-emancipatory processes where disabled young people developed their own services (e.g. the access audit apprenticeship). The power relations between adult professionals and disabled children and young people were not totally changed but the processes of negotiation and partnership were beginning to develop.

This project provides evidence to support Bailey's (2004) view that participatory projects can enable emancipatory agendas. It suggests that there are benefits from joining the two approaches. However, in Liverpool we were lucky to have strong links with senior managers in local authorities who had the power to act on the wishes of participants and to bring together a multi-agency group. This experience appears to reinforce Kirkby with Bryson's (2001) view that the success of participatory projects is dependent on the way they are supported and organised. John Hogan's local contacts and knowledge meant that the participants treated us like insiders. Unlike many university-based projects, we did not parachute into the community. This meant that we received little resistance from children and young people. Indeed, the Deaf children who participated commented that they only chose to speak to us because we were accompanied by an experienced BSL interpreter already well known to them. This recognition of the local social/cultural context is a very important aspect in planning participatory projects.

This means that, like other writers, we believe that there is no one way to do participatory or emancipatory projects (Davis 1998; Hill 2003). Many of the texts that promote emancipatory research show little awareness of the need to take account of local circumstances and cultures (Davis 2000). A variety of approaches might have value. For example, sometimes disabled children and young people want to take full control of projects, policy developments, or service planning/delivery; on other occasions they ask for support from adults or expect adults to provide various services. Therefore, it is important to provide opportunities for disabled children and young people to say what they think about emancipatory and participatory projects and ensure that the processes of project evaluation are better scrutinised by funding providers.

We also have to recognise the dangers of using participatory and emancipatory approaches with children and young people. Firstly, it would be unwise to assume that children and young people are only able to gain control of their lives through 'projects'. Indeed, the children's rights perspective appears to assume that most children don't already carry out citizenship/responsible roles despite contrary evidence from, for example, many studies of families. Very often children successfully combine responsible roles, including supporting parents in health settings and acting as interpreters during negotiations between adult service providers and their parents, with the everyday processes of childhood, such as leisure time and playing with friends (Backett et al. 2000; Candappa and Egharevba 2001). Indeed, in terms of childhood theory, there is a danger that writers on children's rights reproduce the 'passive' discourse they try so hard to refute (Davis et al. 2003). For if we truly believe that children and young people are active/creative social agents then we must also accept they can achieve self-emancipation without the intervention of over-bearing adults. This argument can be linked to the development of post-structural theory in disability studies (Corker and Shakespeare 2002). It is claimed that we should move beyond modernist preoccupations with categorising groups of people to recognise that children and young people (disabled or not) have multiple identities and abilities, and that these cannot be reduced to simple notions of class, 'race', impairment, or age (Davis 2000; Corker and Davis 2001; Davis 2003). On a daily basis these abilities enable them to challenge, resist and overcome the barriers they encounter in their lives.

Secondly, we should recognise that the 'projects' based approach can be too rigid and not what all children and young people want. Some writers argue that most of the pressure for children and young people to attend participatory projects comes from adults (Hill 2003). We are aware that some participatory projects have led to the creation of a 'professional child' who is constantly involved in pseudo-consultation (Hogan 2002). It is important that participatory projects balance the serious topic of socio-political change with creativity and fun. Otherwise, we run the danger of organising projects that corral, discipline, examine and over regulate the everyday experiences of childhood. Indeed, participatory projects may enable professional and service provider agendas to take precedence over the agendas of disabled people (Finkelstein 1999; Mercer 2004).

Finally, we should not assume that the outputs of successful participatory and emancipatory projects can always be fully controlled by the participants or the organisers. As Tom Shakespeare (1996) has pointed out, the idea of independent living was very usefully adopted by Thatcherites hell bent on cutting public expenditure. Yet, when this happens we should not be overly critical if the benefits of experiencing the participation process outweigh the failure to achieve specific outcomes and/or goals. For, in keeping with Friere (1972), Bailey (2004) and Mercer (2004), we consider the educational and social processes of participatory and emancipatory projects to be as important as any of the project's findings and outcomes.

Bibliography

Adams, J., Swain, J. and Clark, J. 2000: What's So Special? Teachers' Models and Their Realisation in Practice in Segragated Schools. *Disability and Society,* 15 (2), 233-246.

Alderson, P. 2002: Student Rights in British Schools: trust, automony, connection and regulation. In R Edwards (ed.), *Children, Home and School: Autonomy, Connection or Regulation.* London: Falmer Press.

Alderson, P. 1999: Civic rights in schools. *Youth and Policy,* 56-73.

Backett-Milburn, K., Davis, J. M. and Cunningham-Burley, S. 2000: Discussion of the social and cultural context of children's lifestyles and the production of health variations relevant to adult risk of CVD. NHF 'Young at Heart' Summit Meeting.

Bailey, K. 2004: Learning More from the Social Model: linking experience, participation and knowledge production. In C.Barnes and G. Mercer (eds), *Implementing the Social Model of Disability: Theory and Research.* Leeds: The Disability Press.

Barnes, C. 1992: Qualitative Research: Valuable or irrelevant? *Disability, Handicap and Society,* 7 (2), 115-124.

Barnes, C. 1996: Disability and the Myth of the Independent Researcher, *Disability and Society,* 11 (1), 107-110.

Barnes, C. 2003: What a Difference a Decade Makes: Reflections on Doing 'Emancipatory' Disability Research. Disability and Society, 18 (1), 3–17.

Beresford, P. 2004: Madness, Distress, Research and the Social Model. In C.Barnes and G. Mercer (eds), *Implementing the Social Model of Disability: Theory and Research.* Leeds: The Disability Press.

Candappa, M. and Egharevba, I. 2001: Negotiating Boundaries: Tensions within home and school life for refugee children. In R Edwards (ed.), *Children, Home and School: Regulation, Autonomy or Connection.* London: Routledge.

Cairns, L. 2001: Investing in Children: Learning how to promote the rights of all children. *Children and Society,* 15 (5), 347-360.

Cockburn, T. 1998: Children and Citizenship in Britain. *Childhood,* 5 (1), 99-118.

Christensen, P. 1999: It Hurts: Children's cultural Learning about everyday illness. *ETNOFOOR.* XII (1), 39-52.

Corker, M. and Davis, J. M. 2001: Portrait of Callum: the disabling of a childhood. In R Edwards (ed.), *Children, Home and School: Regulation, Autonomy or Connection.* London: Routledge.

Corker, M. 1999: Differences, Conflations and Foundations: The limits to 'accurate' theoretical representation of disabled people's experiences. *Disability and Society,* 14 (5), 627-642.

Corker, M. and Shakespeare, T. (eds.) 2002: *Disability and Postmodernity.* London: Continuum

Corsaro, W. 1997: *The Sociology of Childhood.* London: Pine Forge.

Davis, J. M. 1998: Understanding The Meanings of Children: A Reflexive Process. *Children and Society,* 12 (5), 325-335.

Davis, J. M. 2000: Disability studies as ethnographic research and text: Research strategies and roles for promoting social change? *Disability and Society,* 15 (2), 191-206.

Davis, J. M. 2002: Reconstructing 'Health Promotion' with children and young people. Presented at European Conference: Reducing Social Inequalities in Health Among Children and Young People. December, Copenhagen.

Davis, J. M. 2003: Engaging Children and Disability Through Ethnography: Negotiating Everyday Identities With Adults And Children. In D. Kasnitz and R. Shuttleworth (eds), *Engaging Anthropology in Disability Studies.*

Davis, J.M. and Hogan, J. 2002: Diversity and Difference: Consultation and Involvement of Disabled Children and Young People in Policy Planning

and Development in Liverpool Quality Protects/Children's Fund/Liverpool
Bureau for Children and Young People. Unpublished paper.

Davis, J.M. and Watson, N. 2001: Theories Of Social Exclusion In Childhood.
5th European Sociological Association Conference Visions And
Divisions. Helsinki, Finland. Aug. 28-Sept. 1, 2001.

Davis, J.M., Watson, N., Corker, M., and Shakespeare, T. 2003: Reconstructing
Disabled Childhoods and Social Policy in the UK. In A. Prout and C.
Hallet (eds), *Hearing the Voices of Children.* London: Falmer Press.

De Winter, M. 1997: Children as Fellow Citizens: participation and
commitment. Oxford: Radcliff Medical Press.

Friere, P. 1972: *Pedagogy of the Oppressed.* Harmondsworth: Penguin.

Finkelstein, V. 1999: Doing disability research. Disability and Society, 14
(6), 859-67.

Grieg, A. and Taylor, J. 1999: Doing research With Children. London: Sage.

Hargreaves, A. 1989: *Curriculum and Assessment Reform.* Oxford: Oxford
University Press.

Hart, R. 1997: *Children's Participation.* London: Earthscan, in association
with UNICEF.

Hill, M. 2003: Children's Voices On Ways Of Having A Voice. ESRC Seminar
Series: Challenging 'Social Inclusion' Perspectives For and From Young
People. April: Glasgow.

Hogan, J. 2002: Rhetoric or Reality. Unpublished MA Thesis. University
of Liverpool.

Kirby, P. with Bryson, S. 2002: *Measuring the Magic? Evaluating and researching
young people's participation in public decision making.* London:
Carnegie Young People Initiative.

Kirby, P. 2001: Involving Young People in Research. In B. Franklin (ed.),
The New Handbook of Children's Rights: Contemporary Policy and Practice.
London: Routledge.

Mayall, B. 1994: *Negotiating health: Primary School Children at Home and
School.* London: Cassell.

Mercer, G. 2004: From Critique to Practice: emancipatory disability research.
In C.Barnes and G. Mercer (eds), *Implementing the Social Model of
Disability: Theory and Research.* Leeds: The Disability Press.

Middleton, S. 1999: *Disabled Children: Challenging Social Exclusion.* Oxford:
Blackwell.

Mitchell, R.C. 2001: Implementing Children's Rights in Brittish Columbia:
Using The Population Health Framework. *International Journal of
Children's Rights,* 8, 333-349.

Moss, P. and Petrie, P. 2002: *From Children's Services to Children's Spaces:
Public Policy, Children and Childhood.* London: Routledge.

Morris, J. 1999: *Hurtling Into A Void. Transition to Adulthood for Young Disabled People.* York: Joseph Rowntree Foundation.

Morrow, G. 2000: 'It's cool...cos' you can't give us detentions and things, can you?': Reflections on research with children. In P. Milner and B. Carolin (eds), *Time to Listen to Children.* London: Routledge.

Oliver, M. 1992: Changing the Social Relations of Research Production. *Disability, Handicap and Society,* 7 (2), 101-114.

Oliver, M. 1996: *Understanding Disability: From theory to practice.* Basingstoke: Macmillan.

Oliver, M. 1999: Final accounts and The Parasite People. In M. Corker and S. French (eds), *Disability Discourse.* Buckingham: Open University Press.

Prout, A. 2000: Children's Participation: Control and Self-Realisation in British Late Modernity. *Children and Society,* 14 (4), 304-15.

Roche, J. 1997: Children's Rights: Participation and Dialogue. In J. Roche and S. Tucker (eds), *Youth in Society.* London: Sage

Roche, J. 1999: Childhood: rights, participation and citizenship. *Childhood,* 6 (4), 475-94.

Shakespeare, T. 1996: Rules of Engagement: Doing disability research. *Disability and Society.* 11 (1), 115-119.

Shakespeare, T. 1997: Researching Disabled Sexuality. In C. Barnes and G. Mercer (eds), *Doing Disability Research.* Leeds: The Disability Press.

Shakespeare, T. and Watson, N. 1998: Theoretical Perspectives on Disabled Childhood. In C. Robinson and K. Stalker (eds), *Growing Up With Disability.* London: Jessica Kingsley.

Stone, E. and Priestley, M. 1996: Parasites, pawns and partners: disability research and the role of non-disabled researchers. British Journal of Sociology, 47 (4), 699-716.

Tisdall, K. and Davis, J. M. 2003: Making A Difference, Bringing Children And Young People's Views Into Policy Making. ESRC Seminar: Challenging 'Social Inclusion'. April: Glasgow.

Zarb, G. 1992: On The Road to Damascus: First steps towards changing the relations of disability research production. *Disability, Handicap and Society,* 7 (2), 125-138.

CHAPTER 12

The Social Model, the Emancipatory Paradigm and User Involvement

Angie Carmichael

Introduction

> It is only the disabled person who can satisfactorily define his
> or her needs in terms of the enabling of equal opportunity.
> This is the basis of demanding consultation and it is the
> purpose of consultation (HCIL 1990: unpaged)

Since this statement was made in 1990, there has been a mushrooming in
the number and type of user/consumer consultation and research exercises
carried out by service providers and policy makers, often in response to
legislation. In 2002, I carried out a study which was prompted by concerns
that service user involvement (UI), instead of providing a voice for disabled
people, had served instead to legitimise the aims of service providers and
policy makers. In addition, it was suggested, UI had distracted people's
attention and energies from the main disability agenda - the emancipation
of disabled people through full human and civil rights including the right
to participate in society on equal terms with others. But were these fair
criticisms? In broad terms, I attempted to examine whether UI is a
worthwhile exercise, that is, were there any tangible signs of change as a
result of disabled people's participation, how people involved perceived
it and finally, had it had an empowering effect? Put another way, does UI
as it is currently practiced sit comfortably with the struggle for equality implicit
in the social model, does it fulfil or dissipate the vision of those disability
rights campaigners who originally called for disabled people to have a real
and effective voice in service provision?

This chapter is based on that study and will review the methods
used, provide an analysis of the key findings and emerging themes, and
conclude by reflecting on my research practices within the emancipatory
paradigm.

The social model

Although the first stirrings of disability protest had begun in the 19th century, it was not until the 1960s that disabled people started to come together collectively and to challenge the role of paternalistic impairment-specific charities like the RNID and SCOPE (formerly the Spastics Society) who, together with the growing body of welfare professionals, sought to speak on behalf of and had significant influence over the lives of disabled people (Campbell and Oliver 1996). By breaking away from these traditional charities and forming new pressure groups, disabled people were able to question their position in society, how they wished to be perceived and to develop the roles they would play in the wider struggle against their oppression.

The social model is accredited as originating from within UPIAS in the 1970s (Campbell and Oliver 1996), and later formalised by Oliver (1983:23). It redefines disabled people's position and status, by framing the causes of disability in social terms rather than viewing the person's impairment or pathology as the problem: that is, the ways in which the physical, cultural and social environments exclude or disadvantage those labeled as disabled. In this way disabled people have been able to express their situation in terms of human rights and as an issue of equality, aligning themselves with other oppressed groups. However, for disabled people the biggest obstacles to their inclusion in society are negative public attitudes and material considerations such as the economy and the way it is organised by the mode of production (Barnes 1991; Oliver 1996). Furthermore, for disabled people, the dynamics of oppression are deeply rooted in the social and welfare policies of the state: they are evident in the power relationships present in UI for example, which include issues of control and the roles assigned to users in research formulation (Fisher 2002). Notwithstanding these differences, alignment with other oppressed groups has allowed disabled people to draw on the experience and thinking of feminist and anti-racist theorists in many areas, including that of research.

The emancipatory research paradigm

There has been much examination of the role of disabled people in research (for example, Hunt 1981; Oliver 1987; Barnes, 1996; Stone and Priestley 1996). Since the 1960s, as the 'business' of disability research has continued to grow, there have been calls by disabled people and disability theorists for the social and material relationships of research production to change (Barton 1992; Oliver 1992; Barnes 1996). Central to the criticisms of disability research projects is that they have been carried out in a non-partisan and objective manner using empirical methodologies, which is said to have compounded disabled people's oppression through:

> The misunderstanding of the nature of disability, the [projects']
> distortion of the experience of disability, their failure to involve
> disabled people and the lack of any real improvements in the
> lives of disabled people (Barton 1992:99).

To provide an alternative to the empirical research model, the emancipatory
paradigm has been put forward by Oliver (1992) and others (Barnes 1992;
Finkelstein 1992). This approach seeks to advance the interests of 'subordinate'
or oppressed groups in society (Guba 1990), in line with feminist and anti-
racist research methods. Its key feature is the rebuttal of positivist and
interpretative claims to objectivity and assertions about the political positions
of the researcher (Stone and Priestley 1996). Moreover, emancipatory
disability research must be located within the social model of disability and
should aim to change the world, not just describe it, if it is to provide a radical
alternative to mainstream theory and methods (Oliver 1992). Furthermore,
it is argued, that unless disabled people are involved in determining the aims,
methods and use of research, then clearly such research neither empowers
nor has transformative potential (Zarb 1992). However, this emphasis on
the importance of disabled people's central role within a project is very different,
I believe, from the assumption that only disabled people should carry out
such research. As Barnes (1992) has argued, emancipatory disability research
is not about biology but about commitment and researchers (with or without
impairments) putting their knowledge and skills at the disposal of disabled
people and their organisations, and the 'generation and production of
accessible and useable knowledge' (Barnes 2003:6). There are now a number
of academics who do much to promote disabled people's interests.

Within critical or emancipatory social research it is necessary for the researcher
to see beyond the dominant ideologies in order for the truth to be revealed
(Harvey 1990). Through this approach feminists, for example, have been able
to demonstrate that housework is real work, that it has been devalued by a
male dominated society and consequently by revealing oppressive structures,
have encouraged social change in the roles of women (Oakley 1974).
Emancipatory disability research then, whilst seeking new hypothesis, bases
itself upon the methods and methodologies used within the feminist paradigm
of 'reciprocity', 'gain' and 'empowerment' (Lather 1987; Ribbens 1990)
and more recently, from within disability studies itself, the requirement of
the researchers for 'reflexivity' (Oliver 1992).

Of course, the emancipatory paradigm has not been without its critics.
For example, it has been argued that by focusing on one oppressed group
the research may conflict with the interests of other oppressed groups who
have not been considered legitimate objects for study (Hammersley 1992;

Silverman 1998). Other academics, (Stone and Priestley 1996; Stone 1997; Barnes and Mercer 1997; Oliver 1997; Shakespeare 1997), who are in the main supportive of the principles of emancipatory research, have raised questions about the practicality and effectiveness of doing emancipatory disability research.

Nevertheless, it is the emancipatory paradigm that has informed much of disability research in recent years. The integrating theme running through this application of social model thinking is its transformative aim: that is 'the removal of barriers and the promotion of disabled people's individual and collective empowerment' (Barnes 2003: 5). For Oliver (1992, 1996), the value of research can be gauged by asking how far the process of participation has made a contribution to individual or collective empowerment and whether improvements in the lives of disabled people have been achieved in any measure as a result. From this perspective the role of the researcher is to help facilitate these goals through the research process. It is this standpoint and these principles, which I attempted to use as a yardstick in studying user involvement projects, and also to apply to my own research in carrying out that study.

Recent developments in user involvement and associated research
In response to disabled people's campaigning for improved representation (and also to the wider development of consumer and citizens rights), over the past two decades there have been major changes to the way health, social services and the benefits system have developed policies which focus on the housing and support needs of disabled people (Means and Smith 1998; Cameron et al. 2001). Legislation and policy statements now stress the importance of enabling those who are in receipt of services to have their say in how those services are run (Beresford and Campbell, 1994; Barnes, Mercer and Morgan 2002) and during the 1990s consultation exercises became an increasingly common element of policy reviews affecting services for disabled people.

The form and quality of these exercises varied widely: for example, some involved only the occasional input while others were on a much larger scale. Some initiatives, indeed, have appeared to be going further towards giving control over research to disabled people who are service users through the development of 'user-led' reviews (Evans and Carmichael 2002). Notwithstanding these general advances, the question of involving people with learning difficulties in the process of research (and in user consultations) has invariably been viewed as too complex to resolve, and until recently they have tended to remain on the periphery (Richards 1984; Aspis 1997).

Within the past few years, however, a small number of projects have aimed to address these issues, for example (Baines et al. 2001; Gramilch et al. 2002).

User or consumer involvement then, is now seen as an essential part of the policy making process and lends credibility to the decisions made as a result of policy review. In essence, for disabled people, UI has become the process whereby they contribute in some way to the decisions made within the statutory and voluntary service sectors to provision that may have a profound effect on their lives. Indeed, thousands of disabled people are now participating in a range of such activities.

The focus of my study (which was carried out for an MA dissertation at the University of Leeds) was to evaluate disabled people's experiences of being involved (as service users) in research and consultation projects and to assess from their perspective, the impact of UI practices over the past two decades by identifying tangible signs of change. A literature review was undertaken and data were collected using methods appropriate to both emancipatory and participatory research.

The research project

In order to maximise the validity of the data, it was decided to use both qualitative and quantitative methods. The qualitative part of the study involved in depth interviews of participants in two research projects and a focus group discussion. The quantitative part consisted of a questionnaire-based survey of disability organisations regarding their experience of UI over the past five years.

Qualitative methods

Two recent projects, which were viewed as originating from disabled people and/or as 'user led', were identified as case studies: the first was a local authority best value review of the Direct Payments scheme and its support service, while the second project aimed to map the current and future use of services provided for people with learning difficulties across a rural county. Both studies had involved disabled people in a variety of ways (principally as researchers and contributors) and findings from these had been disseminated through public launches to their constituents and interested agencies, and by the circulation of summary reports.

In line with the principles of emancipatory methods and to avoid the research being viewed as oppressive, participants were asked how they preferred to be interviewed: individually, in pairs or as a focus group. Those who opted for individual interviews were then offered a choice of face-to-face, telephone or email interviews. As a result, data was collected by means of three semi-

structured telephone interviews and a small focus group discussion. In order
to facilitate the meaningful participation of people with learning difficulties
(who had conducted the majority of the fieldwork in the second sample project
under review) participants were asked how they would like to be involved
and by whom (if anyone) they would like to be supported. Following a brief
discussion among the potential group, it was agreed that participants would
be most at their ease if the meeting were held in their organisation's office
over lunch. Supporters were chosen by the participants and were people with
whom they were familiar (a paid worker and an advisor to the organisation).

The researcher recognises that it is accepted practice to acknowledge the
value of disabled people's participation in research by offering a nominal fee.
However, all of those involved in the focus group and individual interviews
stated they were happy to assist without payment as the study was funded
by the researcher and was for academic rather than commercial purposes.
The members of the focus group agreed to accept payment for a sandwich
lunch, as this enabled people to attend who would usually have been
elsewhere at this time.

After an initial informal discussion with the researcher, during which the
aims and objectives of the study were outlined, participants were given the
opportunity to ask questions and clarify their roles within this exercise. The
researcher gave assurances that all information received would be treated with
confidence and sensitivity and would not be attributable to any individuals
or organisations. An information sheet was provided setting out the aims and
objectives and a copy of the proposed interview questions (in plain text and
pictures) was circulated in advance to the focus group and their supporters,
to enable participants to be prepared for the meeting.

A time convenient to the interviewees was arranged and consent was given
either verbally or in writing before the interviews/group discussion took place,
and again at the start of interview, with an opportunity to withdraw at any
time. The interviews and the surveys were structured around the key
themes of previous experiences of UI, current experiences of a specific research
project including access issues, training, ownership, influence and outcomes.
The focus group discussion was less structured but followed a similar pattern
to the individual interviews as well as providing an opportunity to talk about
emerging issues and concerns.

Quantitative methods

In order to survey the experiences of both established groups as well as those that
have emerged over the last ten years, nine organisations that had participated in
similar, recent research (Barnes, Morgan and Mercer 2001) were selected for inclusion,

the sampling criteria was according to that report, based on the year of establishment, size of membership, geographic location, and range of services offered. However, as the response to this first survey attempt was low, further organisations were included, in order to provide a wider collection of data to be analysed. The second tranche were all members of BCODP and, as far as possible, fulfilled the same sampling criteria as the first group. Initial contact was made with organisations by telephone and email, to explain the study and enquire if they would be willing to participate. After receiving agreement, surveys and covering letters were sent out either by email or mail, according to the organisations' preferences. In total, 22 organisations were contacted and eleven surveys returned, providing data on 44 projects.

Research findings and analysis

The following sections highlight a number of significant issues and themes that emerged from the analysis of both the results of the fieldwork exercises and the literature and policy review that was undertaken regarding the impact of user involvement.

A means of changing policies?

This admittedly small-scale study revealed that, over the past five years, organisations of disabled people and their members have been involved in a wide variety of UI activities, with a number of different agencies (for example, health authorities, community trading exchange schemes, national care standards commission, research projects) and at varying levels of participation. However, the primary focus of UI activity remains on disabled people's relationships with Social Services Departments and the provision of essential support arrangements.

As observers of the disability movement have acknowledged (Campbell and Oliver 1996; Drake 1999), it is difficult to quantify the impact that disabled people's involvement has had on changing policy, particularly where there is sparse evidence on which to base any assessment. Marx and Adam's (1994) criteria for gauging the progress of (new) social movements put an emphasis on concrete change: political, economic, legislative, attitudinal and behavioural. Although this study found that only a minority of projects resulted in visible outcomes, the significance of these changes should not be underestimated. As noted by survey respondents:

> We now have a CIL, run by disabled people, providing a range of services.
>
> A Day Centre 'warehouse' run by a large charity under contract will close, the service will re-tender with a new specification to more appropriately reflect the varying needs of service users.

In a wider context, UI can be seen as part of an increasing ability to influence policy. As a result of disabled people's redefinition of their situation in terms of human rights and equality, together with their increased visibility in society, it has been possible for disabled people and their organisations to effect changes, particularly in local health and social services policies. Although some of these have been relatively small changes at local levels, others have been more visible. For example, as a consequence of the success of the Direct Payments legislation and the growth of the Independent Living Movement, disabled people once regarded simply as the passive recipients of services now have greater choice and control over how their support needs are met (Begum and Fletcher 1995; Wood 1991).

Contributing to empowerment?

Campbell and Oliver (1996) specify other standards that may be used as a measure of the success of UI. These include raising the consciousness and supporting the empowerment of disabled people and the promotion of disability as a civil and human rights issue. These aspects are fundamental to the emancipation of disabled people, and empowerment in particular proved to be an aspect of UI about which participants in the study tended to be most enthusiastic:

> Participating users gain confidence, new skills and knowledge.
> (survey respondent)

> I personally got a lot from it (the research project). I felt much
> more confident both in myself and what I could do. (interviewee)

Sometimes this empowerment took the form of knowing better how to play the game next time:

> We will be better prepared and know what questions to ask before
> we do anything like this again!   (focus group participant)

Although some have questioned the reach of UI into the community, it seems undeniable that UI draws in those who were previously unpoliticised and raises their consciousness of inequality:

> I have become more aware that Direct Payment users and disabled
> people who rely on services, are expected to be accountable
> in all things, all of the time.... which wouldn't be accepted
> by non disabled people. (interviewee)

With regard to raising disability issues, this study looked primarily at local initiatives. At this level most organisations felt that their efforts had been effective, reporting 'increased Social Services awareness of disability issues' but most found it difficult to quantify any benefit from their UI activities in terms of civil rights or the wider agenda. In summary, while the large majority of participants in this study perceived UI to be beneficial, they also highlighted some less positive aspects of the process.

Consultation fatigue, disillusionment and setting priorities

Consultation fatigue was also raised as an issue by the majority of participants in the study. As noted elsewhere, (Barnes, Mercer and Morgan 2002) disabled people have become tired of being asked for their views in all sorts of surveys, especially when there appears to be few improvements arising from it. Again, in this study, survey respondents commented that:

> Lack of resources and inaccessible structures most often mean that consultation becomes ineffective.
>
> We are asked regularly to 'supply' disabled people for research, UI etc.... people have their own lives and do not just get involved in UI unless it's going to make a difference to them.

A significant cause for concern noted by participants in both of the research projects examined during this study, was the feeling that their work had been to some extent misused, distorted or even ignored if it challenged the status quo.

> It's disappointing as we were very strong …Seems like they have cherry picked and have taken up some of the recommendations which they could do without too much hassle or cost. (interviewee)

As a result of consultation fatigue and a (healthy) degree of scepticism regarding agencies' motivation, it appears that disabled people (as service users) are becoming much more selective than in the past in deciding to whom they will give their views and in which activities they will participate. There was evidence that organisations and individuals are beginning to set priorities that reflect perceptions of which project is likely to be of most benefit to them or their cause. When disabled people's experience is that the value of UI is doubtful and that the outcomes have the potential to become distorted or the findings to be manipulated to fulfill another party's agenda, it is not surprising that they tend to be more reluctant to enter into dialogue, or will even refuse to take part.

As UI is still a relatively recent activity, certainly in the amount that is currently being practiced, disabled people are understandably starting to re-examine the role they play within it. Accountability and control of projects were the key determinants of satisfaction levels expressed by organisations of disabled people: they gave noticeably higher ratings to exercises in which they had taken a leading role, or when they had been the initiators. One survey respondent highlighted the reason for the success of such self-initiated UI:

Then there is an expectation that [members'] views will be acted
upon as the organisation is accountable to its users/members.

Observations like these, drawn from practical experience in the current
'UI industry', are contributing to the formulation of 'rules of engagement'.
It is to be expected that these principles will solidify and sharpen disabled
people's involvement, particularly if they are disseminated to new or less
experienced groups.

Facilitation and inclusion

As Walmsey (1997) stresses, facilitating the inclusion of people with learning
difficulties in service reviews and research projects can be more complex than
that of meeting the general access needs of other disabled people. If people
who are labeled as having learning difficulties are to be enabled to understand
complex ideas and to articulate their views, they will require facilitation which
is, to a considerable extent, reliant on human intermediaries in the form of
skilled supporters and advisors.

Furthermore, as identified in other studies (for example Barnes, Mercer
and Morgan, 2000; Vernon, 2002) and echoed in my own, more effort is
needed to include disabled people from minority ethnic communities and
the wider community of unpoliticised disabled people. As a survey respondent
commented:

What usually tends to happen is that a small core group of disabled
people become involved in a range of different initiatives and the real voice
and experiences of disabled people then become muted.

However, when attempts are made to be more representative and the
access and support needs are met in an appropriate manner, the benefits of
UI to both service users and providers have regularly been shown to be significant
(Lindow and Morris 1995, 2001; Morris 1995). Satisfaction with facilitation
and participants' ability to influence the conduct of projects was rated as average
or above for 34 of the 44 projects surveyed in my study. Exceptions
occurred where facilitation was organised exclusively by professionals or by
inexperienced non-disabled people from the voluntary sector. Some disabled
service users themselves frankly acknowledged their own initial lack of
understanding of the needs of others. They also emphasised that effective
involvement requires commitment, not only of resources, but also of time.

Building alliances and funding

For the past decade disability theorists have criticised the material relations
of research production, and the power relationships inherent within (Oliver
1992). Similarly, the validity of a large number of UI projects must be questionable

when the subject of the consultation is also the funding body, which often controls the purse strings of the organisations participating (Pagel 1988; Barnes, Harrison, Mort and Shardlow 1999; Barnes, Morgan and Mercer 2001). Those who contributed to this study were keenly aware of these tensions.

Looking back, we can see that campaigning for changes to the way society is structured and for equal rights was the mobilising force behind the emergence of the disability movement: recent studies (Barnes, Morgan and Mercer 2001) demonstrate that, although there may be differing views on the shape of such activities, this remains a key function for the majority of organisations of disabled people. However, as a consequence of the uncertainties surrounding the resourcing of organisations and therefore UI, it is perhaps inevitable that disabled people have tackled issues in a 'piecemeal' way, most often at local levels. This may be a factor contributing to the difficulty of assessing the impact that disabled people's involvement has had on influencing policies and services. Until alternative forms of funding are made available to promote citizenship participation, there will always remain an imbalance of power and a limit as to how far disabled people can effect changes through UI alone. Furthermore, it is important to remember that user involvement is a means to an end and not an end in itself (Campbell and Oliver 1996). This end is the emancipation of disabled people through full human and civil rights, and the right to participate in society on equal terms with others.

The future for disabled people's involvement

If UI is to be viewed as a valuable resource and worthwhile activity, as seen from the researchers own small study, it will require a commitment from all concerned, an investment in time and resources and it must be relevant to the lives and needs of all disabled people. Furthermore, the future for UI has to be one of equal partnerships between disabled people and the agencies and other professionals involved. Having employed the principles of the social model and empancipatory research in order to develop a critique of recent examples of UI in research and wider activities, how then did my own research practices measure up?

Reflections on the project

This research was undertaken as part of an academic project, and as such, it was subject to limitations in terms of accountability, time, resources and the extent to which the researcher was able to fulfill her intention to work within the emancipatory research paradigm. Although the researcher was a disabled person, and was committed to the social theory of disability, which provided a framework in which to contextualise disabled people's experiences and position, it would be inappropriate to claim that disabled people had initiated the topic or that the fieldwork undertaken for this study was user-led. However, every effort was made to ensure that participants did not find the research process oppressive and, wherever possible, the methods employed respected individual preferences and opinions. It was also hoped that the subject of disabled people's involvement would be one of wider interest and practical use, to those who took part and a summary report of the key findings were made available to those who requested a copy.

The projects and groups under study were, of necessity, selected by the researcher and the participants (both in the focus group and individual interviewees) were self-selected, introducing the possibility of sample bias. Nevertheless, this was principally an explorative study, from a disability perspective, which sought to highlight emerging issues and themes, as well as providing some pointers towards possible further research in this area.

In order to maximise participants' control over the collection of data both through the interviews and focus group discussion and also, although to a lesser degree, with regard to the surveys, informed consent was sought. To this effect, information sheets, draft interview schedules in accessible formats and covering letters were provided which clearly set out the aims and objectives of the study. Participants were given the opportunity to decline or withdraw from interviews at any time. Furthermore, participants were able to amend or change their answers as individual's contributions were read back to them before being written up. However, due to the timescale and nature of the study it was not possible for participants to comment on the researcher's commentary or final analysis, although one disability activist and researcher advised on the survey design and gave some useful insights into the results of the initial findings. In future research projects, attempts will be made to undertake more in-depth analysis and so help validate the findings more fully.

Empowerment and accountability

Within emancipatory disability research there is a focus on empowerment of the research subjects through ownership of projects and their outcomes as well as by the process of data collection. To some extent this was achieved within my research, if initial feedback to me from participants can be counted as suitably objective! However, as Oliver (1997: 20) has pointed out, empowerment is a process that requires people to do something for themselves: empowerment cannot be given.

Additionally, in the debate over changing the relationships of disability research, Shakespeare (1997) argues that there is a difference between loyalty to a cause or movement and accountability to research subjects. He also raises the question of the extent to which 'independent' researchers can, or should, commit themselves to causes like the disability movement, if this will inhibit constructive analysis or debates, which may at times appear to undermine their positions.

Regarding accountability to the research 'subjects' within my study, I feel that I went some way towards enabling participants to have a degree of control over the process, that they decided on the level and method of their involvement and that I reflected accurately their experiences, in the final analysis. Despite being mindful of the barriers that disadvantage disabled people, having a commitment to the 'movement' and striving to work in an anti-oppressive manner that would not alienate people from the research process, I could not claim to have 'equalised' the research relationship to any great extent. As others have recognised (Barton 1992), regardless of how much effort you make to remedy power imbalances, or are committed to a cause, it is ultimately the researcher's view of the world which is produced and which carries the intellectual weight, whatever value that may have. Furthermore, when undertaking research of concern to oppressed groups the researcher cannot be 'independent' in researching oppression, but is either on the side of the oppressor or the oppressed (Barnes 1996).

In conclusion, within any study there will be aspects of the research process which could be improved upon or done differently, especially with the benefit of hindsight, and mine was no exception. Was it emancipatory or participatory research? I think that my project was a hybrid of both: I believe a number of the fundamental principles within the emancipatory paradigm were upheld and that the outcomes will be of practical use to those concerned. However, it was undoubtedly 'my' project in which disabled people were participants: I did not put my skills at their disposal to use as they wished; they were not the initiators; and the end results were mine.

Conclusion

I have used my study on disabled people's participation in research and policy reviews to illustrate a number of the key principles and issues surrounding the social model and carrying out emancipatory research, from what might be termed both 'inside' and 'outside' perspectives. As experienced by other researchers the path of disability research is never a simple formulaic process and nor should it be: it requires a variety of skills, access to resources and a commitment to challenge the oppression experienced by disabled people.

In common with other civil rights movements, the disability movement has developed to encompass diverging strands of opinion on how best to effect political and social change. While it appears that there have been a number of advances towards emancipation as a result of disabled people's participation in research and in other areas of policy formation, the emerging themes arising from my small scale study and the wider experience of the last few decades indicates that the emancipation of disabled people will not come about by research and reformist methods alone, but through a combination of methods, some of them revolutionary. I suggest that the way forward will require a degree of pragmatism in the choice of tactics to be employed, but that these are very likely to include direct action in the form of civil disobedience; campaigning and lobbying at different levels; underpinned by rigorous academic research, evidence and argument. Ultimately, as for all civil rights struggles, success will lie in the strength and solidarity of a disability movement that is inclusive and remains relevant to all.

Bibliography

Aspis, S. 1997: Personal Communication. In L. Barton and M. Oliver (eds), *Disability Studies: Past, Present and Future.* Leeds: The Disability Press.

Baines, M., Brayshay, M., Norman, D., Roy, D., Wallis, M., Walsh, P., Wintersgill, C. and Lindsay, S. 2001: *Making Your Days Better: Helping Each Other for a Better World.* Bristol: Norah Fry Research Centre.

Barnes, C. 1991: *Disabled People in Britain and Discrimination.* London: Hurst and Co., in association with the British Council of Organisations of Disabled People.

Barnes, C. 1992: Qualitative Research: Valuable Or Irrelevant? *Disability Handicap & Society,* 7 (2), 115-24.

Barnes, C. 1996: Disability and the Myth of the Independent Researcher. *Disability and Society,* 11(1), 107-10.

Barnes, C. 2003: What A Difference A Decade Makes: Reflections On Doing 'Emancipatory' Disability Research. *Disability and Society,* 18 (1), 3-18.

Barnes C., and Mercer, G. (eds) 1997: Doing Disability Research. Leeds: The Disability Press.

Barnes, C., Mercer, G. and Morgan, H. 2000: *Creating Independent Futures: An Evaluation Of Services Led By Disabled People, Stage One Report.* Leeds: The Disability Press.

Barnes, C., Mercer, G. and Morgan, H. 2002: *Creating Independent Futures: Conference Report, Preliminary Findings and Policy Implications.* Leeds: The Disability Press.

Barnes, C., Morgan, H. and Mercer, G. 2001: *Creating Independent Futures: An Evaluation of Services Led by Disabled People, Stage Two Report.* Leeds: The Disability Press.

Barnes, M., Harrison, S., Mort, M. and Shardlow, P. 1999: *Unequal Partners: User Groups and Community Care.* Bristol: The Policy Press.

Barton, L. 1992: Introduction. *Disability, Handicap and Society,* 7 (2), 99.

Begum, N. and Fletcher, S. 1995: *Improving Health and Social Services for Disabled People.* London: Kings Fund.

Beresford, P. and Campbell, J. 1994: Disabled People, Service Users User Involvement and Representation. *Disability and Society,* 9 (3), 315-325.

Cameron, A., Harrison, L., Burton, P. and Marsh, A. 2001: *Crossing the Housing and Care Divide.* Bristol: Policy Press.

Campbell, J. and Oliver, M. 1996: *Disability Politics: Understanding Our Past, Changing Our Future.* London: Routledge.

Drake, F. 1999: *Understanding Disability Policies.* Basingstoke: Macmillan.

Evans, C, Carmichael, A. 2002: *Users Best Value: A Guide to User Involvement Good Practice in Best Value Reviews.* York: Joseph Rowntree Foundation.

Fisher, M. 2002: The Role of Service Users in Problem Formulation and Technical Aspects of Social Research. *Social Work Education,* 21 (3), 305-12.

Finkelstein, V. 1992: Setting Future Agendas. Keynote address given at the Disability Research National Conference, London: 1 June.

Gramilch, S., McBride, G., Snelham, N. and Myers, B., Williams, V., Simons, K. 2002: *Journey To Independence: What Self Advocates Tell Us About Direct Payments.* Bild publications, Plymouth.

Guba, E.G. (ed.) 1990: *The Paradigm Dialogue.* Newbury Park, CA: Sage.

Hammersley, M. 1992: *What's Wrong With Ethnography?* London: Routledge.

Harvey, L. 1990: *Critical Social Research.* London: Unwin Hyman.

HCIL. 1990: *Consumer Consultation.* Hampshire Centre for Integrated Living. Also available at: http://www.leeds.ac.uk/disability-studies/archiveuk/index.html

Hunt, P. 1981: Settling Accounts with the Parasite People. *Disability Challenge,* 2, 37-50.

Lather, P. 1987: Research as Praxis. *Harvard Educational Review,* 56 (3), 257-73.

Lindow, V. and Morris, J. 1995: Service User Involvement; Synthesis of Findings and Experience in the Field of Community Care. York: Joseph Rowntree Foundation.

Lindow V. and Morris, J. 2001: *Evaluation of the National User Involvement Project.* Findings, 129. York: Joseph Rowntree Foundation.

Marx G. and Adams, D. 1994: *Collective Behaviour and Social Movements.* Englewood Cliffs, NJ: Prentice Hall.

Means, R. and Smith, R. 1998: Community Care: Policy and Practice. 2nd edn. Basingstoke: Macmillan.

Morris, J. 1995: User Involvement Ideas into Action. Unpublished seminar report. London: Kings Fund.

Oakley, A. 1974: *The Sociology of Housework.* Oxford: Martin Robertson.

Oliver, M. 1983: *Social Work with Disabled People.* Basingstoke: Macmillan.

Oliver, M. 1987: Redefining Disability: Some Issues In Research. *Research, Polity And Planning,* 5, 9-13.

Oliver, M. 1992: Changing the Social Relations of Research Production. *Disability Handicap and Society,* 7 (2), 101 –114.

Oliver, M. 1996: *Understanding Disability: From Theory To Practice.* Basingstoke: Macmillan.

Oliver, M. 1997: Emancipatory Research: Realistic Goal or Impossible Dream. In C. Barnes and G. Mercer (eds), *Doing Disability Research.* Leeds: The Disability Press.

Pagel, M. 1988: *On Our Own Behalf; an Introduction to the Self – Organisation of Disabled People.* Manchester: GMCDP Publications.

Ribbens, J. 1990: Interviewing - An Unnatural Situation. *Women's Studies International Forum,* 12 (6), 579-92.

Richards, S. 1984: *Community Care of the Mentally Handicapped: Consumer Perspectives.* Birmingham: University of Birmingham.

Silverman, D. 1998: Research and Social Theory. In C. Seale (ed.), *Researching Sociology and Culture.* London: Sage.

Stone, E., and Priestley, M. 1996: Parasites, Pawns and Partners: Disability Research and the Role of the Non-Disabled Researcher. *British Journal of Sociology,* 47 (4), 699-716.

Stone, E. 1997: From The Research Notes Of A Foreign Devil: Disability Research In China. In C. Barnes and G. Mercer (eds), *Doing Disability Research.* Leeds: The Disability Press.

Shakespeare, T. 1997: Rules Of Engagement: Changing Disability Research. In L. Barton and M. Oliver (eds), *Disability Studies: Past, Present and Future.* Leeds: The Disability Press.

Vernon, A. 2002: *Users Views of Community Care Services for Asian Disabled People.* Findings, No 752. York: Joseph Rowntree Foundation.

Walmsey, J. 1997: Including People With Learning Difficulties: Theory And Practice. In L. Barton and M. Oliver (eds), *Disability Studies: Past, Present and Future.* Leeds: The Disability Press.

Wood, R. 1991: Care Of Disabled People. In G. Dalley (ed.), *Disability and Social Policy.* London: Policy Studies Institute.

Zarb, G. 1992: On the Road to Damascus: First Steps Toward Changing the Relations of Research Production. *Disability, Handicap and Society,* 7 (2), 125-38.

CHAPTER 13

Madness, Distress, Research and a Social Model

Peter Beresford

Introduction

The focus of this chapter is on research and a social model approach from the perspectives of mental health service users/survivors. Three major points need to be made by way of introduction to this discussion.

First, it is important to remember that the initial attempt made by people, as subjects of and categorised by social policy, to develop a social approach to and understanding of their situation and identity, from their own perspectives, came from disabled people and the disabled people's movement. It is also important to be aware that while this is a relatively recent development, emerging in the 1970s, in another sense it is now well established. It is thus a development that already has its own history, body of written and recorded knowledge and wider legacy in the consciousness of disabled people. This means that a social model approach is particularly associated with disability and disabled people and tends to be understood primarily from these perspectives.

Second, it needs to be said that mental health service users/survivors have never been central to the social model of disability. The corollary of this has been that for a long time, the social model of disability has not had any particular significance for most mental health service users/survivors. The social model of disability grew from and has primarily been concerned with the experience of people with physical and sensory impairments. Over time, awareness of it has grown among other groups of people subject to or eligible for health and social care policies and services, including older people, people with learning difficulties, Deaf people, black people and members of minority ethnic groups and mental health service users. There has been some critical debate from these different groupings about both the degree to which the social model of disability has taken account of their situations and perspectives and how applicable it might be to them (Morris 1996; Corker 1998; Docherty et al. 2003). It cannot really be said that there has been a strong sense of shared ownership of the social model or that it originated with the concerns of mental health service users/survivors specifically in mind.

Third, it is necessary to make clear the dynamic state of discussion about the social model of disability. From the time since Liz Crow first wrote critically about the social model as a disabled woman, it has been subjected to considerable review and re-evaluation from within the disabled people's movement and by disabled people (Crow 1996). Such discussion and analysis has been more and less supportive of the social model. It has questioned its capacity to address issues of difference in relation to gender, ethnicity, culture and sexuality (Walmsley and Downer, 1997; Gillespie-Sells et al. 1998; Vernon 1998; Goodley 2000). It has called into question the ability of the proponents of the social model to address equally and to inter-relate its twin focus on (perceived) impairment and disability and on direct experience and social barriers. The social model of disability has been critiqued from feminist, cultural, postmodern and poststructural perspectives (Thomas 2002).

Thus it is important that any discussion as in this chapter that advances on the social model of disability from a different perspective must guard against approaching it with a simplistic understanding of the model. It is also helpful to remember that the social model did not originate with a concern to address the issues of mental health service users/survivors and therefore should not automatically be assumed to relate to it directly. There has been some confusion about this because of the lack of clarity and agreement about the definition of 'disabled' and 'disability' by disabled people and the disabled people's movement themselves. The terms have been used both narrowly to include people with physical and sensory impairments and more broadly to include a much wider range of groups, including mental health service users/survivors.

Issues of terminology

It may also be helpful at this stage in a volume whose focus is disability studies and the social model of disability, to say something about the language and definitions used in this chapter where the discussion concentrates on 'mental health' issues and mental health service users/ survivors.

There is as yet no agreement among mental health service users/survivors about terminology. It has become common for people with a mental illness diagnosis to be described as 'service users' or simply 'users' – certainly in the mental health field. But, in reality, the identity and naming of people included in this category is much more problematic, both to themselves and to others in society. The proliferation of descriptions and self-descriptions in current use, for example – consumer, sufferer, service user, survivor, recipient, mad – is testimony to the uncertainties involved. Most of these terms, while familiar to mental health professionals, would not find easy recognition among non-professionals. On United Kingdom's streets currently, terms like 'mentally ill' and 'mental patient' would be more common and more easily understood. The description 'mad', repossessed and re-valued by some activists, would be widely understood as a negative term, seen by many as bordering on political incorrectness. But mental patient and ex-mental patient, characterizations from which many activists are seeking to escape, are likely to be viewed as realistic and acceptable by many people in broader society.

The two terms most often used by people actively involved in collective action are service user and survivor. Although they are often used simultaneously and are not always intended to have profound and contrasting meanings, service user and survivor are not the same term. At the very least, the term service user is neutral about the mental patient experience whereas the term survivor is taking a definite and critical position. Some commentators, building on this difference, have claimed that self-described service users are reformist while survivors are radical, even seeking the overthrow of a mental health service dominated by psychiatry. Whether or not this is true, it is clear that service user/survivor activists may have different priorities. Survivor, which has become shorthand for 'psychiatric system survivor', seeks to denote people's survival of mental health services rather than of 'mental illness'. It is often preferred to 'service user' because people reject the passivity denoted by that term and its tendency to define them primarily in terms of mental health services rather than their own independent qualities and characteristics. For some 'service users', however, the term survivor is too aggressive and predictive. Because there is no agreement and all terms cause some offence, the term service user/survivor is used here in an attempt to be as inclusive and unpejorative as possible (Beresford and Campbell 2003).

Putting this discussion in context
To develop the discussion on madness, distress, research and a social model, it is helpful to make three initial connections. These are with:
- the recent history of mental health service user/survivor research;
- the mental health service user/survivor movement;
- the dominance of partnership approaches in the field of mental health service user involvement.

Each of these has important ramifications both for the development of the discussion and for understanding it.

Recent history of mental health service user/survivor research

In the context of disability research, research by mental health service user/survivor organisations and individual service user/researchers has been a late arrival. If we take 1997 as a reference point, at that stage there were barely any large-scale research projects and little contact with the broader disabled people's movement. Much research was small scale with limited or in some cases no funding. Service user/survivor researchers were generally working with very limited resources and little status or recognition. Furthermore there were relatively few such researchers and only a small number of service users/survivors with research training (Beresford and Wallcraft 1997).

Mental health service user/survivor movement

We can only make sense of mental health service users'/survivors' approaches to research (and as we shall see 'social models') through prior consideration of the mental health service user/survivor movement. There is both an old and modern history of service user/survivor organisations. During the eighteenth and nineteenth century there were examples of people (predominantly men), who were the equivalent of today's service users/survivors, who provided written accounts of their views and experience, calling for inquiries and reform. There were campaigning organisations like the Society for the Protection of Alleged Lunatics and the Alleged Lunatics' Friend Society (Porter 1987; Showalter 1987; Campbell 1996). Since the 1980s, there has been an enormous growth in the mental health service user/survivor movement. Many local and national organisations have developed. Some still question whether there is such a movement (Beresford and Campbell 2003), nonetheless, unprecedented numbers of service users/survivors have 'got involved'. Service user/survivor organisations have been contrasted with disabled people's organisations; the latter seen as being citizens rights based; the former as based on a consumerist approach (Barnes and Shardlow 1996; Barnes et al. 1999; Beresford 2000). Mental health service users/survivors and their organisations operate in a context of grossly inadequate and often inappropriate, unreliable and unsafe support services and arrangements and an increasing media and political emphasis on them as 'dangerous' and 'threatening' (Sayce 2000). This has been exacerbated by current government commitment to the extension of compulsory powers in new mental health legislation. This has overshadowed the activities of mental health service users/survivors. It has also significantly influenced resource allocation and diverted attention from the support needs of service users/survivors.

Dominance of partnership approaches, rather than separatism in 'mental health'
While there has tended to be some oversimplification in external accounts
of the development of collective action by mental health service
users/survivors, contrasted with that of disabled people, there have been
some significant differences. These are relevant for understanding service
user/survivor research and its relation with a social approach.

The emergence of the disabled people's movement has been characterised
by:

1. the development of social approaches to disability;
2. the identification of strategies and goals following from the development
   of social understandings of disability;
3. the development of rights based approaches to disability consistent with
   such social approaches to disability;
4. the idea and practice of 'independent living' based on 'the social model'.
   This has led disabled people to prioritise the development of their own
   proactive approaches to support and change (rather than paying
   primary attention to the reform of traditional services) They have then
   sought to mainstream their own independent developments – notably
   through 'direct payment', self run assistance schemes and action based
   on anti-discrimination. (Campbell and Oliver 1996; Oliver 1996)

While it might not be appropriate to characterise the UK disabled
people's movement as 'separatist', it has certainly deliberately developed its
own agenda and for a long time has placed much more emphasis on
independent development than partnership approaches. The process adopted
by the mental health service user/survivor movement has been significantly
different to this. It has followed much more from a partnership model
where:

- activity has mainly been concentrated in the mental health/psychiatric
  system with its structures and requirements for 'user involvement;
- there have been strong pressures for mental health service users'/survivors'
  involvement to be in mental health service based initiatives;
- most of the effort and energy of mental health service users who become
  involved has been focused on reforming traditional mental health services;
- much of the involvement of mental health service users has been related
  to the service, policy and practice system(s) rather than their own agendas;
- much of the funded activity of mental health service users/survivors
  has been in non-user controlled voluntary and statutory organisations.

Significantly, the best known campaigning and most radical of the
national service user/survivor organisations established in the 1980s,

Survivors Speak Out, experienced the most difficulties gaining and maintaining funding and in recent years has been very restricted in its profile and activities. More recently Mad Pride has emerged as a champion of direct action in the mental health service user/survivor movement. However, even they have sometimes felt constrained by the massive pressures and discriminations facing mental health service users. Pete Shaughnessy, one of its founders, writing in relation to the mental health alliance established to challenge the extension of compulsory 'treatment' beyond hospital, argued:

> We think that (mental health charities) are too soft and trying
> to pander to the Government and middle England…to show
> a united front we have limited our public attacks on Sane, and
> saying Mind are a mixed bunch (Shaughnessy 2002).

Thus, while some mental health service users/survivors have taken a more radical and separatist position, developing their own initiatives rather than acting in partnership with professionals (O'Hagan 1993), this has not been the main thrust of activity. The approach advocated by the American survivor and activist, Judy Chamberlin, doing things 'On Our Own', has been the exception, rather than the rule in the UK (Chamberlin 1988).

The philosophical underpinnings of the mental health service user/survivor movement

There seem to be a set of shared values and beliefs underpinning the mental health service user/survivor movement. However, the movement does not seem to have developed explicit philosophies or theories comparable to those of the social model of disability or independent living developed by the disabled people's movement. The reasons for this appear to be various and complex. They seem to relate to two concerns which mental health service users/survivors seem to have. The first of these relates to challenging the underpinning medical model of 'mental illness' when service users'/survivors' intellects are inherently perceived as 'defective' or 'pathological' and the fear that rejecting a medicalised individual model of their situation and identity would lead to them being ruled out and discounted as simplistic and irrational (Campbell 1996). The second relates to service users/survivors worries about signing up to any kind of monolithic theory or set of principles for fear that these dominate and subordinate them and demand an orthodoxy in the same way as professional psychiatric thinking has done for so long. There is a strong libertarian strand in much mental health service user/survivor thinking.

Social approaches and mental health service users/survivors

There can be no question that the mental health service user/survivor movement and related groups and organisations are very conscious of 'the social' in their thinking and activities. Service user/survivor organisations have frequently been characterised by their twin emphasis on mutual aid/personal support and campaigning and action for broader (social and political) change. While as has been said, their activities have frequently had to focus on the (mental health) service system – because this is where they have been able to access resources – their concern has been much broader. The large and growing body of mental health service user/literature highlights an approach which is holistic and both crosses and goes beyond policy divisions. Service user/survivor discourses address both material and spiritual issues; the personal as well as the political. However, this still did not lead to the widespread development of any equivalent of the social model of disability.

It may be helpful at this point to restate the idea at the heart of the social model of disability, while reiterating that this has become the jumping off point for a wide range of critical discussions. The social model rejects the medicalised individual model that understands disability in terms of the deficiencies and incapacities occasioned by personal physical, sensory and intellectual impairment. Instead it asserts that the capacities of people with (perceived) impairment(s) are constrained and prejudiced by the creation and perpetuation of disabling physical and attitudinal 'barriers by the non-disabled majority' (Thomas 2002: 38). Thus disability is a form of social oppression and the social model highlights both social oppression and social understanding in relation to disability.

There is no doubt that most if not all mental health service users/survivors are well aware of the discrimination and oppression which they face, for example, as parents, and in terms of negative stereotyping and their exclusion from employment. But this still has not led to any equivalent of the social model of disability playing a central role in their developing discussions or collective action.

Similarly, there is also a history of social approaches in the fields of psychiatry and 'mental health'. This can be traced to the post-war social psychiatrists and perhaps most significantly, the 'anti-psychiatrists', like Thomas Szasz and notably R.D. Laing and David Cooper. These certainly sought to move from traditional medicalised understandings, to social approaches, which explored social issues, for example, the role of the nuclear family in mental distress. (Laing 1965; Coppick and Hopton 2000). Michel Foucault also developed an influential critique of people's confinement and the emergence of medical psychiatry (Foucault 1967). However, while service users/survivors have sometimes found these helpful and in some cases, as having a contributory role to their own thinking and activities, the anti-psychiatrists came from a professional standpoint and service users played little or no part in the development of their ideas. Also they did not parallel or prefigure the concern with discrimination, social oppression and civil rights embodied in the social model of disability. The interest that some service users/survivors have had in these approaches can be seen as origins for the continuing alliances that have developed between them and organisations and groupings of radical professionals, like critical psychiatrists and critical psychologists. It is difficult, however, to see the social approaches of the anti-psychiatrists prefiguring any equivalent of the social model of disability. So while in one sense it can be said that social understandings have long played a part in the field of mental health and the thinking of mental health service users/survivors, they have not as yet developed to have a central role in the development of a strategy, objectives or coherent philosophy for the service user/survivor movement.

Exploring the location of major service user/survivor research projects

There has been a considerable increase in funded service user/survivor led research in the last few years. Some highly visible and prestigious research activities have emerged. However, major mental health service user/survivor led research projects developing in the last few years have generally been based in non-user controlled organisations. Such organisations (which include the Sainsbury Centre for Mental Health, Mental Health Foundation, Institute of Psychiatry) are themselves generally based on a medicalised model of madness and distress. While some of these projects are internally run by service users/survivors, they face the stresses and tensions of being based in different kinds of organisations. This is in sharp contrast to initiatives from the disabled people's movement (for example, focusing on discrimination, user-led services, independent living, direct payments and the history of the disabled people's movement) which have either been based in organisations controlled by disabled people or undertaken by independent disabled researchers (Barnes 1991; Barnes, Morgan and Mercer 2001; Morris 1993). Viv Lindow has highlighted some of the issues facing 'partnership research':

> It is important to clarify different levels of survivor participation in research...Care must be taken, especially in partnership and user-focussed research that the process is not wittingly or unwittingly highjacked by the more powerful partner (Lindow 2001: 139).

Key examples of such large mental health service user/survivor projects are:

- The User-led Monitoring project (based at the Sainsbury Centre for Mental Health) which sought to measure and evaluate service users views of the nature and quality of mental health services. Mental health service users/survivors have developed interview schedules for use and adapt locally to monitor a range of mental health service settings. Local service users/survivors are trained as interviewers (Muijen 1998; Rose 2001).

- The two Strategies for Living three year programmes (based at the Mental Health Foundation) supporting and undertaking user led research locally and nationally. These have been managed by skilled and experienced service user/survivor researchers and were shaped from the start by service user/survivor researchers and broader consultation and involvement of mental health service users/survivors. This work has placed an emphasis on the coping strategies which survivors develop for themselves and on research and information-gathering to support service users' empowerment. It is currently supporting 15 local projects, as well as supporting the training of user researchers and has placed an emphasis on exploring complementary and alternative approaches to support as well as more holistic and spiritual approaches to madness and distress (Faulkner and Nicholls 1999; Faulkner and Layzell 2000; Nicholls 2001).

- The Service Users Research Enterprises (SURE) is an initiative based at the Institute of Psychiatry, King's College London, which has successfully bid for and undertaken major user led research projects. SURE is made up of a team of mental health service user/survivor researchers. Its activities so far include projects on 'consumer perspectives on ECT' (electro convulsive therapy), users and carers perspectives on continuity of care and a literature review on 'user involvement in change management in organisations funded by NHSE R & D SDO monies' (SURE 2002).

To the best of my knowledge, none of these initiatives has sought to base its activities explicitly on 'a social model of madness and distress', or explicitly and completely rejected traditional ('mental health') understandings and models. The 'social' has figured in their work. The Strategies for Living project in particular is based on a much more social approach than traditional 'mental health' research activities. Much (but not all) of the work of two of these initiatives can be seen, so far, to have been focused mainly on traditional service based approaches. Much good work is coming from these initiatives but they still raise worrying questions. The involvement of service users in non-user controlled research and development organisations may strengthen the latter's legitimacy and at a time when 'user involvement in research' is prioritised increase their capacity to secure research funding. However, it may actually make it more difficult for user controlled organisations to compete successfully on their own for such funding and therefore making if more difficult to advance service users' own research agenda and priorities. This needs to be monitored.

Mental health service user/survivor views of research priorities

In 2002, the Department of Health (DoH) undertook a strategic review of mental health research and development priorities. As part of this initiative they included two service users/survivors in the review group and set up a consultation meeting with a wider range of service users/survivors in response to their request. This provides an initial picture of service users'/survivors' views of appropriate research priorities in this field. These were in sharp contrast to existing DoH priorities that were narrowly focused on the psychiatric system and individual 'mental health'. Participants' proposals for priorities were very different to existing ones. These included:

- A more holistic research approach.
- Challenged the medicalisation of research and dominance of a medicalised individual model of 'mental health issues'.
- Recognition of the importance of self management as a research focus.
- A real focus on issues of race equality.
- The importance of effective user involvement in the research process.
- A conception of mental health research which was concerned with improving the overall wellbeing of service users and which took account of the wide range of policies, issues and considerations (such as social, economic, financial, employment related, housing and cultural).

Thus participants both highlighted the need for research to have a much more 'joined up' and social approach and for the exploration of alternative social approaches or models as a basis for research rather than prevailing medical models. This discussion represents an important and early explicit indicator of mental health service users'/survivors' and user researchers' interest in and commitment to a 'social model' (Department of Health 2002).

Towards social approaches in 'mental health' research

There is now the beginning of interest in the development of social approaches to understanding, which could provide a framework for survivor led research in the context of mental health. However this development is at a very early stage. In 2002-3, two conferences focusing on a social model of madness and distress were organised by Greater London Action on Disability. There was significant interest in these events from a wide range of service users/survivors. However over the same period, there has also been the development of a parallel (professionalized) national discussion, convened by a new Social Perspectives Network. So far contributions to this discussion have mainly come from professionals and been based on an understanding of 'social' which seeks to take account of social factors in explanation rather than reflecting the rights based approach of the social model of disability. (Duggan et al. 2002) This network has also been publicly described (by the person in the Department of Health responsible for Mental Health Legislation generally and specifically for taking forward the new Mental Health Bill with extended provisions for compulsion) as:

> a network of professionals funded over two years to ensure a
> social care presence in the National Institute for Mental Health
> England (NIMHE) (Sieff 2003).

This seems some distance from many service users'/survivors' understanding of a social approach.

What might a social model of madness and distress look like

While discussion is still at an early stage, some key issues have been highlighted (Beresford 2002). First there is an interest among service users/survivors in a social model which is located within a framework of the social model of disability, but which would also have transformatory implications for the social model of disability itself. It would highlight both issues of personal experience and social oppression. There is an unwillingness among many survivors to see 'impairment' as an objective part of their condition, so the discussion demands consideration of the socially constructed nature of 'impairment'. Such a model would also have to take account of the strong sense that many survivors have that their processing in the psychiatric system is related not only to them being seen as defective but also frequently dissident, non-conformist and different in their values from dominant societal values (Plumb 1994, 1999). These are all issues that require further discussion among mental health service users/survivors.

Strategies for the future

A few years ago, two of us (Beresford and Wallcraft 1997) wrote that for the disabled people's movement the social model provided a starting point for thinking, strategy, and action. In contrast, for survivors it might be the other way round, as they came at a model to inform and increase the effectiveness of their activities much later. There are now renewed threats facing both social understandings of madness and distress and the rights of mental health service users. These notably relate to the emphasis on 'dangerousness' and demand for increased compulsory restriction of mental health service users/survivors rights. Second is a return in emphasis to the idea of 'recovery' which is likely greatly to reinforce medicalised understandings of service users' experience and situation.

One encouraging development has been the recent strengthening of contact, links and understandings between survivors and the disabled people's movement (Beresford, Harrison, Wilson 2002). This has been encouraged by further recognition of the shared aspects of their identity relating to the Disability Discrimination Act, the Disability Rights Commission, Human Rights Act and Direct Payments. All should be supportive of the reinforcement of interest and activity around a social model of madness and distress. It also seems important to explore the increased development of truly user-controlled research. It will be helpful to examine systematically both the barriers in the way of and possible supports for taking this forward. It is only likely to be through truly user/survivor controlled research that service users interests and agendas are effectively advanced. Moreover, the development of a social model is most likely to take place within this framework (as well as helping to take it forward). We can expect that a social model of madness and distress will be as contentious and contested an idea as the social model of disability. This is certainly not a reason for seeing its development as anything but an urgent priority.

Bibliography

Barnes, C. 1991: *Disabled People in Britain and Discrimination.* London: Hurst and Co., in association with the British Council of Organisations of Disabled People.

Barnes, C., Morgan, H. and Mercer, G. 2001: *Creating Independent Lives: An evaluation of services led by disabled people, Stage 3 Report.* Leeds: Disability Press.

Barnes, M. Harrison, S., Mort, M. and Shardlow, P. 1999: *Unequal Partners: User groups and community care.* Bristol: The Policy Press.

Barnes, M. and Shardlow, P. 1996: Effective Consumers And Active Citizens: Strategies for users' influence on service and beyond. *Research, Policy and Planning,* 11 (1), 3-38.

Beresford, P. 2000: Review of: Barnes, M. et al. Unequal Partners: User groups and community care. *Disability and Society,* 15 (3), 540-542.

Beresford, P., Harrison, C. and Wilson, A. 2002: Mental Health, Service Users And Disability: Implications for future strategies. *Policy and Politics,* 30 (3), 387-396.

Beresford, P. 2002: Thinking About 'Mental Health': Towards a social model. *Journal of Mental Health,* 11 (6), 581-584.

Beresford, P and Campbell, C. 2003 forthcoming: Participation and Protest: Mental health service users /survivors. In G. Taylor and M. Todd (eds), **Democracy And Protest.** London: Merlin Press.

Beresford, P and Wallcraft, J: 1997: Psychiatric System Survivors and Emancipatory Research: Issues, Overlaps and Differences. In C. Barnes and G. Mercer (eds), **Doing Disability Research.** Leeds: The Disability Press.

Campbell, J. and Oliver, M. 1996: **Disability Politics: Understanding our past, changing our future.** London: Routledge.

Campbell, P. 1996: The History of the User Movement in the United Kingdom. In T. Heller, J. Reynolds, R. Gomm, R. Muston, and S. Pattison (eds), **Mental Health Matters: A Reader.** Basingstoke: Macmillan in association with the Open University.

Chamberlin, J. 1988: **On Our Own: Patient controlled alternatives to the mental health system.** London: Mind.

Coppick, V. and Hopton, J. 2000: **Critical Perspectives On Mental Health,** London: Tavistock.

Corker, M. 1998: **Deaf and Disabled, Or Deafness Disabled?** Buckingham: Open University Press.

Crow, L. 1996: Renewing the Social Model of Disability, **Coalition,** July, 5-9.

Department of Health, 2002: **Report of the Service User Panel, Appendix 5, Strategic Reviews Of Research And Development – Mental Health Report Appendices.** Leeds: Department of Health.

Docherty, D., Hughes, R., Phillips, P., Corbett, D., Regan, B., Barber, A., Adams, M., Boxall, K., Kaplan, I. and Izzidien, S. 2003 forthcoming: This Is What We Think, **Disability Studies Quarterly.**

Duggan, M. with Cooper, A. and Foster, J. 2002: Modernising the Social Model in Mental Health: A Discussion Paper, Social Perspectives Network, Leeds: Training Organisation for the Personal Social Services.

Faulkner, A. and Layzell, S. 2000: *Strategies For Living: A report of user-led research into people's strategies for living with mental distress.* London: The Mental Health Foundation.

Faulkner, A. and Nicholls, V. 1999: *The DIY Guide To Survivor Research.* London: The Mental Health Foundation.

Foucault, M. 1967: *Madness and Civilisation.* London: Tavistock.

Gillespie-Sells, K., Hill, M. and Robbins, B. 1998: *She Dances To Different Dreams: Research into disabled women's sexuality.* London: King's Fund.

Goodley, D. 2000: *Self-Advocacy In The Lives Of People With Learning Difficulties.* Buckingham: Open University Press.

Laing, R.D. 1965: *The Divided Self.* Harmondsworth: Pelican.

Lindow, V. 2001: Survivor Research. In C.Newnes, G. Holmes and C. Dunn (eds), *This is Madness Too.* Ross on Wye: PCCS Books.

Morris, J. 1993: *Independent Lives? Community care and disabled people.* Basingstoke: Macmillan.

Morris, J. (ed.) 1996: *Encounters With Strangers: Feminism and disability.* London: Women's Press.

Muijen, M. 1998: Users Monitoring Mental Health Services, *Q-Net,* 6, 1.

Nicholls, V. 2001: *Doing Research Ourselves.* London: Mental Health Foundation.

O'Hagan, M. 1993: *Stopovers On My Way Home From Mars: A Winston Churchill Fellowship report on the psychiatric survivor movement in the USA, Britain and the Netherlands.* London: Survivors Speak Out.

Oliver, M. 1996: *Understanding Disability.* Basingstoke: Macmillan.

Porter, R, 1987: *A Social History of Madness: Stories of the Insane.* London: Weidenfeld and Nicolson.

Plumb, A. 1994: *Distress or Disability? A discussion document.* Manchester: Greater Manchester Coalition of Disabled People.

Plumb, A. 1999: New Mental Health Legislation: A lifesaver? Changing paradigm and practice, *Social Work Education,* 18 (4), 450-478.

Rose, D. 2001: *Users' Voices.* London: Sainsbury Centre for Mental Health.

Sayce, L. 2000: *From Psychiatric Patient to Citizen: Overcoming discrimination and social exclusion.* Basingstoke: Macmillan.

Shaughnessy, P. 2002: On Community Treatment Orders (CTOs) And Injustice. *S.U.N. Newsletter,* Manchester: Survivors' United Network, December: p. 2.

Showalter, E. 1987: *The Female Malady: Women, madness and English culture 1830-1980.* London: Virago.

Sieff, A. 2003: The Mental Health Bill – The right prescription? Conference paper, Community Care Live, London: 21 May.

SURE. 2002: *Service User Research Enterprise, Annual Report, 2001–2002,* London: SURE, Health Service Research, Institute of Psychiatry.

Thomas, C. 2002: Disability Theory: Key ideas, issues and theories. In C. Barnes, M. Oliver, and L. Barton (eds), *Disability Studies Today.* Cambridge: Polity Press.

Vernon, A. 1998: Multiple Oppression and the Disabled People's Movement. In T. Shakespeare (ed.), *The Disability Reader: Social science perspectives.* London: Cassell.

Walmsley, J. and Downer, J. 1997: Shouting the Loudest: Self-advocacy, power and diversity. In P. Ramcharan, G. Roberts, G. Grant, G. and J. Borland (eds), *Empowerment In Everyday Life: Learning Disability.* London: Jessica Kingsley.

INDEX (Compiled by Marie Ross)

Disability Discrimination Act,
27, 29, 78, 90, 219

Disability Equality Training, 3,
10, 15, 22, 91

Disability Movement, 16, 18, 22,
24-25, 31-32

Disability Rights Commission, 5,
14, 20, 24, 90, 219

Disability Studies Today, 41, 44,
47, 152, 154, 171, 221

Disabled Advice Line, 181

Disabled Living Allowance, 91

Disabled People's International,
5, 140

disablement, 3, 10-11, 22-23, 25,
49, 51, 54, 61, 103, 106, 108-
113

disablism, 10, 11, 33, 34, 36, 38,
41-42, 83-90, 92-97, 112

discourse, 48, 54, 103, 109, 111-
112, 130-131, 133, 147, 158,
163, 169, 172, 186

discrimination, 1, 2, 29, 48, 53,
67, 90, 94, 102, 105, 109, 130-
131, 142, 176, 179, 182, 214-
215, 221

disease, 60

Docherty, D., 209, 220

Dockery, G., 141, 147, 153

domination, 45, 55, 107, 118

Douard, J.W., 66, 80

Drake, F., 147, 153, 197, 205

Drake, R., 147, 153, 197, 205

Duggan, M., 218, 220

education, 2, 6, 12, 20-21, 30,
33-34, 38, 73, 79, 102, 124,
126, 136, 159, 167, 177, 182

emancipatory research, 11, 105,
118-119, 121-122, 124-126,
131-132, 142, 144, 146, 148,
150, 175, 184, 186, 192, 194,
201, 203

Emanuel, J., 162, 170

employment, 20-21, 29, 33-34,
52-54, 78, 102, 111, 181, 214,
217

empowerment, 9, 28, 78, 99, 120,
122, 124, 132, 147, 193-194,
198, 202, 216

environment, 5, 12, 20-21, 53,
70, 85, 90, 102, 112, 147

equality, 29, 33, 56, 76, 78, 191-
192, 198, 217

ethics: of listening, 75

ethnicity, 8, 34, 39, 65, 67, 79, 89,
103, 108, 112-113, 120, 129,
209

eugenics, 48

Evans, C., 118, 124, 125, 128,
133, 194, 205

exclusion, 11, 33-34, 52-53, 60,
65-66, 77, 80, 86, 90, 94, 96,
99, 132, 162, 182, 214

experience, 39, 59, 86, 88, 90, 93,
97, 101, 103-104, 110, 119,
121, 128, 138, 142, 145, 168,
192; and non-disabled, 74, 76;
children, 179; collectivisation,
157, 162; Deaf, 168;
difference, 85; disability, 42,
74, 78, 93, 94, 96, 106, 113,
132, 138-139, 141, 143, 149-
150, 153, 193; gender, 23, 36;
impairment, 85, 87, 120, 208,
209; individual, 13, 22, 108,
124, 131, 146, 218; mental
health service user, 210-211,
218; oppression, 37, 95, 104,
120, 151; psycho-emotional,
85, 89-90, 92; shared, 22, 103,
108-109, 139, 141, 147

experiential studies, 84, 158

experts, 1, 27, 104, 125, 128, 134

exploitation, 48, 50, 56-57, 74